ARGO

HOW THE CIA AND HOLLYWOOD PULLED OFF THE MOST AUDACIOUS RESCUE IN HISTORY

Antonio J. Mendez
and Matt Baglio

PENGUIN BOOKS

PENGUIN BOOKS

Published by the Penguin Group
Penguin Group (USA) Inc., 375 Hudson Street,
New York, New York 10014, USA

USA | Canada | UK | Ireland | Australia | New Zealand | India | South Africa | China
Penguin Books Ltd, Registered Offices: 80 Strand, London WC2R 0RL, England
For more information about the Penguin Group visit penguin.com

Penguin Books Ltd, Registered Offices:
80 Strand, London WC2R 0RL, England

First published in the United States of America by Viking Penguin,
a member of Penguin Group (USA) Inc., 2012
Published in Penguin Books 2013

THE LIBRARY OF CONGRESS HAS CATALOGED THE HARDCOVER EDITION AS FOLLOWS:
Mendez, Antonio J.
    Argo : how the CIA and Hollywood pulled off the most audacious rescue in history / Antonio
J. Mendez and Matt Baglio.
        p. cm.
    ISBN 978-0-670-02622-7 (hc.)
    ISBN 978-0-14-750973-4 (pbk.)
    1. Iran Hostage Crisis, 1979–1981.   2. United States. Central Intelligence Agency.   3. Canada—
Foreign relations—Iran.   4 Iran—Foreign relations—Canada.   5. Mendez, Antonio J.
6. Diplomats—United States—History—20th century.   I. Baglio, Matt.   II. Title.
    E183.8.I55M46 2012
    955.05'42—dc23
    2012014991

Printed in the United States of America
10 9 8 7 6 5 4 3 2 1

Set in ITC Galliard Std
Designed by Alissa Amell

Praise for *Argo*

"Besides being a talented spy, Mendez is also a gifted storyteller. . . . His latest book is a page-turner." —Associated Press

"Fascinating story . . . This book is an exciting read." —*Deseret News*

"*Argo* is a mesmerizing book; a fast-paced, irresistible read that's equal parts politics, history, and espionage." —*Shelf Awareness*

"This is an amazing and dramatic story of intrigue and deception set against the backdrop of international tension." —*Booklist*

"Fresh and engaging . . . A solid choice for fans of thrillers and international intrigue." —*Kirkus Reviews*

"[A] fast-paced account of a 1979 rescue operation during the Iran hostage crisis of 1979–1981. . . . Details of this dangerous operation inject strong suspense and excitement into the closing chapters."
—*Publishers Weekly*

"One of the most daring and courageous clandestine operations during my career involved efforts to rescue Americans taken hostage in Tehran after our embassy was seized on November 4, 1979. Six Americans managed to escape the U.S. compound and flee to the Canadian embassy, where they were hidden. A very brave CIA officer, Tony Mendez, using commercial cover, entered Iran with false identities for the six and, using techniques that ought to remain secret so they can be used again, managed to get them out of Iran."
—Robert M. Gates, former director of the Central Intelligence Agency and former U.S. Secretary of Defense, in his book *From the Shadows*

"This is a fascinating story about how Tony Mendez and the CIA used a bit of technical expertise and a lot of daring and courage to rescue American hostages in Iran. Tony is emblematic of the extraordinary men and women of the CIA. Most of their stories cannot be told—but fortunately, in *Argo*, Tony has been able to lift the veil of secrecy—just a bit."
—George J. Tenet, former director of the Central Intelligence Agency

"Forget your spy novels, here's how this stuff really works: Two secret agents quietly enter the enemy camp, unarmed but for their wits and experience. Hiding in plain sight, they rescue six virtual hostages under the eyes of their captors, a covert operation seemingly devised in central casting. Now their story can be told—and it makes for one hell of a read."　　—Peter Earnest, retired CIA officer and executive director, International Spy Museum

"This true spy story has it all: guile, audacity, and bravery in a struggle with a fanatic and lethal enemy, a crucial role played by a loyal ally, and a marvelous conspiracy with Hollywood."
　　　　　　　　—R. James Woolsey, former director of the Central Intelligence Agency

"Artist-spy Tony Mendez paints a dramatic portrait of unlikely collaborators—Hollywood, the CIA, and Canada—allied in the common cause of freedom. Mendez fills *Argo* with the drama, pressure, and tension of one of the CIA's most spectacular rescue operations. *Argo* is proof that espionage reality is more riveting than spy fiction."
　　—Robert Wallace, former director, CIA Office of Technical Service

"Tony Mendez is a spy's spy. His work saved my neck on numerous occasions. I laugh quietly to myself when I watch Hollywood's version of disguise technology in today's spy movies—because Tony did it better. What he did in the Argo operation was spine-tingling espionage at its very best."
　　—James M. Olson, former director of CIA Counterintelligence

"*Argo* is a must-read to understand how dangerous risks have been successfully managed by men and women like Tony Mendez operating in secrecy for our protection."
　　　　　　　　—William H. Webster, former director, Central Intelligence and Federal Bureau of Investigation

PENGUIN BOOKS

ARGO

Antonio Mendez served in the CIA for twenty-five years and is a highly decorated officer, one of the top fifty officers in its first fifty years, and a recipient of the Intelligence Star for Valor for the ARGO operation. Author of *The Master of Disguise* and *Spy Dust*, Mendez lives with his family in rural Maryland outside Washington, D.C.

Matt Baglio has worked for a variety of news organizations and magazines. Author of the bestselling book *The Rite: The Making of a Modern Exorcist*, he divides his time between Italy and California.

To Jonna

Some names have been changed to protect the privacy of the individuals involved.

CONTENTS

Contents

INTRODUCTION

Late that Saturday afternoon I was painting in my studio. Outside, the sun was just beginning to fall behind the hills, casting a long dark shadow that covered the valley like a curtain. I liked the half-light in the room.

"Come Rain or Come Shine" poured from the radio. I often listened to music while I worked. It was almost as important to me as the light. I had installed a fine stereo system and if I painted late enough into Saturday night, I could catch Rob Bamberger's Hot Jazz Saturday Night on NPR.

I had been painting since my early childhood, and was working as an artist when the CIA hired me in 1965. I still considered myself to be a painter first and a spy second. Painting had always been an outlet for the tensions that came with my job at the Agency. While there were occasional bureaucrats whose antics brought me to the point of wanting to throttle them, if I could get into my studio and pick up a brush then those pent-up hostilities would melt away.

My studio sat perched above the garage, up a steeply angled set of stairs. It was a large room with windows on three sides. The room had diagonal yellow pine floors covered with a variety of oriental carpets and was furnished with a huge white sofa and some antique pieces that my wife, Karen, had acquired for her interior design business. It was a comfortable space and, most important, it was mine. You needed permission, which I gave pretty freely, to enter. Friends and family knew, however, that when I was in the middle of a project, they should tread lightly.

I had built the studio as I had built the house. Upon returning from a posting overseas in 1974, Karen and I had decided it would be best to raise our three kids away from the grit and crime of Washington, D.C. We'd chosen a forty-acre plot of land in the foothills of the Blue Ridge Mountains, and after clearing a section of woods, I'd spent the better part of three summers constructing the main house while the family and I lived in a log cabin I had also built. The land had a long history. Antietam Battlefield was just up the road and every now and then we would find Civil War relics—buttons, bullets, breastplates—discarded among the leaves and fallen trees bordering our property.

The painting I was working on that afternoon had been triggered by a phrase associated with my job: "Wolf Rain." It had the haunted sound of blue, dreary, dank weather, and spoke to the depths of the wooded landscape, just outside my window, on a winter's night. It conveyed a kind of sorrow that I couldn't explain, but felt that I could paint.

Working on "Wolf Rain" was one of those things you hope happens in your career as an artist—the painting just emerges from nowhere. Perhaps like a character who shoulders his way into a book to take over the narrative. The figure of the wolf was recognizable only by the eyes—it was a floating image in a rain-soaked forest, and you could sense the anguish in its gaze.

If my painting was going well, my brain would instantly go into "alpha" mode, the subjective, creative right-brain state where the breakthroughs happen. Einstein said that the definition of genius is not that you are smarter than everyone else, it's that you're ready to receive the inspiration. That was the definition of "alpha" for me. I would start the painting session by ridding myself of all the assholes at work and then leap to moments of clarity where I would find solutions to problems that I had never considered before. I would be ready to receive.

It was December 19, 1979, and there was much on my mind. Earlier in the week I had been given a memorandum from the U.S. State Department that contained some startling news. Six American diplomats had escaped from the militant-overrun U.S. embassy in Tehran and were hiding out at the residences of the Canadian ambassador, Ken Taylor, and his senior immigration officer, John Sheardown. The six appeared to be safe for the moment, but there was no guarantee they would remain so; in the wake of the embassy takeover, militants were combing the city looking for any American they could find. The six Americans had been in hiding for almost two months. How much longer could they hold out?

The news of their escape had come as a bit of a surprise to me. I had spent the previous month down at the CIA engrossed in the wider problem. On November 4, a group of Iranian militants had stormed the U.S. embassy in Tehran and taken more than sixty-six Americans hostage. The militants accused the Americans of "spying" and trying to undermine the country's nascent Islamic Revolution, all of this while the Iranian government, led by the Ayatollah Khomeini, lent its support.

At the time of the takeover, I was working as the chief of the CIA's worldwide disguise operations in the Office of Technical

Services (OTS). Over the course of my then fourteen-year career, I had conducted numerous clandestine operations in far-flung places, disguised agents and case officers, and helped to rescue defectors and refugees from behind the Iron Curtain.

In the immediate aftermath of the attack, my team and I had been working on preparing the disguises, false documents, and cover stories for the various aliases that any advance team would need in order to infiltrate Iran. Then, in the midst of these preparations, the memo from the State Department arrived.

As I applied a dark glaze across the underpainting of the canvas, it immediately transformed the mood of the work. The piercing eyes of the wolf suddenly came alive like two golden orbs. I stared, transfixed. The image had triggered something. The State Department appeared to be taking a wait-and-see approach with the six Americans, which I found to be problematic. I had recently been to Iran on a covert operation and I knew the dangers firsthand. At any moment they could be discovered. The city was full of eyes, watching, searching. If the six Americans had to run, where would they go? The crowds of thousands of people chanting outside the American embassy in Tehran each day gave no doubt that, if captured, the six would almost certainly be thrown in jail and perhaps even lined up in front of a firing squad. I had always told my team that there are two kinds of exfiltrations: those with hostile pursuit and those without. We couldn't afford to wait until the six Americans were on the run. It would be almost impossible to get them out then.

My son Ian walked into the studio. "What's up?" he asked. He walked over to the painting and scrutinized it as only the seventeen-year-old son of the artist could. "Nice, Dad," he pronounced, stepping back to get a better perspective. "But it needs more blue." He'd barely noticed the eyes of the wolf.

"Get your butt out of here, Ian. I'll be in for dinner in about thirty minutes. Tell your mom, will you?"

On the radio Ella broke into a rendition of "Just One of Those Things," an early version, and I began to clean my brushes in the turpentine and put the caps back on the oil paints. My palette, which had built up over the years, resembled a bunch of brightly colored stalagmites sitting on an oval board with a thumbhole through it. At this point it was too heavy to pick up, but it contained fragments of every painting done in my studio.

As I put away my brushes, the initial stages of a plan began to emerge. Not only would we need to create new identities as well as disguises for the six Americans, but someone would have to infiltrate Iran, link up with them, and assess their ability to carry it off.

A million questions began running through my mind. How was I going to convince six innocent American diplomats who had no covert training that they could successfully escape from Iran? How was I going to create a cover story that would account for the presence of this group in a country caught up in the throes of a revolution? Despite having done dozens of "exfiltrations," I could see that this was going to be one of my most challenging missions to date.

I turned off the radio and the lights and stood for a moment in the darkness, looking out the window and through the night to the glow of the chandelier in the greenhouse. Espionage is an instrument of statecraft, I mused. If conducted properly and professionally, there are international rules of engagement. In the case of the revolutionary government of Iran, however, the only rule was that there weren't any.

1

WELCOME TO THE REVOLUTION

The call went out over the radio network a little after ten o'clock in the morning: "Recall! Recall! All marines to Post One!" The voice was that of Al Golacinski, the chief security officer of the U.S. embassy in Tehran. The date was November 4, 1979, and a large crowd of "militant students" had just broken through the front gates and was pouring into the compound.

The embassy was massive. It took up nearly twenty-seven acres and was surrounded by a high brick wall. Inside, there were dozens of buildings and warehouses, the ambassador's residence, an athletic field, tennis courts, even a swimming pool. In addition, the compound was located right in the heart of downtown Tehran, and was bordered on all sides by some of the city's most heavily trafficked streets. When you added it all up, it meant that the embassy was a security nightmare. Nearly a dozen U.S. Marines were stationed at the compound, but their job was mainly to provide internal protection.

For this reason, the security plan hatched by Golacinski called for all personnel to head toward the chancery, a large three-story building that had been fortified with window grills, blast shields, and time-coded locks. The second floor could be sealed off by a thick steel door, which would theoretically allow the Americans to hold out for several hours. Every embassy in the world is dependent on the host government to provide external security, and it was hoped that these precautions would give the Iranian government enough time to organize a response and send help.

The embassy had been attacked once before, nine months previously, on February 14, 1979, just one month after Mohammad Reza Pahlavi, the shah of Iran, had fled the country. During that attack, a group of Marxist guerrillas had stormed the embassy in a hail of gunfire and held the staffers hostage for four hours.

At the time, Iran was a chaotic mess. The Ayatollah Khomeini had returned triumphantly from exile in Paris and the shah's government had quickly collapsed. The army soon followed suit and in the vacuum the diverse factions who had banded together to oust the shah (leftists, nationalists, Soviet-sponsored communists, hard-line Islamicists) had splintered and were now fighting it out among each other. Armed men roamed the streets and revenge killings were rampant. Small gangs called *komiteh* (committees) sprang up across the country, carving out territories of control. Beholden to no one except whatever mullah they claimed allegiance to, these gangs amounted to little more than thugs, and began enforcing their own brand of revolutionary justice at the barrel of a gun. Amid this confusion, Khomeini and his inner circle had installed a provisional government to manage the country while the Assembly of Experts worked diligently behind the scenes to draft a new constitution.

It wasn't long before the provisional government had sent a

ragtag group of men to kick the occupiers out, but the Valentine's Day takeover would have important repercussions for the events to follow. For one, the U.S. embassy staff was drastically reduced (at full strength the embassy employed nearly a thousand people). Second, and perhaps even more important, it gave the impression that the Iranian government would honor its commitment to protect the embassy and the diplomats working inside.

After the Marxist guerrillas were evicted, the protection of the embassy was assigned to a group of komiteh, who took over one of the small buildings near the front of the compound and patrolled the grounds. It wasn't until the summer that a more permanent security force was assigned to guard the embassy, but even by the most optimistic of assessments it was only token.

In light of the danger exposed by this first attack, one might ask why the embassy wasn't simply closed down. For starters, Iran was just too important to the strategic interests of the United States. Not only did the country hold vast oil reserves, but for more than twenty-five years it had served as a staunch ally and buffer against the Soviet Union, which shared a sixteen-hundred-mile border with Iran. It was no secret that the Soviets desired a warm-water port and wished to increase their influence in the Persian Gulf. So rather than sever ties, the Carter administration began cautiously working with the provisional government and the U.S. embassy in Iran remained open for business.

I t may seem odd today to think that Iran and the United States were once allies, but everything must be understood in terms of the Great Game waged between the Soviet Union and America.

In earlier times, the United States seemed content to observe Iran from the sidelines. Then known as Persia (it wouldn't be named Iran until 1935), the country was like the knot in the center of a tug-of-war match between Russia and Great Britain—a role that Iran managed with great skill, playing one nation off the other. Then World War II happened and the geopolitics of the region were upended. Suddenly Moscow and London were allies, and in their quest to protect oil and overland shipping routes into Russia, they decided to jointly occupy the country. Worried that the Iranian monarch, Reza Shah, was leaning toward an alliance with Nazi Germany, the two nations had him deposed and installed his twenty-one-year-old son, Mohammad Reza Pahlavi, to the throne.

After the war, the United States invested heavily in Iran, both economically and militarily. Stalin had only reluctantly withdrawn his troops from northern Iran in 1946, and the thinking in Washington was that he would use the slightest pretext to invade again. Just as concerning was the potential for the Soviets to undermine the shah's government through clandestine means. Iran's communist Tudeh Party was growing in power and openly supported the aims of Moscow.

As a result, it was with trepidation that America watched in 1951 as the shah's power was slowly stripped away by an Iranian lawyer named Mohammed Mosaddeq. Mosaddeq had risen to prominence on the back of a campaign to nationalize the British-owned Anglo-Iranian Oil Company (AIOC), a popular move among Iranians who had long felt exploited by the British. Caught up in a wave of nationalism, Mosaddeq became a hero and was eventually nominated prime minister.

As one would expect, in response to the Iranians' attempt to nationalize the AIOC, the British soon instigated what amounted to a boycott of Iranian oil, which sent the local economy into a tailspin. In the ensuing turmoil, the coalition that had supported Mosaddeq began to splinter.

Nobody in Washington believed that Mosaddeq was a communist, but concern began to mount when he aligned himself with the Tudeh Party. The final straw for the Eisenhower administration came when intelligence uncovered that the Soviets were about to give Mosaddeq twenty million dollars in aid.

In light of these threats, the White House ordered CIA director Allen Dulles to work with the British to overthrow Mosaddeq.

With the benefit of hindsight, it's easy to say that the Eisenhower administration overreacted. However, in the heat of the Cold War, America's leaders saw a very different world than the one that exists today. In it, the Soviets were on the march everywhere, installing puppet regimes in Eastern Europe and supporting uprisings in Italy, France, and Greece. It's also important to remember that the United States was involved in a bloody war at the time in Korea, which Eisenhower had inherited from Truman. Iran could just as easily become another front.

In the spring of 1953, Kermit "Kim" Roosevelt, chief of the Near East Division of the CIA's Directorate of Plans, was granted one million dollars and tasked with carrying out the operation to overthrow Mosaddeq, known as TPAJAX, or Operation AJAX.

The plan called for the use of propaganda and political action to undermine Mosaddeq's support, but, as usual, things didn't go according to plan. Mosaddeq had been warned of the countercoup and had some of the plotters arrested even before the operation could get under way. However, with the help of massive public demonstrations, many of them organized by Roosevelt, Mosaddeq was forced to resign and the shah was swept to power.

In terms of its Cold War strategy of containment, Washington considered the operation to be a massive foreign policy success, and Kermit Roosevelt was heralded as a hero. Upon meeting him, the shah famously said, "I owe my throne to God, my people, the army—and you!"

In the wake of the operation the shah quickly worked out an agreement with the oil giant AIOC, and Iran became a stable, pro-Western ally, providing the United States with a steady flow of oil as well as a series of listening posts along the Soviet-Iran border that allowed it to eavesdrop on Russian intercontinental ballistic missile launches.

Regardless of these strategic advantages, however, there is no denying that the 1953 countercoup had major consequences for the long-term relations between the United States and Iran.

Many opponents of Operation AJAX blamed the United States for acting selfishly to protect its own interests, to the detriment of Iran and its people. Ironically, as the historical record shows, the countercoup would not have succeeded if it hadn't been for the support of a sizable faction of Iranians who'd also had much to gain by securing the shah's power. However, the popular myth in 1979 among Iranians, ever distrustful of foreign intervention, was that the CIA had single-handedly ousted a democratic leader while imposing a tyrant in his place. While not entirely accurate, it painted a picture that many Iranians were eager to believe.

After returning to power, the shah aligned himself with the West and immediately set about trying to legitimize his reign. He ushered in a series of Westernized reforms and spent lavishly to create a well-trained and modern military. Both efforts would put him at odds with his people, who would later claim he had destroyed their traditional way of life and at the same time squandered the nation's wealth in an attempt to appease Washington.

Over time he grew more and more autocratic, tamping down any form of dissent with the help of his brutal secret police known by the acronym SAVAK.

As tended to happen during the Great Game, however, successive American administrations decided to take the good with the bad and outwardly supported the shah, even while privately encouraging him to cut the systemic corruption of his regime and curb the abuses of SAVAK.

The shah seemed neither willing nor capable to do either.

With most avenues for political dissent gone, the masses had turned to the mullahs for support, and the clergy used their newfound power to denounce the shah as a tool of the West. The most outspoken of these critics was a cleric by the name of Ruhollah Khomeini. Born in 1902, Khomeini had made a name for himself among the religious community of Iran by authoring numerous tracts against Iran's secular leadership, including the shah's father, Reza. Then in 1961, he would take on the shah directly, decrying the shah's pro-Western policies—specifically those enfranchising women and non-Muslims—as being antithetical to the true spirit of Islam. However, unknown even to his own followers, who believed he would support a moderate Islamic democracy once the shah had abdicated, Khomeini's real aim was to create a government that was strictly beholden to Islamic law and was ruled unquestionably by him.

Too powerful to arrest or kill, Khomeini was exiled by the shah to Turkey in 1964 and then eventually to Najaf, in southern Iraq. From there the cleric would prove to be a resourceful political operator. For the next fourteen years he would continue to give sermons lambasting the evils of the shah and America, which were smuggled back into Iran and sold in the bazaars as cassette tapes.

By the fall of 1978, the country was on the brink of collapse. A succession of riots and strikes had led to violent clashes between the shah's security forces and Khomeini's supporters. After a series of last-ditch measures—including a military government—had failed to stem the tide, the shah was finally forced to leave Iran on January 16, 1979. In his wake he left a country teetering on the edge, and it would take only ten days for the remnants of his government and the army to fall apart.

While there had been many signs that the shah's regime was on the verge of crumbling, the suddenness with which it happened caught the White House, as well as the intelligence community, completely off guard. Even as late as August of 1978, a National Intelligence Estimate famously reported that Iran was not in a "revolutionary or even a pre-revolutionary situation." As to how we at the CIA and the White House could have been so wildly off the mark, there is no easy answer. The shah had maintained an iron grip on his country for nearly twenty-five years, and the common wisdom was that despite the unrest he would weather the storm. After the fact, it was revealed that many in Washington had assumed the shah would use any force necessary to save his regime, and they were baffled when he failed to do so. Even the U.S. ambassador to Iran at the time, Bill Sullivan, believed the shah's government would survive; by the time he changed his tune, on

November 9, 1978, there was little that could be done. Through-out the struggles of 1978, there was no clear strategy for meeting with the opposition groups, partly because of the fear that it might undermine the shah's regime. In the end, though, perhaps the big-gest reason for the intelligence failure was that the U.S. govern-ment had invested too much importance in the person of the shah and not enough in the people of Iran. So when the cracks in the regime began to appear, the policy makers in Washington refused to acknowledge them because they simply had no other alternative than to support the shah.

Ironically, the shah was said to be somewhat nervous about the election of Jimmy Carter. The shah's main concern, it seems, had been Carter's stated goal of making human rights a central tenet of his presidency. Sensitive to public opinion, the shah was apparently concerned that Carter might think he was a tyrant. He needn't have worried. As late as New Year's Eve 1978, just one week before a series of violent clashes would touch off the revolution, President Carter visited Tehran and reassured the shah of America's firm commitment by calling Iran an "island of stability in one of the more troubled areas of the world." While Carter may have had good reasons to support the shah, or he had no alternative given the strategic alliance created under the necessities of the Cold War, this perceived hypocrisy did not go unnoticed by the masses in Iran. The American president was now considered to be a close friend of the shah, and it wasn't long before crowds of angry dem-onstrators began denouncing Carter's name alongside that of the shah's.

Despite the Iranians' rhetoric, there seemed to be some com-mon ground between the two countries. The shah, for one, had purchased vast amounts of American military equipment during the Nixon and Ford administrations, some of which still had to be delivered. In addition, Iran had several billion dollars deposited in U.S. banks, money the revolutionary government would desperately need to stay afloat. During the fall of 1979, Khomeini had yet to solidify his power, and the country was being loosely run by the relatively "moderate" government of Prime Minister Mehdi Bazargan. In June of 1979, the Iranians accepted the appointment of Bruce Laingen as the U.S. embassy's chargé d'affaires, and it appeared the two countries were on track to normalize relations.

Fleeing Iran, the shah spent several months as an international "fugitive," until President Carter was persuaded to admit the deposed ruler for humanitarian reasons, when it was discovered he was suffering from lymphoma and needed emergency medical treatment. Yet even as he admitted the shah, Carter knew he was taking a risk. Khomeini had been calling for the shah to return to face "crimes," and Carter was worried about reprisals. In a breakfast meeting at the White House with his staff, he reiterated his concerns, asking them, "What course of action will you recommend to me if the Americans in Iran are seized or killed?" No one had an answer.

News of the shah's arrival in America immediately touched off a wave of anger and paranoia among the Iranian population, which feared the United States was conspiring to reinstall him. For months, Iranian newspapers had been running fabricated stories claiming the United States was behind every setback that befell the country. Khomeini, searching for a way to strengthen his control, added fuel to the flames, calling on students to expand their attacks on America in the hopes that the United States would be pressured to return the deposed ruler. Predictably, Iranians set their sights on the most obvious target they could find: the American embassy in Tehran.

The morning of November 4, 1979, had started off just like any other, and for the Americans heading to work that day there was no reason to suspect that the embassy was in the crosshairs of a massive assault. Bruce Laingen had chaired a morning meeting of the department heads, after which he, along with Vic Tomseth and Mike Howland, had gone to Iran's foreign ministry to discuss obtaining diplomatic immunity for American military personnel stationed in Iran.

One of the first people to see the militants enter the compound was John Graves, who was the public affairs officer. Graves had been in Iran for more than a year and had been through the Valentine's Day attack.

The press office was located just off the motor pool near the front gate. Somebody had cut the chain looped through the gate, and a large crowd of demonstrators came surging in. Most of them were women carrying signs that read, DON'T BE AFRAID and WE ONLY WANT TO SET IN—mistakenly using the English "set" instead of "sit" in the latter. The preponderance of females in the first wave was actually by design, as the militants felt that the U.S. Marines would be hesitant to fire on the women. As Graves stood by the window he watched one of the militants approach an Iranian policeman who was supposed to be protecting the embassy, and the two men embraced. Graves wasn't surprised.

As the militants dispersed throughout the compound, the rest of the embassy personnel were slow to react. Demonstrations and crowds shouting "Death to America" and "Down with the shah" had become an almost daily occurrence, so much so that the Americans working inside referred to them as background noise. To complicate matters, the militants had chosen to launch their attack on National Students Day, an event commemorating the death of a group of students killed by the shah's forces during a demonstration at the University of Tehran the year before. The demonstration had drawn several million students, and the planners were able to use this larger crowd to camouflage their assault.

In a matter of minutes, the militants were able to completely cut off the chancery. Staffers and embassy personnel, now fully aware of what was going on, stood on chairs to peer out windows. Some crowded around closed-circuit monitors located down in the security room. What they saw startled them. The embassy grounds were swarming with militants who were waving signs and chanting, "We only want to set in!" Then, one by one, the closed-circuit monitors went blank as the cameras were yanked out of the walls.

Most of the embassy personnel were calm, some even annoyed. It seemed as if the students were just going to march around the embassy grounds chanting and cheering until it was time to go home. Over and over, voices rose above the din—some with the aid of megaphones—shouting, "We mean you no harm! We only want to set in!"

Unbeknownst to the Americans, this was not some overzealous protest march but a well-coordinated assault. Calling themselves

Muslim Students Following the Imam's Line, the students had cased the embassy for many days and had drawn up detailed maps. They'd cut strips of cloth to use as blindfolds for nearly one hundred hostages and had even stockpiled food to feed their captives.

The plan was to occupy the embassy for three days, at which point they would read a list of grievances against the shah and America. Their principal hope was that the attack would weaken the position of the moderate Bazargan government by forcing it into a tough situation. If Bazargan came to the rescue of the Americans, then Iranians would see him and other moderates in the government for what they were: puppets of the West.

Some of the militants carried makeshift weapons such as bike chains, boards, even hammers. At least a few carried pistols, contradicting later claims that the assault was completely nonviolent.

After locking down the chancery, the marines quickly donned their riot gear. They loaded pistols and shotguns and took up positions throughout the embassy. The adrenaline was pumping and some seemed eager for a fight. One lay down in one of the offices on his belly with ammunition easily within reach, sighting down the barrel of his shotgun sniper-style as he scanned the window.

Meanwhile Laingen, Tomseth, and Howland were in a car on their way back from their meeting at the foreign ministry. They had just pulled out into traffic when Al Golacinski called on the radio and told them to turn around. "There's hundreds of people swarming all over the embassy grounds," he said. The three realized that even if they reached the embassy, they probably wouldn't be able to make it inside. They quickly decided that the best course of action would be to head back to the foreign ministry and try to organize help from there.

The last thing Laingen told Golacinski before signing off was to make sure that the marines didn't open fire. If even one of the marines fired, then they would likely have a bloodbath on their hands.

"What about tear gas?" Golacinski asked him.

"Only as a last resort," Laingen responded.

By this time, the staffers on the second floor of the chancery began to realize that the attack was more serious than they had at first thought. Some of the marines and other Americans, including John Graves, who'd been working in the outer buildings, had already been captured, and the Americans in the chancery watched from the second-floor windows as their colleagues were blindfolded, had their hands tied, and were marched toward the ambassador's residence near the back of the compound.

Don Hohman, an army medic who was at the Bijon apartments across the street from the back gate, radioed Golacinski to tell him that a group of Iranians had broken in over there as well. Up on the fourth floor, he could hear them kicking down doors and searching the apartments below. Golacinski realized there was little he could do; he told Hohman he was on his own. (Hohman would later be captured as he tried to scale down the outside of the building.)

At the moment, Golacinski had bigger problems than Hohman; word had reached him on the radio that the chancery had just been breached. Despite the fact that several million dollars had recently been spent to fortify the building, the militants had found the structure's one weak spot: a basement window that had been left unbarred as a fire escape. In fact, the intruders seemed to know beforehand exactly where it was.

With the militants inside the chancery's basement, Golacinski ordered everyone, including the Iranian staffers waiting on the first floor, up to the second floor. (The second floor was normally considered off-limits to the local employees.) In a fit of bravery or stupidity, depending on how you look at it, Golacinski then asked Laingen over the radio if he could go outside to "reason" with the crowd, which now numbered well over a thousand. Laingen told him he could do so only if he could guarantee his own safety, which he could not. Golacinski went anyway, and he was soon captured and marched back to the chancery at gunpoint.

On the second floor of the chancery, marines and staffers began piling up furniture behind the steel door. The central hallway was crowded now and everyone shared worried glances. Some of the Iranian employees started crying. Marines walked among everyone handing out gas masks. Other marines cocked and recocked their shotguns. The mood was tense.

Elsewhere in the building, a small group of Americans was busy destroying documents and dismantling sensitive communications equipment so it couldn't fall into the hands of the militants. The order to do so had been slow in coming from Laingen, since it was hoped that the demonstration would end without incident. A few of the more enterprising staff members had already begun destroying documents inside the embassy's ultrasecure communications room, referred to as the "vault" because it could be sealed off by a large steel safelike door. Besides housing the communications equipment, the vault, which was about twelve feet by twelve feet, also contained a barrel-like device used to pulverize documents. However, the machine often jammed, so somebody had brought in a commercial shredder that cut papers into long strips. But the going was slow, and rather than destroying the documents completely, it left a pile of strips on the floor.

The situation was deteriorating fast. The militants led Al Gola-cinski into the basement of the chancery and then marched him up to the second floor, where the Americans had barricaded them-selves behind the reinforced door. The stairwell was filling with tear gas and his eyes stung. Someone waved a burning magazine in front of his face and he recoiled in fear. "Don't burn me!" he shouted. Then the barrel of a gun was shoved to the back of his head and he was given an ultimatum: tell them to open this door or you die.

Golacinski shouted through the metal door, telling his col-leagues that there was no point resisting. He said the militants had already captured eight Americans (this was his own assessment) and that they only wanted to read a statement and then leave. "This is just like February 14," he said.

John Limbert, a political officer who spoke fluent Farsi, volun-teered to go outside and see if he could persuade them to free Go-lacinski. At first the militants were surprised when he admonished them like children in their own language, telling them that the Revolutionary Guard was on the way to kick them out. They knew he was bluffing, and in a matter of minutes he was captured and given the same option as Golacinski: get your friends to open this door or we shoot you.

Laingen had by now realized that resisting further was hopeless. Despite their best efforts at the Iranian foreign ministry, he and Tomseth had been unable get the Iranian government to help. Us-ing the telephone in the foreign minister's office, he called the U.S. embassy and told Ann Swift, the embassy's senior political officer, to surrender. Swift and two other staffers were manning a bank of phones in Bruce Laingen's outer office. As the most senior official present at the embassy, she was doing her best to keep the lines of communication open. Early in the assault, she had called the Operations Center at the U.S. State Department and had been put through to three senior officials, including Hal Saunders, the assistant secretary of state for Near Eastern and South Asian Affairs. Saunders was still on the phone with Swift an hour later when Laingen told her it was time to give up. "We're going to let them in," she told Saunders over the phone.

Realizing the seriousness of the situation, Saunders then relayed this information to President Carter's national security adviser, Zbigniew Brzezinski, who then called the president at four in the morning. Carter was "deeply disturbed but reasonably confident" that the Iranian government would quickly remove the militants, much as it had on February 14.

After surrendering, the Americans in the chancery resigned themselves to their fate. When the steel door was finally opened, the breathless mob flooded in. The staffers inside the vault would continue to hold out for another hour or so destroying documents, but in the end they too would be forced to give up.

The original security plan had called for the embassy staff to hold on for two hours until the Iranian government could send help. As it turned out, the plan had worked to perfection. The only problem, of course, was that the help never came.

News of the embassy attack reached me on Sunday morning while I was standing at the kitchen counter sipping my first cup of coffee. This was my favorite part of the weekend— when my family was still asleep and the house was quiet. I had a small transistor radio tuned to NPR and I half listened to it as I flipped through the Sunday newspaper. Outside, a light dusting of snow covered the ground and the sky was cold and gray. I was wondering how much firewood I was going to have to cut before I could get into my studio to paint. We had a large greenhouse attached to the front of the house and I was just about to step into it to watch the snow when the NPR broadcast was interrupted by news of the attack.

Events were still unfolding, but the overall picture was clear. A mob had stormed the embassy and the lives of nearly seventy American diplomats were in danger.

My mind flashed back to April 1979, the last time I had set foot inside the U.S. embassy in Tehran. As a technical officer in the CIA's Office of Technical Services with more than fourteen years of experience at the time, I had been asked to infiltrate Iran in the midst of the revolution to help rescue a "blue striper," or top Iranian agent, code-named RAPTOR. As the chief of the disguise branch, I was charged with coming up with a convincing disguise that would allow the agent, a former colonel in the Iranian army, to walk past the security controls at Mehrabad Airport and onto a commercial flight.

The operation was similar to countless others I'd done in Southeast Asia and other distant parts of the world, but it was far from routine. Violence had exploded all across the country and revolutionaries were hunting down former members of the shah's regime. Time was running out for the colonel. He'd spent the winter hiding in his grandmother's tin-roofed attic, where snow dripped down on him while a group of Revolutionary Guards rifled through the apartment below. By the time I got to him he was badly shaken.

I had used the library in the embassy as part of my research for his disguise. Then I spent the better part of a week preparing him, training him, using all the tricks I'd learned over the course of my career to get him out of the country alive.

After listening to the news for a few minutes, I tiptoed into the bedroom and quietly picked up my car keys and my Agency badge. I stopped in the kitchen to scribble a note to Karen explaining where I had gone, then picked up the phone and called the duty officer for my section. On the weekends it would be his job to monitor all the cable traffic and let me know if I needed to come in. The details of the attack were still sketchy, but cables were flooding in by the minute. All of us at the CIA were aware of the dangers that the embassy personnel were up against in a place as unpredictable as revolutionary Iran. Among the Americans were three CIA colleagues of mine who no doubt would be singled out for special treatment if the Iranians were able to identify them. I only hoped that the staffers had had enough time to destroy all the sensitive documents inside the embassy. When I finally got the duty officer on the line, he only confirmed what I had already suspected. Things were rolling down at the office. It was time to go to work.

2

PICKING UP THE PIECES

In 1979, the headquarters for OTS was located in Foggy Bottom, on a small hill on the District side of the Teddy Roosevelt Bridge, just north of the John F. Kennedy Center for the Performing Arts. The small collection of neoclassical limestone and brick buildings was unremarkable by most accounts. Once a part of the original Naval Observatory in the late 1800s, the buildings were eventually taken over during World War II by America's first intelligence agency, the Office of Strategic Services (OSS). Commanded by Major General William "Wild Bill" Donovan, the OSS had been staffed by some of the most colorful characters in the history of espionage, including con artists, second-story men, experts in counterfeiting, magicians, even actors and Ivy League blue bloods. World War II is full of the exploits of these daring operatives. The fledgling spy service sent operatives behind German and Japanese lines and created ingenious devices such as cigarette pistols, matchbox cameras, even exploding flour. It also paved the way for the

CIA. In fact, much of the structure, operational methods, and procedures that the CIA would later come to use evolved directly from the OSS.

OTS, meanwhile, sprang from the research and development branch of the OSS. Originally headed by a chemist, Stanley Lovell, the R&D branch would play an integral role in developing and pushing the capabilities of OSS operatives, while paving the way for future techs such as myself.

Perhaps one of the most important legacies that the R&D branch left to later generations of OTS techs was the way in which it worked with outside contractors in order to develop new technologies. This allowed the OSS to take full advantage of the modern manufacturing and technological capacity of the U.S. private sector, which was very different from the way that other foreign services, such as MI6 or the KGB, went about developing their new technologies. Eventually this gave us a huge advantage when it came to defeating our Soviet counterparts, who relied on state-run facilities and bureaucratic thinking. Part of the reason for this outsourcing was necessity, since Lovell didn't have the funds necessary to build laboratories from scratch. By taking full advantage of the private sector, however, OTS was able to stay on the cutting edge.

In 1965, when I entered on duty at the CIA's Technical Services Division, or TSD (it would be renamed OTS in 1973), we characterized our office and our work as mirroring the character Q from the James Bond films. We were the CIA's gadget makers, the suppliers of the technical wherewithal necessary for our operations officers to successfully steal our enemies' secrets.

Our organization was part of the operational element of the CIA called the Directorate of Operations, or DO. There were three other directorates—Administration, Science and Technology, and Intelligence. The work of the DO was primarily overseas, which meant our equipment and our expertise were exercised around the world, though typically not in the United States.

There were essentially two groups that made up our office. Half of the officers in our development and engineering division were chemists, physicists, mechanical and electrical engineers, and an assortment of PhD scientists who specialized in extremely narrow fields, such as batteries, hot air balloons, special inks, you name it. These were the folks who designed and built our gadgetry. The other half were part of the operations division, the people who operated the equipment and who taught our case officers and foreign agents how to use it.

A listing of the capabilities will give a hint of the robust possibilities at the beck and call of the CIA. In no particular order, those capabilities were audio, photo/video, disguise, documents, and concealments. We also had experts in graphology, psychology and parapsychology, forensics, and many other esoteric disciplines. If you needed technical support for your operation, we would provide it, and if it didn't exist, we could invent it.

My office was located in Central Building, which also housed the authentication branch, the disguise labs, the artists' bullpen, and the documents section. Across a small courtyard stood the imposing neoclassical South Building, the location of OTS headquarters. On November 4, 1979, my title was "chief of disguise," but I was actually in the process of being promoted to "chief, authentication branch," a job that would put me in charge of the CIA's worldwide disguise operations, as well as any cases involving false documentation and the forensic monitoring of these documents for counterterrorism purposes.

Moving from chief of disguise to chief of authentication was a big step, and I was eager to make the transition. I was well grounded in disguise, and felt perfectly capable of moving on. When it came to my professional abilities and knowledge, I honestly felt that there was probably nobody else as good as me, with the exception of somebody in the KGB whom I didn't know about yet. "Cocky but confident" is probably how I was seen by my peers, "up-and-coming" by my bosses. As for me, I hadn't yet encountered a situation or a foe that I didn't feel up to tackling.

I had never set out to become a spy. There was never a little voice in my ear suggesting I sign up for a job in the clandestine services. In fact, I was convinced that my life's career would be as a fine artist. In several ways that career materialized, just not in the form that I had anticipated.

I was born poor in Eureka, Nevada—according to *National Geographic*, the loneliest town on the loneliest road in America. It's probably a good thing I didn't know that when I was growing up. I thought things were just fine.

My mom, Neva June Tognoni, came from an old Nevada family and was the only daughter in a family of boys. Her three brothers had gone on to relative success in this western state: one became a state senator, while the other two were attorneys, often representing mining cases. Her grandfather J. C. Tognoni, an immigrant from the northern Italian town of Chiavenna, had struck it rich with the largest gold strike in the history of the state. As quickly as he made his fortune, however, he lost it. Neva June never got to taste the riches that her grandfather had enjoyed; instead, she was set aside, over and over, as her brothers were given the education and opportunities she was denied.

This was my mom's story. She, in turn, passed her experience on to her family of four girls and two boys. My sisters were favored over my brother and me, in an attempt to right the cosmic wrong that had been her lot.

My dad was named John Mendez. He was incredibly handsome and young when I was born, just twenty-three years old, but I never really knew him. He worked in the copper mines in Nevada, where he was killed when I was three years old, crushed by a cart full of ore. My father's family had a murky background; it's quite possible that my father's actual name was Manuel Gomez. The story was that my dad's mother was killed in a car accident in Los Angeles, and in a custody dispute between my grandfather and the sister of his deceased wife, my grandfather took his two boys, ran away, and changed the family name.

My mom talked about my dad constantly when we were growing up. She had been madly in love with him, and they were both so young when she lost him.

My brother John and I worked long and hard in the barren desert surrounding Eureka, hauling wood through the snow in a little red wagon during the winter, selling newspapers on the train that made a nine-minute stop in our town once a day, and harvesting and selling bat guano to the Mormon ladies on the other side of town, as fertilizer for their gardens. We made enough money for the occasional movie for the six of us, and sometimes an ice cream at the local confectionery. My mom had no extra money for such luxuries.

From an early age I had loved to draw. Since we were so poor I had to make do with what I could find. I used a sharpened stick to scratch figures into the ground, a lump of coal on an old board or piece of cardboard, a pencil on a brown paper bag. When I was five or six, my mom came home from town with a package for each of us. My gift was a small watercolor kit, the most basic kind. My mom said, "Tony, you're going to be an artist." It was not a suggestion. Remarkably, during my future career at the CIA, I would often carry a similar watercolor kit on my world travels, just one of the many tools I used over the course of my espionage career.

After high school, I attended the University of Colorado at Boulder for a year, but took time off to work as a plumber's assistant to help support the family. It was around this time that I met my wife, Karen Smith, and five years later we'd had three children: the oldest, Amanda, followed by Toby, and later Ian. By then I was in Denver working for Martin Marietta as a tool designer/artist-illustrator and running my own design studio. The work was mundane—drawing the wiring diagrams for the Titan missiles that were being installed in silos across America—but it paid the bills. Then one day in 1965 I saw something that would forever change my life. It was an ad in the *Denver Post* looking for applicants to work as artists overseas for the U.S. Navy. I sent in a response with some samples to the P.O. box in Salt Lake City. I told Karen that it might be refreshing to try something new.

When I met with the representative from the government, it was not in the federal building in downtown Denver, but in a motel room on Colfax Avenue on the west side of the city. The blinds were closed. My meeting was with a somewhat shady-looking character who wore his snap-brim hat indoors like an old-time detective. He flashed a government credential at me and hefted a bottle of Jim Beam up onto the table.

"Son," he said, pouring each of us a glass of bourbon, "this is not the navy."

No kidding! I thought.

In fact, he told me, he was from the CIA. I didn't know what the CIA was at the time, but tried to look interested as I listened to his sales pitch.

"I don't know what kind of artist they're looking for," he said. "I sent them a few résumés, but they didn't seem quite right. Here—look at this. You will understand it better than I do."

I read through the (classified!) recruitment guide and understood immediately that the kind of artist this CIA recruiter had in mind would quickly be locked up in a federal prison if he tried to practice this kind of "art" on his own. What they were looking for were old-fashioned forgers. Technically, this was not a problem for me. It was a matter of hand-eye coordination, along with an ability to manipulate the materials, and I could surely do that.

I went home and read up on the CIA, and the more I read the more interested I became. I could serve my country, see the world, and possibly make an impact on the events of the day. I put together an artist's sample of my work, including a Bulgarian postage stamp, part of a U.S. dollar bill, and some Chinese grass writing, and mailed it off to the Agency recruiter in Salt Lake City. The summons to Washington came within a few weeks.

In D.C., I had several levels of interviews. It was clear that they liked my samples, and the quality of my work was never a problem. In the end, the question became a moral issue. I met with the deputy director of TSD, Sidney Gottlieb, who conducted my last interview.

"You know, Tony," he said, "there are some people who might have a problem doing what we will be asking you to do. Breaking the laws of foreign governments. Lying to your friends and family, who will want to know where you work and what you do. Will you have a problem with that? Over a long period of time?"

I seriously considered what he was saying. This would be a new way of living, a new way of working, a shutting down of some avenues and the opening of doors that I could only imagine. I didn't hesitate. "I think, Dr. Gottlieb, that the truth is not necessarily everyone's business," I said, "especially when your country is relying on you to keep its secrets."

He stood to shake my hand. "You'll do just fine here, Tony," he said.

My first job at the Agency was in the graphics branch, working in the artists' bullpen, learning to work with linguists and experts who had studied foreign travel and security controls. When I arrived at the bullpen, I was the low man on the totem pole. The office was headed by Franco, a heavy-set, jovial, often demanding guy who was also very fair. If you wanted to work a little harder, he made sure you got credit. If you solved problems, you got rewarded. He was a great first boss. His deputy, Ricardo, on the other hand, was very competitive with his staff. If he saw a weakness, he would pounce.

I had many challenging projects over the twenty-two months I worked in the headquarters bullpen. Perhaps the most difficult of these, though, was dealing with Ricardo. Everyone would leave their artwork mounted down on their desk at the end of each day, and Ricardo would come in early the next morning to check everyone's progress, going around to each desk to see how the artist was doing. After he did his inspection he would make very small blue arrows on each artist's work indicating the areas they needed to work on. So first thing in the morning you would come in and see your artwork from the day before and find these small arrows all over it. It seemed he would get a certain pleasure from making those small blue marks. To the artists it was infuriating.

In order to break the tension, we had installed a dartboard, which we would use during breaks. Instead of throwing three darts a standard distance of nine feet, we developed a more macho, high-pressure game—one dart, at a distance of eighteen feet, for a dollar a throw. Ricardo proved to be a master, and could launch a dart with the cool accuracy of a scorpion flicking its tail. What he would love to do was get you in a dart game and take your money in front of the others. When I finally beat him, I wouldn't give him a rematch, and for a time I feared for my life. But he did appreciate my work enough that when he left for an assignment to be chief of graphics at our Far East base a year later, he specifically requested me to be his subordinate, ahead of other artists with more seniority.

As artists we were reproducing mostly personal identity documents that could be used for operational purposes such as travel, renting safe houses or hotel rooms. They could also be used for exfiltrations, false flag recruitment, entrapment, or crossing international borders. The forgeries sometimes were designed to discredit individuals and governments, just like the KGB did to us. Their program was called Special Measures. Our program had no name—we just called it covert action. Other documents that we produced could take the form of disinformation, letters in diaries, bumper stickers, or any other graphics item that could influence events of the day. We were able to reproduce almost anything that was put in front of us; the only restrictions were matters of state-craft, such as currency. Making the other guy's money at that time was considered to be an act of war. But bombing a country with leaflets instead of munitions was a capability that we gladly pro-vided.

After my time in the bullpen, I spent the next seven years, from 1967 to 1974, living and working in Okinawa and Bangkok and other far-off places, traveling the world as an undercover CIA tech-nical officer. Throughout that time I continued to work as an artist-validator, but I also branched out into other areas such as dis-guise and exfiltration, helping to rescue defectors and refugees from behind the Iron Curtain. A big part of this was due to the fact that I had helped to usher in a new "generalist" program, which cross-trained technical officers in various disciplines like disguise or documents or whatever was required for the particular region they would be working in. Not only did this give us a new skill set as technical officers, but it also allowed us to be more agile in re-sponding to the potential needs of our station chiefs and case offi-cers, who often asked techs to do a little bit of everything in the field.

Then, in 1974, I was promoted to chief of disguise and asked to come back to headquarters to run the disguise section. At the time I was only thirty-three years old, and some people didn't take kindly to a young upstart such as myself coming in and telling them what to do.

In the wake of Watergate, morale was near an all-time low in the Agency. Nixon had just left the White House and the Senate was preparing an investigation of the CIA. Blood was in the water. My attitude was that there were still good people working in the Agency and a lot of work to be done. I was eager to get to it.

The 1970s were smack in the middle of the Cold War and there were numerous ongoing cases in the works. The Soviet Union was spreading out into the third world, and as they extended their reach we had greater access to their personnel.

As I pushed through the doors of Central Building on the morning of November 4, 1979, I could see that the crisis was garnering everyone's full attention. Despite the fact that it was a Sunday, the building seemed to be under a state of siege, with people hurrying in every direction. Several carried red-striped secret files; everyone carried grim expressions. I had never seen the building so frenetic—it was as though a silent alarm had gone off. The weekend was officially over.

I headed up to my suite of offices and labs, located on the third floor, to read the cable traffic and meet with my team.

First I popped my head into the office of the deputy chief of OTS operations. Matt, an intense, conservative, but polite man, was sitting behind his desk, handing out cables and talking on the phone.

"Hi, Tony. Welcome. Glad you could make it in," he said, covering the mouthpiece of the phone in his hand and motioning me to a chair with his jacket balled up on it. It was the first time I had seen Matt without his tie. His trademark red hair was uncombed and he didn't look up from the heap of paperwork on his desk.

"Sounds like we've got something to do," I said when he got off the phone.

"Yeah, we are expecting that it's going to get even more hectic around here. Why don't you get caught up and we'll touch base later."

I continued on to my section. Most of my team was already there, some working on other projects unrelated to the hostage crisis. Tim, my deputy, came striding in and yanked off his tie; he'd been coming back from church. Without so much as a hello he began brewing a pot of coffee. I paused at the door to the disguise labs, to see who else had made it in.

When I was first promoted to run the disguise section in 1974, the chief of operations had pulled me aside and tasked me with making the disguise capability of OTS the best it could possibly be, and I set out to make that a reality. At the time, most people thought the disguise branch was nothing more than a group of cosmetologists. The whole concept of disguise wasn't given great merit within the Agency, especially by officers who'd come of age when disguises amounted to nothing more than ill-fitting wigs, mustaches, and hats. There were people who worked at the CIA during that time whose approach to disguise amounted to sitting a case officer in a barber's chair and lecturing him or her on the art of disguise, while providing nothing in the way of materials.

That all changed once I began working with a Hollywood makeup artist in the early 1970s and started to show them what they could accomplish with a little creative thinking. The first such operation involved turning an African American case officer and a Lao cabinet minister into two Caucasians so they could meet in Vientiane, Laos, in 1972. The disguises had been so convincing

that the two men had been able to pass through a roadblock undetected. The episode had opened up the floodgates and changed
everything as far as operational disguise was concerned.

By the mid-1970s, everybody in the disguise branch had to learn
to do a facial impression. Some people who worked there for twenty
years were no longer qualified. But by 1979, we had totally revolu-
tionized the department, creating numerous disguises that could
completely alter a person's appearance and be applied in the dark in
a matter of seconds. As I stood in the doorway and watched the
professionalism of my team at work, I was reminded of just how far
we'd come. They were motivated and ready, and I felt confident that
no matter what challenge lay ahead, they could get the job done.

As I entered my office that morning, I saw a neat stack of about
two hundred cables waiting for me on my desk. This was not unusual; what immediately caught my attention, however, was that a
good number were marked FLASH. This was the highest level of
priority the CIA used (the others being IMMEDIATE, PRIORITY, and
the lowest, ROUTINE). FLASH cables were serious business, and only
ever used in wartime or when U.S. lives were in immediate danger.
Some communicators went their whole careers without ever even
seeing one. In this case I wasn't looking at one, but several dozen.
It was then that the gravity of the situation began to sink in.

That morning, most of us were still confident that the embassy
occupiers would stay only a few hours, as had the group of Marxist
guerrillas on February 14.

In the meantime, our first order of business was a tall one. Now
that the embassy had been overrun, we would need to try to reestablish some kind of human intelligence network in Iran. Normally, when you have a nation in flux, or are in a denied area such

as Moscow, you build a network of stay-behind agents, citizens who agree to stay in contact with the West after any untoward incident and will advise on the current situation. We had such a network set up in Tehran before the attack. Our agents, however, seemed to have melted into the landscape. They may have stayed put, but most of them "unrecruited" themselves when they realized the danger they and their families might be in.

The plan then was to assemble a group of trained intelligence officers who could infiltrate Iran to reconnoiter the situation and start building an infrastructure for any potential rescue. Such a scenario involved our first asking several questions: What would their documents and disguise materials look like? What would their nationalities be? We began looking for candidates who could carry the foreign personas that we had document intel and inventory to support. These individuals would need to have the language capability to pass themselves off as non-American. They also needed to look the part. A Latin American businessman has to look Latin. A German student needs to speak German.

Once the candidates were identified, we could then build their cover legends. Who was coming and going from Iran at this time in history? Businessmen? Journalists? The world was watching and the media was certainly all over the story.

As for disguise, the same rules applied. Did we already have things on the shelf? Would an officer need to look older? Could we make them look like Iranians? What about creating the insignia for Iranian uniforms? We were scrambling, running hard to stay ahead of whatever requirement we might be asked to fulfill. We were apprehensive but we weren't scared. Whatever needed to be done, we could do it, I thought, but it was going to take time.

Although the mood in the Central Building was anxious during that first week, there was no shortage of ideas, but not many of them were very well thought out. In one instance I had an ex–special forces operator step into my office and tell me that he was going to solve the whole damn thing if I could just outfit him with a rubber "stunt double" mask and give him an AK47.

Another time, a senior CIA officer I had worked with in South Asia showed up in my doorway, looking lost. "Hey, Jack. What can I do for you?" I asked. He explained how the director of operations had seen him walking down the hallway over at the headquarters building and told him to get his ass over to Central Building to be outfitted to go into Iran. Jack was an Asian American, and the thinking went that it would probably be easier for a non-Caucasian to slip into Iran inconspicuously. There was just one important element missing in order to make this scenario a reality.

"They told me to come and see you," he said. "But there's no way I can do this—I don't speak Japanese."

In another part of OTS, Mike Dougherty, an Irish mercenary in another life, ran his division roughshod and high-spirited. He was putting together his paramilitary capabilities to form a task force that would oversee the larger office response. His task force and my team coordinated our efforts with the operations directorate at CIA headquarters and the Pentagon. Mike and I had a series of meetings over the next four days, with attendance varying according to the topic. Mike loved a meeting, and so there were perhaps more meetings than I would have hoped. At one point we even had a meeting about meetings. There was an overwhelming amount of cable traffic, but that was pretty much an administrative chore that we were already set up to handle—there was not that much difference between two hundred and four hundred cables per day. But the meetings chewed up time, and time was precious. At the end of four days we were exhausted. Things were in the works. Plans had been made. But the Pentagon was in disarray because there was no special operations command; thus they had no way of marshaling resources. The White House was so timid in its response that President Jimmy Carter didn't even want to call the hostages "hostages," for fear of offending Iran's revolutionary government, an oxymoronic term.

I came dragging home on Thursday night, exhausted after working eighteen-hour days for the past four days. I was drained, and took off my coat as I walked through the greenhouse, which served as a vestibule attached to our kitchen. We often had formal dinners in there in the winter and hoped for snow each time. It was a magical place at night with the snow and a little candlelight. I loosened my tie and sank into my favorite chair in the living room, removing my shoes. Karen came to meet me with a beer and a hug. She sat down next to me on the sofa and listened while I rattled on about the job, the office, the Pentagon, everything. It was beginning to look more and more like the crisis was going to drag out indefinitely. On November 5, the Ayatollah Khomeini's son Ahmad had praised the takeover as being in the name of the people. After that, the entire religious leadership of Iran had thrown its support behind the militants. Mehdi Bazargan, Iran's prime minister, was forced to resign in protest, and this meant that there was only one person left for President Carter and his administration to deal with: the Ayatollah Khomeini.

I paused long enough to take a sip of beer and felt her looking closely at me. Glancing up, I saw that she had been waiting for me to stop talking so that she could tell me something.

"What?" I said. I thought on some subconscious level that she was having a problem with one of the kids.

"Honey, I've been thinking," she began. "I've been thinking of how to get those Iranians to leave the embassy and free the hostages. How to end the crisis. And I've got an idea . . ."

"Okay," I said. "Tell me your idea." I leaned back into my chair. The truth was that I was only half listening—I was that tired.

"You have to kill the shah," she said.

I turned to face her. "I'm all ears," I said.

3

DIPLOMACY

The first few weeks of November became something of a blur for me at the CIA as we worked on getting the advance team up and running. We were meeting with the chief of the Near East Division, Chuck Cogan, his deputy, Eric Neff, and his branch chiefs to get organized and figure out what the U.S. options were. Out of those meetings evolved the division of labor. In a crisis situation such as this, a nation has four options to review: overt diplomacy, or trying to engage the government of revolutionary Iran; military assault; secret diplomacy; or covert action.

From the beginning, the Carter administration faced a number of challenges. When Khomeini and the Revolutionary Council threw their support behind the takeover, there was basically nobody for the U.S. government to negotiate with. Carter tried sending two emissaries, but Khomeini refused to allow them to even enter the country. With overt diplomacy off the table, Carter then turned to his military planners, who gave him a similarly bleak assessment. If the United States were to launch a retaliatory strike, the Iranians might execute the hostages. The chance of rescue also seemed remote. Geographically, Iran was extremely isolated and the U.S. embassy compound was located in the heart of the capital city. It appeared there would be no way to get the rescuers in and back out without the Iranians knowing.

At that point the president settled on a two-track strategy of trying to ramp up diplomatic pressure, while giving the military the green light to work on contingency planning for a rescue. Under no condition would the United States hand over the shah.

In keeping with the first part of his strategy, on November 9 the president halted all shipments of military materials and spare parts to Iran. Then, on November 12, he cut off America's importation of oil from the country (about seven hundred thousand barrels a day). And on November 14, when word got out that the Iranians were trying to withdraw the nearly twelve billion dollars in deposits the shah had placed in American banks, Carter signed an executive order freezing the money.

The effect these measures had was minimal. Iran, for its part, escalated the war of words, demanding that the United States return the "criminal" shah and his assets, and warning America that if any rescue attempt was made, the hostages would be executed and the embassy blown up. In a speech given before a roaring crowd of supporters, Khomeini goaded Carter, saying, "Why should we be afraid? . . . Carter does not have the guts to engage in a military action." And if it came to that, Khomeini claimed that the whole nation of Iran was ready to die as martyrs.

One of the biggest problems that Carter would have to soon face was the fact that normal diplomatic maneuvers—international pressure, the threat of being branded an outlaw state, and so on—had no effect on Iran. For Khomeini, a medieval-style prophet convinced that his dream of an Islamic Republic was divinely inspired, no sacrifice was too great to achieve this goal, including sullying the international standing of his country. Faced with such a fatalistic perspective, the career diplomats in Washington were soon at a loss. It was almost like dealing with aliens from another planet.

Understandably, as the days wore on and the impasse continued, it wasn't long before the public began doubting the president's resolve. And while the Carter administration was cautioning restraint, protests and violence toward Iranians erupted all over America. In one surreal instance, Hamilton Jordan, President Carter's chief of staff, remembers driving past a demonstration outside the Iranian embassy in Washington, where American police were holding back an angry crowd. It was the irony of all ironies. Here was the United States protecting Iranian diplomats, while at the same time in Iran, American diplomats were being held captive and abused.

How could the president stand by and do nothing while sixty-six Americans were in danger? There was no shortage of critics, including political foes of Carter who used the moment to score points by decrying him as weak and ineffective.

News coverage of the crisis was relentless. From day one, the event had become a media circus, with hundreds of journalists from all over the world descending on the U.S. embassy in Tehran to point their cameras and pontificate on the nightly news. It's clear that early on the militants viewed the media as an ally and counted on them to beam their message into America's living rooms. This, of course, led to an odd situation in which American journalists roamed freely about the city while sixty-six of their fellow countrymen were being held hostage. Most of the news anchors would set up for their nightly broadcasts right outside the embassy's gates while nearby crowds chanted, "Death to America" and "Down with Carter."

One of the reasons for this frenzied coverage was the highly personalized nature of the crisis. The hostages came from different parts of the country and had friends and family who could be interviewed, all of which gave local news outlets a chance to weigh in on a national story. One local radio station in Ohio was somehow able to call the embassy and speak with one of the militants, who identified himself as "Mr. X." At another radio station in the Midwest, the station manager spent a portion of the day tied to a chair in his studio to better communicate to his listeners what it felt like to be in captivity.

The family members of the hostages were repeat guests on talk shows and radio programs. And with each appearance, the echo chamber increased. Carter was criticized for not being bold enough, and for allowing the shah into the country. One of his most outspoken critics was Dorothea Morefield, the wife of Dick Morefield, who was the embassy's consul general. She repeatedly criticized Carter for not having evacuated the embassy before he had allowed the shah to come to New York.

In one instance, Mike Wallace of *60 Minutes* was granted an interview with Khomeini. The questions had to be submitted beforehand, and when Wallace tried to go off script the imam refused to answer. Throughout the interview Wallace was extremely—almost excessively—respectful of Khomeini, which rubbed the Carter administration the wrong way.

The Iran hostage situation was also the prime subject for Ted Koppel's ABC show *Nightline*, which began four days after the siege of the embassy and continued its coverage throughout the crisis and well beyond.

In a fit of frustration, Carter told his press secretary one day that he was tired of seeing "those bastards holding our people referred to as 'students.' They should be referred to as 'terrorists' or 'captors,' or something that accurately describes what they are."

The militants for their part soon revealed their talents for manipulating the media, who were hungry to gain access to the hostages and willing to tolerate almost anything to get an exclusive. They organized staged events, handed over signed "confessions," and ferreted out the most malleable of the hostages to give false statements about the conditions of their captivity. Thirty-three hostages were made to sign a petition requesting the return of the shah. And the more attention they got, the more emboldened the militants felt.

One of Carter's early strategies was to encourage outside intermediaries with connections or access to Khomeini to try to resolve the crisis. Pope John Paul II sent an emissary to Qom only to have Khomeini lecture the Vatican on the evils of the shah and the hypocrisy of the Catholic Church toward his regime. The imam was reported to have told the emissary that if Jesus were alive today, he would want Carter impeached.

On December 19, NBC aired an interview with Marine Sergeant Billy Gallegos, the first such exclusive with a hostage. The conditions given by the militants, however, stipulated that Nilufar Ebtekar, the militants' spokesperson, otherwise known as "Tehran Mary," be allowed to read an unedited statement before and after the interview. In it, Ebtekar proceeded to lecture the American people about the evils of the shah and the past sins of America's imperialistic agenda, after which a hollow-eyed Gallegos came on the air to demand that the Carter administration hand over the shah.

Naturally, the American population responded to such displays with anger and frustration, which mystified the militants.

Early on the militants were convinced that their actions would cause the "oppressed" in America, namely blacks and other minorities, to rise up and overthrow the government. On one occasion the militants purchased a half-page ad in the *New York Times* calling for America's minorities to revolt. When the revolution didn't come, they assumed it was because of media censorship. For instance, when NBC aired the Gallegos interview, the producer mentioned to Ebtekar that for time constraints they were going to have to edit the segment, which she took to mean that the U.S. government had commanded NBC to censor it. Having grown up in Iran, she had no concept of a press that was not controlled by the state.

When the reality eventually emerged that Americans actually despised the militants for kidnapping and torturing their fellow countrymen, the militants were shocked and saddened. To some of the hostages who interacted with them on a daily basis, it fit perfectly with the militants' skewed worldview. Much like actors in a Hollywood movie, the militants saw themselves as the heroes and expected the whole world to perceive them as such.

Upon taking over the embassy, the militants appeared almost as shocked as the Americans that their plan had succeeded. They had very little idea about how an embassy operated or what the staff did. In their minds, the embassy's sole purpose was for spying. In one press conference they held up a Dictaphone claiming it was a spy apparatus of some sort—this got a laugh from us at the CIA.

They seemed eager to believe any conspiracy theory, no matter how far-fetched. So any name that was found in an address book was considered a conspirator. Some of the political officers who had extensive contacts within the country were terrified that these militants were going to hunt down representatives of some local governments and shoot them for simply having met with an American diplomat. The students seemed not to comprehend the whole purpose of diplomatic relations.

In reality there were only three CIA officers at the embassy when it was taken. But even their involvement was nominal. The revolution had severed most of the ties we had with former agents, and those officers, two of whom had been in the country for less than three months before the embassy fell, had spent the majority of their time building their cover and getting to know the layout of Iran and its government. In the minds of the students, however, everyone at the embassy was somehow connected to the CIA, and they set out to prove this theory, diligently and viciously.

Relatively early on in their confinement, the hostages were subjected to beatings, sleep deprivation, and long periods of painful binding, and they were often made to stay in awkward or uncomfortable positions. They were also repeatedly threatened. Dick Morefield was even made to lie on the floor while a gun was pointed to the back of his head. On another occasion, Colonel Dave Roeder, the assistant defense attaché, was shown a picture of his family and told by the militants that they knew his son's school bus route back in America. If he didn't start cooperating, they told him, they would kidnap his son, cut him up, and send the pieces to his wife.

Other hostages, especially the three CIA officers, were kept in isolation for nearly the entirety of their 444 days of captivity. All of them were undernourished and underfed and would emerge from captivity as shells of their formers selves.

In early November, the conditions under which the hostages were being held were largely unknown to the Carter administration or the public at large. Then, on November 18 and 19, in a deal brokered by representatives from the Palestine Liberation Organization (PLO), a group of thirteen hostages, consisting of women and minorities, was allowed to leave. Before going, they were subjected to a press conference, where they were made to sit in front of a sign that denounced America for harboring the shah. It was upon their return that the White House learned of the extreme conditions that the hostages were being subjected to.

With their release came a statement by Khomeini that the remaining Americans were soon going to be put on trial as spies. Carter immediately warned the Iranian government through back channels that if any such "trials" took place, or if any of the hostages were harmed in any way, Iran would suffer dire consequences. To back up his threat he ordered an aircraft carrier battle group to take up station off the coast of Iran. The USS *Kitty Hawk* joined with another aircraft carrier already on station, the USS *Midway*, to form one of the largest U.S. naval forces ever to be assembled in the region.

By late November the Pentagon had come up with a complex rescue operation called Eagle Claw. The plan called for a small group of Delta Force commandos and Army Rangers to be flown by helicopter to a remote site in the Iranian desert known as Desert One. There, the group would meet up with three C130 Hercules transport planes, refuel, and fly on to a second staging area, Desert Two, located about fifty miles outside of Tehran. At Desert Two, the Delta Force commandos, led by Colonel Charles Beckwith, would disguise themselves and then drive to the U.S. embassy in trucks, where they would storm the compound and rescue the hostages.

With so many moving parts, many of us within the intelligence community felt that the plan's chances for success were low. The Joint Special Operations Command (JSOC) structure in place today that helps the various services work so smoothly together didn't exist back then. This meant that the marine helicopter pilots, air force pilots, army commandos, and navy sailors would have to learn to cooperate on the fly. (In fact, the eventual failure of coordination among these elements was a major factor in the creation of JSOC.)

Whether or not we agreed with the plan, our number one priority was to get our advance party into Iran so that it could establish a staging area outside the city. Ultimately composed of several non-official cover officers drafted from the ranks of the CIA and its Defense counterpart, the DIA, the party was led by a seasoned former OSS officer, "Bob," who got his start in the business working behind enemy lines in World War II. Bob was a legendary figure in the CIA's clandestine history, an invisible hero whose exploits can never be celebrated. The goal of the advance party was to reconnoiter the situation at the U.S. embassy in Tehran and hopefully learn where the hostages were located. They would also case the area around the embassy, looking for landing sites for the rescue helicopters to get the hostages out of Tehran once the assault team had freed them. These urban landing zones were called Bus Stop I and Bus Stop II. The advance party would also need to establish a commo system so that it could communicate with elements of the U.S. government while in enemy territory.

The team would also need to reconnoiter any potential landing sites in the desert, as well as scrounge up trucks for the final assault. Orbital imaging would initially be used to establish a landing site in the desert, but eventually someone would have to go and check it out. Part of that process would require a black flight, carried out by a CIA pilot and copilot along with a U.S. Air Force special operator. The flight, which would take place many months later, went off without a hitch, and the pilots were able to determine that there was no radar in the area. Once the Twin Otter had landed, the air force special operator then unloaded a small motor scooter from the airplane and drove it around taking soil samples throughout the area. Later, once these had been analyzed and it was determined that the location would work as a landing site, one of OTS's many tasks was to fabricate infrared landing lights to mark a runway that could be seen with IR goggles.

With the plans for a rescue operation still developing and overt diplomacy clearly not working, it wasn't long before my colleagues and I at the CIA began analyzing other ways to end the stalemate. Not much was happening in the early days of the crisis in regard to covert action beyond supporting the advance team. But one very interesting idea did surface, and more than once.

My deputy, Tim Small, came into my office early on the morning of November 9. "Tony, do you have a minute?" he asked.

This was unusual behavior for Tim, because his morning routine was to spend the first several hours of the day uninterrupted, reading the cables and assigning action items to the branch. He seldom stepped out of character, and so when he asked for this meeting of course I agreed.

"I was walking my dog last night," he said, "and I had an idea. I don't want to say something crazy, but you tell me—is it possible that we could invent a deception and make it appear that the shah has gone away?"

It was the exact same idea I had heard from Karen the night before. She had reasoned that if the hostages were taken because the shah was in the United States, then if he departed—or died—the hostages might be released. It was amazing to be hearing it a second time, and from Tim.

He and I both knew that when Carter made the decision to admit the shah to the United States for medical treatment, he had been warned he was running the risk of the embassy's being besieged again. And so it made some sense that if we removed the shah, we might remove the problem.

There is a great tradition in espionage operations of using the principles of magic, misdirection, illusion, deception, and denial. The Trojan horse is one well-known example of deception. Winston Churchill is only one of many world leaders who practiced the art of deception—he had a body double, as have many other public figures throughout history. In the world of stage magic, this is known as misdirection. The magician Jasper Maskelyne used the same principles of grand illusion to create battlefield deceptions during World War II. He actually "moved" the city of Alexandria, Egypt, several nights in a row so the Nazis mistakenly bombed an empty harbor. Operation Bodyguard, another British operation, was a deeply elaborate deception used in the invasion of Normandy. Churchill called it his "bodyguard of lies." The fake buildup of forces in another part of England made the Nazis believe the invasion would be launched at Calais instead.

I decided to test the waters and headed out the door and across our courtyard to South Building. I ended up on the second floor, at the office of Matt, the deputy chief of our operations group. He was up to his elbows in the massive flow of cables that the hostage crisis had generated, annotating some, highlighting others, and putting them in his out-box for distribution.

"What is it, Tony?" he asked, not even looking up.

I knew that Matt would immediately see the downside of any proposal, which made him the best devil's advocate in the building.

"If you've got a minute, I've got an idea," I said, stepping farther into his office and closing the door.

"Sure, what is it?" he asked, still not looking up.

"What if we could make it seem that the shah went away and expired?"

Matt paused, reflected, looked at me, and then said, "The shah becomes a nonperson. Pretty good . . ."

For the next ninety hours, this initiative was the only one to be entertained within the U.S. government as a means to deal with the hostage crisis. As chief of disguise I quickly assembled a team of experts to vet the idea. I called on Tim and several members of my disguise branch, as well as one officer from the documents branch. I wanted both seasoned officers and young people, an eclectic mix of ideas that I always preferred when tackling a problem.

"If we can't come up with an operational time line in forty-five minutes, we're going to forget this idea," I said.

Forty minutes later we had the bones of an operational plan. I called Hal, chief of the Near East Division, Iran, on the secure phone and told him I had an idea. I knew Hal well, as he and I had worked together in Tehran to exfiltrate the Iranian agent RAPTOR. The two of us had established a good rapport during and after that operation and I considered him a friend, which would come in handy in the days ahead.

"Come!" he said.

I walked into his office at headquarters thirty minutes later, alone. He got up from his desk to tell me we were going to see Bob McGhee, the deputy chief of the Near East Division. McGhee then picked up the phone and called John McMahon, the deputy director of the CIA. McMahon was in McGhee's office a few minutes later.

"What do you need?" McMahon asked.

"Immediate access to the shah," I said.

"We don't know who's talking to him," he said. "We know who isn't. Can you build it backward?" he asked.

What he meant was, could we carry out our plan without initially engaging with the shah? I told him yes, we could.

"We will need everything we have on him, however—all the records, all the photographs, everything we could possibly learn about what he looks like. Scars, tattoos, blemishes—anything that would be subject to scrutiny in an adverse autopsy."

It was at this moment, oddly enough, that McMahon took a call from Texas billionaire H. Ross Perot in McGhee's office. Perot had exfiltrated two of his employees early in the Iranian revolution with the help of a team of former army commandos. The commandos had infiltrated Iran, then used an overland "black" route to smuggle the employees out of the country and into Turkey. We stood to the side and (covertly) listened. We could hear Perot's scratchy voice across the room without any amplification. "What's the holdup?" he was asking. "Is it red tape? If that's it, I can try and help you out and get things moving. Is it money? I can help you out there too till you get your finances flowing."

McMahon thanked Perot for his call and told him he would call him back if he needed something. He put the phone down and came back across the room to our little group.

"Tell me what you need, Tony," he said, "and I'll make it happen."

Saturday morning I went down to the DDI vault, which belonged to the Deputy Directorate for Intelligence, the analytical arm of the CIA, along with two of my best disguise and documents officers. Mountains of papers, photographs, journals, and files surrounded us. We combed through the paperwork, looking for anything that would help us on this reverse engineering project.

By noon we were ready to move to the next phase, to organize a "cattle call," an invitation to a select group of Agency officers to audition for our starring role. We needed high-level authority to go to the Office of Security's badge office and review the photos of all CIA employees. When we contacted those who seemed a suitable match, all but one were willing to come in on the weekend and work with us.

For those next ninety hours we worked nonstop, sleeping on the floor using our balled-up jackets as pillows. Our Hollywood consultant, a makeup great I'll call "Jerome Calloway," had flown in from LA on Sunday and worked right alongside us. That episode is an amazing story in itself, but the upshot was that by the time we were finished we had not one but two deceptions ready to go.

Unfortunately, by Friday, the president decided against using our plan because he didn't want to appear to be backing down to the Iranians—a decision, I am told, he would later regret. In light of this, our master consultant returned to Hollywood, but I would be calling on him again for another favor in a couple of weeks.

With the end of November came the frustrating realization that while we were making incremental progress toward reestablishing our intelligence capability in Iran, as well as helping to plan a rescue mission, fifty-three American diplomats were still being held hostage. It was a hard fact to swallow, but if anything, it only made us redouble our efforts. There was plenty of work to do, and with other hot spots and ongoing clandestine operations grabbing our attention, we were being tasked with all that much more. Then, in the midst of this activity came a memorandum from the State Department marked URGENT. Surprisingly, not all the Americans working at the embassy in Tehran had been captured. Somehow, a group of six, who had been working at the consulate and at another building, had managed to escape and make their way into the hostile streets of Tehran. For the moment they seemed to be safe, but the Iranians were closing in, and there was a chance they could be discovered at any moment.

4

NOWHERE TO RUN

The consulate had gone relatively unnoticed during the first minutes of the attack. Located on the northeast side of the U.S. embassy compound, the building's squat, two-story concrete structure had recently been renovated to handle the massive influx of visa applicants. So many had come in the wake of the shah's departure that getting the building adequately staffed had been a challenge. On the morning of November 4, there were ten Americans, along with about twenty Iranian employees, working inside. Among the Americans were Consul General Dick Morefield, vice consuls Richard Queen and Don Cooke, consul officers Robert Anders and Bob Ode, as well as the building's only security officer, Marine Sergeant James Lopez, known among the staff as Jimmy. There were also two young married couples, Mark and Cora Lijek, and Joe and Kathy Stafford (an eleventh American, Gary Lee, would later join this group during the assault).

The Lijeks and Staffords were particularly close. Mark and Joe, both twenty-nine years old, had met the previous year in Washington while attending language school at the Foreign Service Institute. Despite being nearly polar opposites, the two had become good friends. Mark's straight blond hair and boyish appearance was accentuated by a pair of large glasses that somehow made him appear even more youthful and innocent than he was. He was a guy you could talk to about anything, and he did like to talk. Joe, meanwhile, was the serious and quiet type. With a receding hairline and a neatly trimmed mustache, Joe was slightly shorter than his wife, and cultivated the look of an economics professor, complete with glasses, a sweater vest, and sport coat. The two friends had spent nearly seven hours a day together for six months and had gotten to know each other quite well. To Mark, who had a hard time figuring him out at first, Joe was a reserved, hardworking guy who would suddenly surprise you with his deadpan sense of humor. He liked pushing Mark's buttons, and it was only after the fact that Mark would realize Joe had just been pulling his leg.

Fortunately for Mark and Joe, Cora and Kathy had hit it off as well. They were all young, eager, and for the most part excited to be in Tehran, which was their first posting. (And in fact they were not alone—many of the diplomats working at the Tehran embassy had been drawn there specifically for the sense of excitement, and danger, that the posting offered.)

Mark had thought about joining the Foreign Service during his sophomore year in high school when a friend had turned him on to the idea. Originally from Detroit but raised in Seattle, he headed east after high school to attend Georgetown University in Washington, D.C., on a ROTC scholarship. After graduating in 1974, he spent the next four years in the army, two of them working as a speechwriter for a high-ranking general. He eventually made it into the Foreign Service in 1978. His first choice of posting had been South America, but then he'd gotten a call from a junior officer asking him to volunteer for Iran. He thought about it. The shah was still in power at that point and it seemed like it might be an adventure. He said yes.

Cora, a vivacious twenty-five-year-old Asian American, had also been excited when she heard the news. Her parents had lived in Iran for four years when she was nineteen and she had visited twice. She thought it was an exotic place. She hadn't been following the news and thought it was going to be a lot of fun to go back. By the time she'd landed at Mehrabad Airport, however, her opinion had changed significantly. By then the country was in the midst of the revolution and under the strict rule of Khomeini. Things had changed dramatically. The biggest difference for her was now seeing all the women in their black veils, or chadors. She remembered how before the revolution only a few women wore them, and even then they were always colorful, some with floral prints. Now everyone was covered head to toe in black.

Her friendship with Kathy had grown in Iran. Outgoing and sweet, with a small-town librarian's wholesomeness, Kathy, who was twenty-eight and nearly a head taller than Cora, had studied art in college and hoped to one day become an artist.

Like the Lijeks and Staffords, most of the staff at the consulate were recent replacements or acquisitions. Almost all of them had been in the country for less than four months. None of these Americans had been in Iran for the February 14 attack, but they'd all heard about it. When the shah had been allowed into the United States, everyone had been briefed on the new security measures and was told to keep a low profile. The consulate had been attacked by rocket-propelled grenades during the summer, but it had been fortified since then. The building's main entrance was from the street, but on the day of the attack Morefield had decided to close the consulate so some graffiti on the outside wall could be removed. Instead of the normal crush that morning, there were only about sixty Iranians who'd been permitted to keep their appointments.

Upstairs, Robert "Bob" Anders was in his office helping an older Iranian couple with their immigrant visas. On the tall side with bushy gray hair, Anders had the handsome looks of a B-level actor and was always ready with a smile (in fact, he'd even once played a priest as an extra in the film *The Exorcist*). At fifty-four, he was considered a bit of an old hand as far as the other consular officers were concerned. The Milwaukee native had served as a messenger for the Seventh Army during World War II, where he was wounded in the hand during a mortar attack around the time of the Battle of the Bulge. Upon returning home after the war, he attended Georgetown University and graduated in 1950. After failing to pass the foreign language part of the Foreign Service exam, he bounced around doing a variety of odd jobs until he was able to get a second chance. He took a probationary appointment and served for a time in Burma and Manila. Marital troubles, however, forced him out of the service. After a divorce and several more years of wandering the economic highway, Anders made it back into the Foreign Service working in the passport office as a GS5, the same level he'd started at more than twenty-five years earlier. A few years and several promotions later, he'd inquired about the chance to serve overseas once again. "How about Tehran?" they'd asked him. At that point the shah was still in power, and to Anders it seemed as good a place as any. But by the time he'd set out for the post, Khomeini had taken over, and by then it was too late to turn back.

News of the attack on November 4 reached the consulate when some female Iranian employees who'd gone to get cookies suddenly rushed back into the building. The ex-husband of one of the women was a policeman at the gate and he'd told her to get back inside. As they were hurrying back, the mob was already entering the compound.

While she was reporting back to the others what she'd heard, Jimmy Lopez's radio suddenly squawked to life: "They are coming over the walls!"

It wasn't long before the militants had converged on the consulate. A group rushed to the building's back door and tried to smash it down. The door was made of bulletproof glass and was electronically sealed. It didn't budge. Lopez watched as the militants fanned out. The consulate's windows were protected by metal bars. Undeterred, the militants smashed through the glass and reached in, grabbing whatever they could off desks and out of file cabinets. Lopez hurried to the windows wielding his nightstick, trying to beat their arms back.

He heard Morefield shout, "Everyone upstairs!"

The staffers and Iranians quickly complied.

Bob Anders was still in his office on the second floor when Morefield hurriedly popped his head in and told him to quickly lock up. The Iranian couple Anders had been helping stood to leave, but Anders reminded the woman that she hadn't yet completed her immigrant visa application. He watched as she signed her name. Her hand shook the entire time.

Everyone huddled on the second floor and waited. Cora was

reassured by the fact that none of the American staffers seemed overly worried, but she noted that the same couldn't be said for the Iranians, who kept their heads down and kept quiet. Like the other Americans, Cora had heard about the February 14 attack and thought it would all be over quickly. She sat down near a Filipina woman who was employed as a secretary, and to pass the time they struck up a conversation. As it turned out, the woman had been working at the embassy during the Valentine's Day attack, and recounted how several Iranians had been shot during that first assault. This immediately sobered Cora up.

As they waited, they heard footsteps racing across the roof, followed by a loud pounding. "They're trying to smash through the roof," Cora heard someone say.

Then the power was cut and the building was thrown into darkness. Some of the Iranians moaned, but for the most part everyone remained calm—something Cora found remarkable. A few minutes later, however, everyone straightened up when they heard glass breaking somewhere on the second floor. It sounded as if a window had just been shattered. Waiting in the hallway, Lopez raced to investigate. A bathroom on the second floor had a window that wasn't secured, so he headed there. Before entering, he pulled out his pistol, popped the spoon on a tear gas canister, and threw open the door. Inside, he found a lone Iranian climbing through the broken window. Seeing the marine, the militant quickly jumped back out through the opening and Lopez threw the canister out after him. He then popped the spoon on a second canister and tossed it into the bathroom, closing the door behind him. There was no way to lock the door, so he used some coat hangers from a nearby storage closet to wire it shut.

At that point, Morefield told everyone that he had just talked to Golacinski on the radio. The plan was for everyone to go out the back door and head over to the chancery as a group.

Mark looked out the window to see what was happening outside. The grounds were swarming with militants. A group of Iranians had smashed open the commissary door with some steel bars and had begun ransacking the place. Going out into that mess didn't seem like a good idea to him.

As soon as they reached the back door, Morefield came to the same conclusion. By this time there was a ring of nearly a thousand militants surrounding the chancery screaming and cheering, and he realized the plan wasn't going to work.

Doubling back, Morefield called the chancery and conferred with Ann Swift on the phone. She told him that someone had called the police, that help was on the way, and that everyone should sit tight and wait it out. Then Lopez got word on his radio that the militants had broken into the chancery. Since the consulate had a door that led out onto the street, at that point they realized their best option was to flee the compound, take their chances in the city streets, and try to make it to a friendly embassy.

Before leaving, Don Cooke smashed the visa plates with a steel bar so that they wouldn't fall into the Iranians' hands. Mark, who was in charge of the cashiering, debated taking all the money and stuffing it into his pockets as he locked up. In the end he decided against it. Much like everyone else, he was still under the assumption that they would all return in a few days and business would be back to usual. Several days later, when he was out on the streets and needed money, he would regret that decision.

The front entrance to the consulate opened onto a small side street far away from the chaos at the chancery. After unlocking the door, Richard Queen poked his head outside and was surprised to see that there were only a couple of Iranian police officers standing around. Other than that, the street was completely empty.

The plan was to let the Iranian visa applicants go first, then the Iranian employees, then the Americans. In order not to attract too much attention, Morefield suggested that the Americans split into two groups. Kim King, an American tourist who had overstayed his visa and had come to the consulate that day to get it sorted out, decided to head off on his own, and instantly disappeared.

Mark, Cora, Joe, Kathy, Bob Ode, and Lorraine, an American woman who had come to the consulate that day to get a visa for her Iranian husband, were all in the first group of Americans to leave. With them was an Iranian employee who said she could act as a guide to help them find the British embassy. Cora remembers that, as they left, for some reason one of the Iranian policemen checked everyone's bags.

As they started off, Ode went back to help a blind Iranian man who said he was waiting for somebody to pick him up. Seeing the first group heading off, Bob Anders hurried after them and caught up.

They walked for about fifteen minutes down one of the side streets toward the British embassy. It was raining pretty heavily and it wasn't long before they were completely soaked. Mark felt particularly conspicuous in the rain, wearing a three-piece suit without a raincoat. Cora and the Iranian woman had gotten out in front a little, and when they rounded a bend they were surprised to see that the British embassy was having its own problems. A huge crowd of demonstrators was out front, shouting and screaming and banging on the gates. The two women headed back to confer with the rest of the group. The British embassy was out. Where should they go now? As they discussed their options, they became increasingly aware that more and more Iranians were beginning to stare at them. The Iranian employee offered to take them to her house, but none of the Americans wanted to impose. Since Anders's apartment was the closest, he suggested they go there to get dry and wait it out. Everyone agreed; the Iranian employee said good-bye and melted into the streets.

After helping the blind man into a car, Ode had joined the second group of Americans, consisting of Morefield, Lopez, Gary Lee, Richard Queen, and Don Cooke. They couldn't have been more obvious. Unlike the first group, they'd decided to turn down a larger street that ran parallel to the embassy. They didn't get far before a crowd of Iranians began shadowing them, shouting, "CIA, CIA!" and "SAVAK!" Finally one of the policemen who had been checking bags outside the consulate ran up and fired his pistol into the air. "Stop!" he shouted. Morefield turned to him and explained that the building was empty and they could do with it whatever they wished. Soon an armed group of komiteh rushed to join the fracas, and they knew that was it. One of the militants grabbed him by the arm. "You are our hostage!" he said. Morefield was stunned. "Hostage for what?" he asked. It was the first inkling that this was more than just a simple demonstration. Much to their horror, they were declared prisoners and marched back to the embassy.

With Anders leading the way, the first group took a circuitous route back to his apartment, walking past a komiteh guard post in single file in order to avoid suspicion. The one-room apartment was on the ground floor of a two-story building, with an entrance right off the street. The street was quiet, however, and when the group got inside they finally felt safe. They dried off and Anders handed out whatever extra clothes he had. Mark received a bright yellow sweater. *Great*, he thought, *they're going to be able to spot me a mile away.*

Next, Anders took some frozen leftover chicken curry out of the refrigerator, heated it up, and made everybody a late lunch.

Like all embassy personnel, he had a small standard-issue "lunchbox" escape-and-evade radio, and everybody crowded around it to listen. Events at the chancery were still unfolding. At this point Golacinski had been captured, but the Americans on the second floor had yet to surrender. Occasionally a voice would come on the net speaking Farsi, indicating that someone's radio had been taken and the person most likely captured as well. They took note how as the day progressed more and more Farsi voices were coming on the net.

Someone calling himself by the code name Palm Tree was relaying information about the assault from somewhere off the compound. "Now they're trying to break the lightning rods on the roof," the voice said. "The idiots must think they're the communications antennas or something."

"Who the heck is that?" everyone wondered.

The voice, they would learn, belonged to Lee Schatz, a lanky northwesterner with a handlebar mustache and a mischievous grin, who was an agricultural attaché working for the Department of Agriculture. Schatz worked in a commercial building about a block and a half down the street from the embassy.

Originally from northern Idaho, Schatz had joined the U.S.

Department of Agriculture after obtaining his master's in agricultural economics from the University of Idaho in 1974. He spent the next several years working at the department in D.C., until in the spring of 1978 he got his first overseas posting to New Delhi. He enjoyed the work, which allowed him to travel. It was supposed to be a two-year posting, but after spending just three months in the country he was offered a post in Tehran, where he'd be in charge of the office. He was only thirty-one years old at the time and the opportunity seemed too good to pass up. Iran had a huge agricultural market for U.S. goods, and he would be right in the thick of it. As with the other Americans, by the time he arrived, however, the country was in the middle of its political spiral. It had gotten so bad that the minister of agriculture refused to allow him to travel outside Tehran to do inspections because he couldn't guarantee his safety.

As the agricultural attaché, Schatz usually attended the morning meeting in the chancery. Then, on his way back, he would play a game with one of his secretaries, telling her he had "forgotten" the mail so she could go over and get it and visit with some of her friends.

On November 4, as he was on his way back from the embassy to his office just down the street, he was forced to wait as a huge demonstration passed by in front of the embassy's main gate. His office was on the second floor, overlooking the embassy's motor pool. After telling his secretary to go get the mail, he sat down at his desk and was surprised a few minutes later when he happened to look up and see her running back across the street toward the building. Then he saw why: a virtual tsunami of Iranians was pouring over the walls and through the gate of the embassy. The assault had just begun.

Alerted now, he stood by the window and watched. He had a small lunch-box radio with him, which immediately began to fill up with the frantic conversations of the day. Soon he heard Al Golacinski shouting, "Recall! Recall! All marines to Post One!"

He was amazed by the coordination of the attack. He noticed how some of the militants would stop at strategic points where they could relay commands to one another in the absence of any radios or communication devices. He also noticed how, rather than being just a spontaneous rush toward the chancery, various groups broke off right away and headed in what appeared to be prearranged directions. He picked up his radio and reported what he saw. Everyone at the embassy had been assigned code names, and his was Palm Tree.

At one point he paused to take lunch orders for his staff and sent his driver out to pick up the food. Later, while they were eating, Cecilia Lithander, a consular officer from the Swedish embassy upstairs, came in and told him the State Department was on the line and was trying to contact him.

Before going, he told his staff to tell anyone who came looking for him that they had seen him leave. Then he wished them all good luck and walked out the door.

Upstairs on the phone, the State Department asked for a running commentary on the assault. The Swedish embassy was on the fourth floor, and with a pair of binoculars he could see just about everything. He stayed on the phone late into the evening. By that time a crowd of nearly a million people had gathered in front of the embassy, clogging the road and sidewalks. The mood seemed festive, like a carnival. There were families, kids. People were chanting and cheering while vendors were milling through the crowd selling steamed beets.

Back in Anders's apartment, the group was getting antsy. Anders and Joe were trying to call the various apartments to see if anyone else had gotten out, when the line suddenly went dead. To make matters worse, the radio net was almost totally dominated by voices speaking Farsi. Palm Tree had long since disappeared. Then, a little after four thirty in the afternoon, they heard the remaining Americans holding out in the vault surrender. They were now on their own.

Near seven o'clock, Lorraine's Iranian husband showed up with some food, and everyone had dinner. Lorraine offered to take them all over to her place, but the Americans declined, not wanting to put her and her husband at further risk. (As it turned out, her husband would later be executed by the revolutionary government for something unrelated to the Americans.)

Without a working phone, Anders decided to go upstairs to make some calls from his landlady's phone. This made Mark even more nervous. A litany of potential scenarios played out in his head. It was rumored that the shah had had an extensive phone tapping operation going on, and nobody knew to what extent the Revolutionary Guard had co-opted it. Besides, were they really safe in Anders's apartment? Most people in the neighborhood would probably know that an American lived in the building. Had somebody seen them enter and possibly called the militants? Mark had met a person working at the embassy who had lived in the apartment prior to Bob, so he knew that it had been in the embassy's housing records for quite some time. He doubted the militants had had time to discover the housing records yet, but who could be certain?

After one of his trips upstairs, Anders returned with some news. He'd been able to get through to Kathryn Koob, a forty-two-year-old devout Catholic who worked for the International Communication Agency (ICA), the branch of the Foreign Service concerned with cultural outreach. In Iran, she was the executive director of the Iran-America Society (IAS), a campuslike center with an auditorium, library, and classrooms located about two miles to the north of the U.S. embassy. Koob had explained to Anders that she and her deputy, Bill Royer, had been on the phone all day to the State Department, and if anyone wanted to they could come over and help to keep the line open. (If the line was dropped, there was no guarantee they could reestablish the connection to the State Department.)

Delighted by the chance to connect with Koob, whom everyone called Kate, both the Lijeks and the Staffords agreed to go. At eleven p.m., Koob's driver pulled up to Anders's house in a tiny Citroën Deux Chevaux, and everyone piled in for the anxious twenty-minute trip across town. Anders had decided to stay behind and take the morning shift.

On the morning of November 4, Koob had been in the middle of a staff meeting when an Iranian employee had interrupted to tell everybody that the embassy was under attack. Following the security protocol established by Golacinski, she didn't call but instead waited by the phone. As late morning turned into afternoon, however, she began to get worried when no one bothered to contact her. Eventually, a little after one o'clock, she couldn't wait any longer and called the general line. An Iranian voice came through the phone. "American embassy," the voice said. She asked for the extension in the public affairs office. "Embassy occupied," came the reply, followed by a click. Finally, after calling a different extension, she was able to reach somebody in the communications vault, who told her to call the State Department, which she did. She then spent the better part of the afternoon talking to the State Department on one line, while Royer stayed on the other line with the staffers in the vault, continuing to get updates.

When the group got to the Iran-America Society a little before midnight, the Lijeks and Staffords took shifts manning the phones. They described their ordeal to State Department officials over and over. Anything to keep the line open.

Mark remembers Joe inexplicably picking up another line at one point and calling the U.S. embassy to speak with one of the hostages. The voice on the other end of the line told him no one was available. "Well, are they being treated fairly?" Mark overheard Joe ask. The voice asked for his name. "My name is Joe Stafford," he said, using his real name. *Click.* The person hung up. Mark shook his head in amazement.

At one point during their time at the IAS they tried to get Koob and Royer to join the group and leave with them, but Koob reasoned that, because they ran a cultural center, they should be safe.

The Lijeks and Staffords left at six o'clock the following morning to avoid rush-hour traffic. Mark didn't want to stay at his and Cora's place because he felt their landlady was crazy. She was happy to take their American dollars but wouldn't let them park their car in her compound for fear that somebody would attach a bomb to it and blow up the building. Koob's driver just made a quick stop at the Lijeks' apartment so Mark and Cora could get some clothes. Afterward they were all dropped off at the Staffords', where they passed the morning getting cleaned up and taking a nap.

Unbeknownst to the Americans, a major drama was now unfolding back at the IAS. Just hours after the couples' departure, Koob and Royer had been back on the phones when a group of militants had arrived. An Iranian staffer was able to warn them, and Koob and Royer quickly walked out the back door and into one of the secretary's cars. In a few minutes they were on the main road in front of the IAS heading for the nearby Goethe Institut, run by the Germans.

They spent about an hour at the Goethe Institut, until they heard that the Iranians had left the IAS, so they returned and reestablished a connection with Washington. The German institute's director had volunteered to shelter Koob and Royer indefinitely, but Koob had declined. An hour or so later, however, the militants returned to IAS, this time surrounding the building. Koob tried hiding in a women's bathroom, but she was soon captured and taken to the embassy, along with Royer and an American secretary who had spent the first night hiding out at the Bijon apartments.

The first person to hear about their capture was Vic Tomseth, who had been on the phone with Koob when the militants returned.

Tomseth, along with Bruce Laingen and Mike Howland, were still at the foreign ministry trying to do everything they could to resolve the crisis. They were also aware that several Americans had gotten out and were on the loose in Tehran. Tomseth had called the consulate from the foreign ministry during the assault and given the staffers there the phone number where he and Laingen could be reached. In fact, one of the first calls that Joe Stafford had made from Anders's apartment was to Tomseth. In the wake of Koob's capture, Tomseth realized that something had to be done about the Lijeks, the Staffords, and Bob Anders. It was clear now that the Iranians were hunting down the Americans and it was only a matter of time before they located the five of them. Realizing that time was of the essence, he set to work on the problem immediately.

Later that morning, the Lijeks and Staffords were startled by the sound of the telephone ringing, but happy when they heard Vic Tomseth's voice on the other end. Tomseth had called the British chargé d'affaires and had some good news. The British had agreed to let the Americans stay at their residential compound known as Gholhak Gardens. A sense of relief washed over everyone. "They'll be over to pick you up in an hour or so," Tomseth explained. Because Anders still didn't have a working phone, Mark used Joe's lunch-box radio to let Anders know that a car would be coming over shortly to pick him up.

Everyone packed what clothes they had and waited. When the scheduled pickup time came and went without any word from Tomseth or the British, the Lijeks and Staffords began to get nervous. Had something gone wrong? Were the militants on their way instead? Finally, at about five o'clock, Joe called the

British embassy only to find out that they were in the midst of their own crisis. "They're coming over the walls!" the chargé d'affaires exclaimed.

The promised car finally arrived at six o'clock, and the Lijeks, along with Joe, were driven over to the residential compound. Kathy, meanwhile, went in a second car to pick up Anders. Anders had spent a fitful night within earshot of the cheering crowds outside the embassy. Normally a relaxed and easygoing type, he found his nerves were beginning to fray. When Mark had told him that a car would be coming to pick him up, he wondered whether it was a trap. Did Mark have a gun to his head? When he recognized one of his colleagues from the British embassy pull up, he understood immediately why Mark hadn't told him over the radio who would be picking him up. Like the others, Anders was relieved to be moving to a place that was across town and away from the embassy.

The drive was nerve-racking for everyone. The traffic was terrible and often the car moved along at a snail's pace. Inexplicably, Mark was still wearing Anders's neon yellow sweater, which suddenly felt like a bull's-eye. At every traffic stop, he was conscious of the stares of the nearby motorists. Each minute made it a greater struggle to remain calm.

Their arrival at the residential compound unleashed a flood of relief. The British were kind hosts, and offered them a house of their own, fed them a warm meal, even prepared cocktails. As a precaution they were told not to turn on any lights and if possible to stay away from the windows. They were also warned about the groundskeeper, who was a member of a local komiteh and an ardent supporter of the revolution. Despite these concerns, that night they slept soundly, for the first time feeling secure to be in the care of the British government.

Lee Schatz, for his part, had spent the night in the Swedish embassy, using the Swedish flag as a blanket to keep warm. The morning of November 5 he had resumed his post at the window, watching and reporting. He'd had some difficulty getting a direct line to Washington, but by late morning he was able to tell them that a car had just pulled up to the embassy and dozens of rifles and machine guns were being unloaded from its trunk. To Schatz it appeared as if a second group was moving in to take over. He had no idea what their agenda was.

Later that afternoon it was decided that, for his own safety and perhaps that of the Swedes as well, he should leave. He was taken in the ambassador's car over to the house of Cecilia Lithander, the Swedish consular officer who had first told him about the phone call. Her house was located in a tranquil neighborhood in northern Tehran, and when Schatz got there he couldn't believe he was in the same city where the embassy attack had taken place. Later that evening he and Cecilia went out for a stroll to the local market. All in all, it was a nice evening.

On the morning of Tuesday, November 6, the Americans at Gholhak Gardens awoke feeling better about their prospects. The grounds were nice, the house spacious, and knowing they had the protection of the British government gave them peace of mind. They had heard from an English diplomat that Prime Minister Bazargan had just resigned, and it was beginning to dawn on them that the crisis was likely going to escalate. Knowing they had found a relatively secure place to hide out, however, mollified their concerns. Of course, they were worried for their colleagues down at the embassy, but at this point word had yet to reach them about how poorly the hostages were being treated. Being diplomats, they assumed that the Iranian government would eventually figure things out and free the hostages. Beyond that, they realized there was little they could do. They made a hearty breakfast and settled in to what they hoped would be a tranquil existence amid the chaos that was unfolding around them.

It didn't last long. A little after noon, Tomseth called to tell them that they would have to move. As it turned out, their relaxing night had nearly been a disaster and they didn't even know it. After the British embassy had been attacked, a second crowd had shown up at Gholhak Gardens. The guard told the crowd that everyone was down at the embassy so there was no one left to capture. It was simple luck that they believed him, and there was no guarantee they wouldn't come back. And the British no longer felt they could keep the Americans safe. (Khomeini eventually ordered the attackers out of the British embassy.) Tomseth received a call from the British chargé d'affaires, who told him that the presence of the Americans was too dangerous for his own people and so they had to move.

It was an immense letdown for everyone. After all their efforts, they were now back to square one. Tomseth hadn't revealed to them that the crowd of Iranians had shown up at Gholhak Gardens the night before, so to the Americans it just felt like they were being kicked out.

At the foreign ministry, meanwhile, things had gone from bad to worse for Laingen, Tomseth, and Howland, who in the wake of the Bazargan resignation felt less like guests and more and more like prisoners. With no living quarters in the ministry, the three spent their time cloistered in the building's diplomatic reception area, a ballroomlike space filled with Czech chandeliers, Persian carpets, and easy chairs. They spent their time watching TV, listening to the radio, reading newspapers and magazines, and doing laundry, which they hung from the chandeliers to dry. Occasionally an Iranian servant would bring in tea. On the morning of November 6, they were told by the chief of protocol, Ali Shokouhian, an old-school Iranian diplomat who sympathized with the Americans' plight, that they should be careful not to make too many local calls. Tomseth had suspected that their phone conversations were possibly being monitored from the beginning, and Shokouhian's warning confirmed his suspicions. From now on they would have to be careful about whom they called, which would complicate things immensely for his communication with the escaped Americans.

Tomseth, however, hit upon an ingenious solution. Thanks to a previous posting, Tomseth could speak Thai, a language he was pretty sure the Iranians wouldn't be able to understand. It just so happened that Kathryn Koob's cook, Somchai "Sam" Sriweawnetr, was a Thai national. Speaking in Thai, he called Sam and the two hatched a plan. Sam's wife worked for John Graves, the embassy's senior public affairs officer who had been captured in the early minutes of the assault. Graves's house was in a relatively quiet part of northern Tehran, far from the embassy, and Sam thought it might be a good place for them to hide out. At the minimum,

Tomseth reasoned, Sam and his wife would be there to help look after the fugitive Americans, which would be a big help.

When the Lijeks, Staffords, and Bob Anders heard about this solution, they were far from thrilled. Once again they would be going back to a house belonging to an American embassy employee. To Mark, it seemed only logical that it wouldn't be long before the militants started searching the houses of the Americans for fugitives or other contraband that could be used as evidence for spying. And yet they had no other choice but to go.

That night they ate dinner at the house of a British diplomat, said good-bye, and were driven by the British over to Graves's house. Sam had told them that there was an old man in the neighborhood who belonged to a komiteh, and as they approached the house they saw someone on the street who happened to get a good look at them. Was this the guy? They couldn't tell for sure.

On its surface, Graves's house seemed like a perfect place to lie low. For one thing, it was a large three- to four-bedroom multilevel structure with servants' quarters, all of it surrounded by a wall. It was also set back from the street far enough that they could move about freely without having to worry about being seen. They were also pampered, in a way. In addition to Sam and his wife, there was an elderly Thai housekeeper who worked at the house, and the three did all the cooking and cleaning for the Americans, which saved them the hassle, and risk, of having to go outside. Since there was no TV or books, in order to pass the time they played poker and slept.

One day, while looking for something to do, they found a 16mm film in one of the closets. Since Graves was the press officer at the embassy, it wasn't out of the ordinary that he might have a projector to show such films. Once they got it up and running, though, they realized that it was a film of the shah's coronation. *This is perfect,* thought Mark. *A group of komiteh is going to come bursting in here and find us all watching a movie about the shah.* They quickly turned off the projector and hid the film in a hole in the ceiling.

After two days, concerns that the militants were right on their heels began to eat at them, and they hatched a plan in case anyone came to the door. Kate Koob's house was only three blocks away, so at the first sign of danger they'd all hurry out the back door and over the wall and try to make it to her house. None of them were familiar with the neighborhood, however, and Anders worried they'd quickly get lost and captured.

To make matters worse, the elderly Thai housekeeper had become more and more irrational as the days wore on. She accused the Americans of drinking all the wine in the house (one bottle), and eating all the food. "What will I say to Mr. Graves when he gets back?" she asked them. It wouldn't do any good, they realized, to tell her that Mr. Graves wouldn't be coming back for quite some time. When she became progressively more difficult, they contemplated locking her up in the basement, but quickly realized that it would only add to their problems.

At night they could hear the old komiteh guard continually passing by the house blowing his whistle, seemingly just to remind the Americans that they were trapped inside. The guard made it almost impossible to relax.

On Thursday, November 8, Laingen called from the foreign ministry to tell them that the Iranian government was cutting off the phone lines and that they wouldn't be able to make any more calls. The Americans were now on their own. "Good luck" was all Laingen could tell them before signing off.

By this time, the tension was beginning to grow unbearable. In addition to Laingen's final call, by this time news of Koob's capture had reached them, causing their morale to plummet. They felt cut off, abandoned, helpless. There was no doubt in their minds that the militants were right outside waiting, biding their time before they came bursting through the front door.

And just when they thought it couldn't get any worse, it did. Sam came home on November 9 and told them that their worst fears had been realized: the militants knew where they were and were coming to get them. Sam had gotten the news from a gardener at one of the apartments of an American who was being held in the embassy. The gardener had been working that morning when a group of militants showed up and ransacked the place. It was Mark's worst-case scenario coming true. Sam told the Americans they had to be ready to move. If anyone showed up, the plan was still to try to make it over to Koob's.

That night, everyone slept in their clothes, ready to bolt at the first sign of danger. Kathy and Cora shared the bedroom, while Mark, Joe, and Bob stayed up most of the night in the living room, talking and thinking. Mark was especially worried about Cora. He thought about the events leading up to his wife's coming to Iran. They'd been college sweethearts and had gotten married soon after she graduated. Initially, once Mark had arrived in Iran and seen how bad things were, he had second thoughts—officials at the State Department, he thought, had painted a much rosier picture than the reality. Cora had told him he was overreacting. Now he wished he'd stood his ground and persuaded her not to come.

Along with Joe and Kathy, they were the only married couples at the embassy in Iran, and his main concern was that he and Cora would be captured and the militants would use them against each other. He thought about the ways they could mistreat her, harm her—anything they wanted to get to him, and vice versa. It made him feel very vulnerable. This wasn't some Hollywood movie, but life. The stakes were high.

As the Americans sat in the living room, outside the lonely komiteh made his nightly rounds, his whistle piercing the calm with its shrill wail. The noose was tightening around them and they knew it. And it felt like there was not a single thing they could do about it.

5

CANADA TO THE RESCUE

Just before sunup on the morning of November 10, the fugitive Americans had already made up their minds. Graves's house just wasn't safe enough anymore. It was time to leave.

They organized themselves quickly, agreeing that it would be better if they made the trip before it got light. They were in such a hurry they even forgot a load of laundry in the washing machine. Sam called an Armenian taxi driver friend, who came over and picked everyone up. Kate Koob's home was the logical choice.

At Koob's house, they sat uneasily in the darkness, too afraid to turn on any lights. When it was finally bright enough to see, they did a quick tour of the house and realized immediately that they wouldn't be able to stay. It was located on the corner and right up against the sidewalk. It also had large floor-to-ceiling windows without any drapes, and they wouldn't even be able to enter the kitchen without the whole world knowing. Despair set in once more; they had to find yet another hideout, and fast. Luckily, Anders had a plan.

Two days earlier, on November 8, after Laingen had called to tell the Americans they were on their own, Anders, who had a few numbers with him, phoned a good friend at the Australian embassy. Delighted to hear that Anders was fine, the friend readily agreed to take him in, but when Anders mentioned the others, the friend begged off, saying he just didn't have the room. Anders then remembered John Sheardown, a colleague at the Canadian embassy whom he'd gotten to know well over the previous months. The two had met at one of the many Western-embassy functions that had become so popular in the absence of any nightlife in the city. They had a lot in common. Like Anders, Sheardown had served in World War II, and at fifty-five he was considered to be an old-timer among the Canadian diplomats in Iran. A distinguished balding man with a penchant for smoking pipes, Sheardown was the chief of the immigration section at the Canadian embassy. Since Bob had been in Iran without his family, John had frequently invited him over to his house for dinner. John's wife, Zena, was not a Canadian citizen but was originally from British Guiana (now the independent nation of Guyana). This meant she didn't have diplomatic immunity. A warm and vivacious person, she loved to entertain but rarely left the house.

After striking out with his Australian friend, Anders picked up the phone again and dialed the Canadian embassy. Sheardown, of course, knew about the attack on the U.S. embassy and had just assumed that Anders had been taken along with everyone else. He was amazed to hear that his friend had gotten out. "Where *are* you?" he asked with incredulity.

Anders tried to explain but gave up after a few minutes. The streets in Tehran were complicated enough, and to make matters worse they'd all been renamed after the revolution. "I don't know where I am exactly," he said.

Sheardown asked him what he needed. This was on Thursday, before the Americans knew they would soon be moving to Koob's house. Anders told him that they were okay for the moment but that they might need to find another place soon. "We're in a bit of a bind," he said.

Sheardown didn't hesitate. "Why didn't you call me before?" he said. "What took you so long?"

Anders explained that he was with four other Americans and that they had decided to remain as a group. Because of this, they'd been reluctant to impose on anyone for fear of putting lives in unnecessary danger. Despite not having official permission to do so, Sheardown told Anders that he'd be happy to help in any way he could. Like most Western diplomats in Tehran, he was incensed when Khomeini had endorsed the embassy takeover. The diplomatic community in Tehran was a tight-knit group, and not only did Sheardown know many of the people who were now being held against their will, but the entire exercise went against the conventions of international law and diplomacy. The fact that it was Anders who was calling only made him all the more willing to break with conventions. "We have plenty of room here," Sheardown said.

Anders thanked him and they agreed to keep in touch if the situation ever changed.

As soon as he had gotten off the phone with Anders, Sheardown walked upstairs to see his boss, Canadian ambassador Ken Taylor. At forty-five and sporting a salt-and-pepper 1970s perm and mod-style glasses, Taylor was a bit of an iconoclast among the senior diplomats in Tehran. Born in 1934, Taylor had entered the Canadian

Foreign Service in 1959 and made his way up the ranks as a trade counselor. Eventually he had become the director of Canada's Trade Commissioner Service in 1974. Taylor had always had a bit of an unorthodox working style that sometimes rubbed the more genteel types in the Canadian diplomatic corps the wrong way. He worked at a table instead of a desk, and refused to use in/out boxes. But whatever his style, he got results. He was a tireless worker and a good manager, and his employees enjoyed working for him.

Taylor had been in Tehran since 1977 and had garnered a reputation for being decisive and calm under pressure for his handling of the evacuation of a sizable contingent of Canadian nationals just weeks before the shah had abdicated.

Sheardown had been relatively certain that Taylor would support his decision to help the Americans. Like Sheardown, Taylor was disgusted by the notion that innocent diplomats should be taken hostage and used by a government as leverage. Almost immediately after the attack, Taylor had begun working with the heads of other foreign embassies in Tehran to try to lodge an official protest of some kind against the Iranian government. In addition, a few days after the takeover, he'd been asked by the U.S. State Department to liaise with Bruce Laingen at the Iranian foreign ministry, which he would eventually do a week later, bringing with him, among other things, books and a bottle of English Leather cologne that was actually filled with single-malt scotch.

Sheardown explained his phone call with Anders and brought Taylor up to speed. He reiterated that the Americans were safe for the moment but would probably need a place to stay very soon. Taylor, to his credit, didn't hesitate, and agreed that they should do whatever they could to help. The two then began discussing the best place to hide the Americans. The Canadian embassy had the benefit of security, but was heavily trafficked and didn't have any living quarters. In addition, it was located downtown, close to the U.S. embassy. In the end they decided they would split the Americans between Sheardown's and Taylor's private residences. Both were in a quiet part of town and, more important, far away from the U.S. embassy. As an added bonus, the houses also fell under the protection of diplomatic immunity, not that that amounted to much in Iran. But it was something.

At that point, Taylor began working on a cable to send back to Ottawa, in the hopes of obtaining his government's official permission. In it he outlined his own opinions on the matter and also the plan that he and Sheardown had just worked out.

Of America's many allies, Canada had been one of the most outspoken in condemning Iran for the embassy attack, and it took only a day for Taylor to get his answer, which arrived the following morning. In the cable from Ottawa, he was told to use discretion, but was given a green light to do whatever he thought necessary to help the Americans. The approval had come directly from the Canadian prime minister, Joseph Clark.

The timing could not have been more fortuitous for the fugitive Americans. Bob Anders called Sheardown a second time from Kate Koob's house Saturday morning just hours after Taylor had received the cable.

"Well, John," Anders said. "I guess now's the time."

"Do you have a way of getting over here?" Sheardown asked.

"Not really," Anders responded. He explained how the two British staffers had driven them over to Graves's house, and Sheardown agreed to track them down.

"Sit tight," he said.

The cars came to pick them up a little after one o'clock in the afternoon. Anders had explained to Sheardown that Koob's was right down the street from Graves's house and the drivers had no trouble finding the place. It wasn't ideal to be navigating the afternoon traffic, but the British staffers knew the roads well and kept off the main avenues.

Sheardown's house was located in the fashionable Shemiran district, Tehran's version of Beverly Hills. Situated on the heights in the northern part of the city, the hilly neighborhood, with its large walled compounds and neatly trimmed gardens, was popular with senior diplomats, wealthy Iranians, and foreign businesspeople.

When the cars carrying the Americans arrived, Sheardown was waiting out front, watering the sidewalk with a garden hose. It might have seemed incongruous, but it gave him a plausible reason to keep an eye on the street. There was a construction site up the road and it was often crowded with young Iranian workers, some milling about with nothing to do. As the cars approached, John waved them into his detached garage and followed in after them, closing the door behind him.

Inside the safety of the garage, the Americans climbed out and John greeted everyone warmly. "It's good to see you again," Anders told him. After Anders had made the introductions, everyone followed Sheardown up a flight of stairs and into the main house.

Once inside, the group was introduced to Zena, as well as Ken Taylor, who had driven up while everyone was still in the garage. The Americans were instantly made to feel welcome. Zena had prepared some snacks and drinks, and everyone took a seat in the living room. They spent a few minutes chatting, relating the events of their escape as well as the news about the hostage crisis. They were told that both of President Carter's envoys, Ramsey Clark and William Miller, had been refused entry into Iran and their plane was sitting on the tarmac in Turkey. At one point Mark embarrassed himself by standing up and asking if the Canadian ambassador was aware of their situation. Mark was concerned that maybe Sheardown was acting on his own and they were in for a repeat of Ghol-hak Gardens if Sheardown lost his nerve. Taylor had introduced himself earlier by name only, and Mark hadn't realized who he was. Sheardown couldn't resist. "Of course the Canadian ambassador knows," he responded. "He's sitting right next you."

Everyone shared a laugh at Mark's expense, but it was a great relief to know that there was a government supporting them. For the first time since their escape they felt truly safe.

As planned, the group was to be divided up between the Sheardown and Taylor residences. The Lijeks and Bob Anders would stay with the Sheardowns while the Staffords would go with Taylor. Taylor explained that he had quite a large domestic staff and any more than two visitors would probably raise some suspicions. The group was somewhat unhappy about splitting up but understood the logic of why it was necessary. At this point, everyone was still thinking that the hostage crisis would be resolved in a matter of weeks, if not days, and they would all be able to go on with their everyday lives.

Cora, Mark, and Bob spent the remainder of the afternoon familiarizing themselves with the layout of the Sheardowns' house. The place was palatial, seventeen rooms by one count. The house sat perched on a hillside, spilling down from a road above through a multitude of levels until it reached the street below. It was actually possible to walk out onto the road above from the top floor, which would provide them with an escape route of sorts. The Americans were given their own rooms on an upper floor, separated from the master suite, which was on the top floor. The best part about the house, however, was that it contained an interior courtyard, which would allow the Americans to spend time outside without having to risk being seen on the street. Cooped up as they were, an hour of sunshine was priceless.

Sheardown explained that there was a local komiteh group that sometimes patrolled the neighborhood, but he told them not to worry as they seldom hassled the residents. However, he did warn them about his gardener, who also belonged to the komiteh. As long as they stayed out of sight when he was around, they should be fine.

Joe and Kathy, meanwhile, were driven by the Canadian ambassador over to his residence, an imposing white mansion with two-story columns marching across its facade, set back from the street and separated from it by an eight-foot wall. Waiting for them inside was Ken's wife, Pat, who'd been born in Australia but was of Chinese ancestry. Pat was a woman with boundless energy, and in addition to her duties as the ambassador's wife, she was a research scientist at Tehran's national blood transfusion service. She showed the Staffords around the house, explaining to the Iranian staff that they were simply guests from out of town. Despite the fact that the house had a spacious back lawn, it was recommended that they stay inside as the neighbors might be able to see them.

The following day, Taylor cabled Ottawa to let them know that the Americans had been taken in and were safe. In order to be as discreet as possible, in the cable he referred to the five simply as the "houseguests."

It wasn't long before the Lijeks and Anders settled into a routine at the Sheardowns'. In the morning, everyone would tend to keep to themselves, waking up at different times and making their own breakfast. Early on this had been a challenge since the only way into the kitchen was past a large window and glass door, through which they could easily be seen by the gardener. Realizing it was going to be a long stay if they couldn't use the kitchen, they devised a solution by smearing shoe polish on the glass, which obscured the view.

After breakfast they would either read or find other ways to pass the time. Anders took to sunning himself and exercising in the courtyard, and developed a surprisingly good tan. Cora, meanwhile, remembers sleeping a lot. Mark decided to try growing a beard, something he'd always wanted to do. In the early afternoon the group would congregate in the den to talk and wait for John to get home. Zena tended to stick to herself in the master bedroom.

The Staffords, for their part, followed a similar routine. After breakfast Joe would invariably gravitate toward the radio in the den, where he would listen to the hourly newscasts and jot down notes. In the afternoon Pat would come home and keep Kathy and Joe company until Ken came home later that evening. Shy at first, the rattled Staffords needed some time before they truly felt comfortable in front of their hosts. And even then, Joe was never quite able to get over the feeling that he and his wife were imposing on them.

In the early days of their stay, John Sheardown had a TV and so the Americans were introduced to the spectacle of the hostage crisis. As Anders and the Lijeks watched footage of their former colleagues being paraded in front of news cameras, the one salient detail that became painfully apparent was how poorly treated the hostages looked. Cora found the images particularly disturbing. It was a real wake-up call—as if they needed one—that they were incredibly lucky to have gotten out.

Among those paraded across the TV screen were some of their colleagues working at the consulate the day it was captured. The other group of six Americans had been marched back to the ambassador's residence, where they spent the first few days of their captivity bound hand and foot to chairs in the mansion's formal dining room. They were not permitted to talk, or lie down, or even bathe, for that matter. Some, including Dick Morefield, were forced to undergo mock executions, while others underwent the indignity of being beaten and made to lie for long periods of time on cold, wet concrete without so much as a blanket. Eventually, one by one, they were brought before a group of militants, where they were interrogated and accused of being spies working for the CIA. Kathryn Koob and Bill Royer fared no better. All of them, with the exception of Richard Queen, who was released in July 1980 for health reasons, would remain in captivity for 444 days.

On November 21, Taylor received a curious phone call from the Swedish ambassador, Kaj Sundberg. The ambassador sheepishly explained that he had a bit of a problem that he was hoping Taylor could help out with.

Around this time, the militants had been able to find two alias passports made for two of the suspected CIA officers stationed at the embassy and were ramping up their rhetoric about trying the captured Americans as spies. The fact that the two passports were found was a huge embarrassment to the U.S. government and the CIA. It was also a cause of great concern to the Swedish ambassador, who began to worry about the repercussions of harboring Lee Schatz. It was then that Sundberg thought of Taylor, and after explaining his situation, asked if the Canadian ambassador would be willing to help. Taylor didn't bat an eye, telling the ambassador that since he already had five Americans, it would be easy to just add Schatz to the group. This news, and Taylor's nonchalance, flustered the Swedish ambassador, who'd had no idea that there were other Americans who had escaped.

While the Americans staying with the Canadians had been on the run, Lee Schatz had passed the time at Cecilia Lithander's high-rise apartment in northern Tehran. He spent his days reading and avoiding the housekeeper, who came practically every morning. Cecilia had explained to the housekeeper that Lee was a friend of hers who was visiting, but he found it awkward to be hanging around every day while she did her cleaning. In the evening, Cecilia would come home and they would eat dinner and talk about any new developments in the hostage crisis. Some days they would take walks in the neighborhood, wandering through the crowded local market. No one ever bothered him, and it didn't occur to Lee that he might be running a risk. "When you are a diplomat, you never think it is going to happen to you," he would later say. He had kept in constant touch with Joe Stafford by phone, and knew the other five Americans had found a home and were safe, but he didn't know where. For security reasons, neither told the other where they were staying. After two weeks, however, what was initially looking like a temporary situation was becoming more and more permanent, and the Swedish government was growing nervous.

Schatz wasn't told about the call between the Swedish ambassador and Ken Taylor, or the fact that he was going to be moved. He remembers being in Cecilia's apartment one day when he suddenly heard a key jiggling in the lock. The sound startled him, since Cecilia had already gone off to work and the cleaning lady had the day off. He braced for the possibility that a crowd of angry Iranians might burst through the door. Instead it was just Cecilia, who told him she had some important news. "We made arrangements for you to leave and I really can't tell you any more than that. Someone will be here in a few minutes and you are to go with them. Don't worry—it's okay," she told him.

Schatz was instantly spooked. *Fuck me,* he thought. *This does not sound good.*

He put the few things he had acquired into a backpack, including a sixteen-foot collapsible ruler, which for some reason he'd had with him on the day of the attack.

John Sheardown, meanwhile, was on his way over from the Canadian embassy, and had decided to play a little joke on Schatz. When Cecilia let him into the apartment, rather than introduce himself, he played the part of the tough guy and simply said, "You got everything?" Schatz looked him up and down and nodded. In his mind he was already beginning to wonder if this mysterious visitor was from the CIA.

Sheardown steered him out of the apartment and down to the waiting car, again without saying a word. When Schatz saw that there was a second car idling behind them, it seemed to prove his suspicions about Sheardown. *I can't believe there are a bunch of CIA guys running around in all this mess,* he thought. Once they were in the car, however, Sheardown turned to him and disabused him of his fantasy by smiling and introducing himself. "You're going to come and stay with me," he said.

Schatz nodded, relaxing a little. "Okay, that sounds good," he replied. He still had no idea that the other Americans were there and was thrilled when he entered the Sheardowns' living room to see Cora and Mark Lijek and Bob Anders waiting for him. He wasn't close with the Lijeks or Anders, but he knew them through embassy functions. It was a great relief to see their faces and to know that he was among friends. Given the circumstances, it seemed like an ideal place to ride out the storm.

News of the houseguests wouldn't reach me until mid-December. Often, the only time to get any work done was after everyone had gone home, and since I lived about an hour's drive outside Washington, sometimes I didn't know whether I was coming or going. All of us were working around the clock, but I never heard anyone down at the office complaining. I was standing at my desk one morning having just come from the washroom, where I'd splashed water on my face, when Max, the chief of graphics, along with my deputy, Tim, showed up in my doorway. Max had a copy of a document in his hand, and he waved it about as he walked in.

"Have you seen this?" he said. "Some Americans have escaped from the embassy in Tehran."

By this time I had been promoted from chief of disguise to chief of the authentication branch, and was now in charge of creating and maintaining the myriad false identities and disguises the CIA was using worldwide. I had a large staff of experts in all phases of identity alteration who could penetrate any border undetected, duplicate almost any document, alter anyone's appearance, even change their gender if that's what the job required.

Historically, the chief of the authentication branch was an officer who'd come from our document analysts' ranks—or what we would have considered to be one of our best and brightest. The joke was that they were the only officers in our midst who could write (or spell). The fact was they were operationally more astute than some of our PhD technical officers and had a broader appreciation of the lifeblood of intelligence, which is communications. The work of our document analysts involved languages, area knowledge, travel, and writing—all skills highly valued in the CIA's culture.

I had decided to put my name in the mix when I heard that the chief of OTS operations, Fred Graves, was looking to replace a branch chief. Graves was a man who, on the surface, appeared to be as hard as nails. You would swear he was a former marine—he certainly swore like one—but he was not. He had been a cadet at the Citadel and had acquired a military bearing and point of view that served him well in a CIA culture that was, in fact, modeled after the U.S. military. Fred needed to replace Ricardo, the chief of the graphics branch, who was retiring. When he asked Ricardo who should be his replacement, Ricardo said it should be me. Quite a compliment, actually, but it was not my cup of tea.

"I have another suggestion," I'd said to Graves, sitting in his office in South Building. The GSA-issued furniture was only a backdrop to Fred's unique brand of decorating. Most visitors walked away the first time with the wording on a shade on his door burned into their mind. THE SALOON IS OPEN, it read—or CLOSED, depending on whether or not he was in a meeting.

"We give a lot of lip service around here to cross-training our future managers. Why not get somebody from authentication down to run graphics and make me chief of the authentication branch— the first guy from graphics to do that?" I had said.

"Not bad," he'd responded, nodding his head. "I'll get back to you, Mendez. But remember, you can't be out on trips, gallivanting around the world. You'll need to be back here, managing the branch."

"Yes, sir!" I'd said, trying to sound like a good marine, resisting the compulsion to snap a salute. Backing out the doorway, I bumped into a brass plaque that read: IF YOU'VE GOT THEM BY THE BALLS, THEIR HEARTS AND MINDS WILL FOLLOW. We all loved Fred Graves; we really did. There was something very tender lurking inside that barrel chest.

Thanks to my new promotion, it seemed as if my workload had nearly tripled in light of the hostage crisis. Because I was immersed in too many meetings at both Langley and Foggy Bottom and had many other matters that required my direct attention, I had instructed my secretary, Elaine, to send copies of important correspondence that required action directly to the line supervisor concerned.

So I was not surprised when Max and Tim walked into my office that morning with a copy of the State Department memo in their hands.

Max handed me the memorandum and took a seat while I looked it over. Tim sat at the conference table in front of my desk, scanning a copy of the same message.

The memo was addressed to CIA's Central Cover staff, which handles all cover requirement. It was requesting the CIA's advice about a potential exfiltration of six American diplomats who had escaped from the U.S. embassy in Tehran and were now in the care of the Canadians. It did not request that we take the lead in any rescue, but that we be available to consult during the planning stages. There was not a lot of information in the memorandum—certainly not enough to make any decisions.

I read it and thought it sounded interesting, but in the context of the hostage crisis it didn't seem like a top-tier requirement. It did not sound urgent. While not stated precisely, by omission it seemed to imply that the six Americans were settled, were safe, and could weather another few weeks or months without danger. I was inclined to put it aside to concentrate on helping to rescue the hostages at the embassy.

The original plan to deal with the houseguests, it seems, had been to sit tight and wait it out. In his early communications with the Canadian government, Taylor had discussed the possibility of creating contingency plans in case the houseguests might have to be evacuated, but once they had been settled, and were relatively safe, the thinking in Ottawa, as well as at the U.S. State Department, was that the situation at the U.S. embassy should take precedence. Once the hostages were released, they reasoned, the problem with the houseguests would work itself out.

After Lee Schatz had joined the other Americans at the Sheardowns', a couple of weeks had passed without incident. They'd spent the majority of their time reading. Sheardown had a pretty extensive library, including many spy thrillers by John le Carré. Occasionally the group would get together to play cards or board games. One of their favorites was Scrabble. A born competitor, Schatz took the game very seriously. His main rival was Anders, who had a knack for the game. After a grueling duel, Schatz pored through a two-volume British dictionary that Sheardown had on the shelf. It wasn't long before he found a killer word—"dzo"—that helped him improve his score. When a skeptical Anders shook his head, Lee pulled out the dictionary. "Here it is," he said triumphantly. "Dzo—a cross between a cow and a yak."

Thanks to a fluke, the house's basement was filled with all manner of beer, wine, and hard liquor, and the houseguests wasted no time depleting the stores. This largesse was because the Canadian embassy had been next in line to host the Friday night party—the weekly bender held at a different Western embassy each week. The tradition was discontinued after the takeover, but not before the liquor had been transferred to Sheardown's house. Eventually, they'd drunk so much that Sheardown had to get creative in disposing of the empties, which had been piling up. His solution was to parcel them out and take them with him to the Canadian embassy.

By all accounts, the highlight of their day was the evening meal, fondly remembered by all as a kind of traditional Norman Rockwell moment each night. John would come home from work and everyone would gather at the dinner table to hear the news. Since Sheardown's TV had broken a week or so after the houseguests had arrived, they relied on John to keep them informed on events happening in the outside world. The vibe got to be so familial that Anders took to calling Sheardown "Big Daddy."

On certain occasions, the Staffords would be driven over, giving the group a chance to catch up. On Thanksgiving, the Canadians threw a traditional dinner for everyone, which went a long way in helping to cheer them up.

They also had visitors. Roger Lucy, the first secretary of the Canadian embassy, was a frequent guest. Lucy, who was then thirty-one, had been in Switzerland visiting friends when the takeover had happened, but had since been brought up to speed on everything. He'd originally arrived in Iran in the fall of 1978, just days before the shah had declared martial law, and had been instrumental in helping Taylor organize the mass exodus of Canadian citizens out of Iran. An adventurous type, Lucy would become an important member of the local team looking out for the houseguests. Anders would later recall the first time he met Lucy at one of these early dinners. He described him as a character right out of Rudyard Kipling, with a bushy mustache and little circular glasses, wearing a pith helmet and carrying a little staff.

Two other frequent visitors would be ambassadors Troels Munk from Denmark and Chris Beeby from New Zealand. Beeby would prove to be especially helpful as the crisis evolved, going above and beyond what anyone had asked of him, including bringing in a case of contraband beer for the houseguests. Coals to Newcastle, perhaps, but welcome nonetheless.

For the most part, however, the houseguests tried to keep a low profile. Despite their living situation, the threat of discovery was still very real. On more than one occasion, the Taylors' staff asked pointed questions about the Staffords, wondering why if they were tourists they always stayed indoors. The worry that an unexpected visitor might suddenly show up unannounced meant that the Americans tended to stay in the back of the house, or often shut up in their rooms. One evening, for instance, Taylor had ABC News correspondent Peter Jennings over for dinner. Jennings was one of the many Western journalists who had come to Iran to cover the hostage crisis. While the two were enjoying their dinner, the Staffords huddled in their room upstairs, worried they might make an inadvertent sound and be discovered.

On certain occasions Roger Lucy was asked to drive the Lijeks, Bob Anders, and Lee Schatz over to his own house. The owner of the house that Sheardown was living in was trying to sell it and would come over with prospective buyers from time to time. Lucy remembers these trips as being tremendously nerve-racking; one time they even got caught in the snow and Lucy had to ask a group of Iranians to help dig them out.

The houseguests were allowed to write letters home once a week, but it wasn't long before they ran out of things to say. In one of his early letters to his parents, Mark wrote, "We are in a safe place but I can't tell you where. If something happens to us you'll probably know because it will be on the TV or you'll get a call from the State Department, but unless something like that happens, you'll know we are okay."

As the weeks stretched on, concern began to grow among the Canadians that the secret of the Americans would get out. Amazingly, the local newspaper in Lee Schatz's hometown of Post Falls, Idaho, ran a story about his hiding out at "at an undisclosed location in Iran" after the State Department told his mother he was safe but apparently forgot to tell her not to tell the press. In another instance, during a telephone interview, an American citizen named Kim King, who had been at the consulate the day of the takeover, told a local reporter that he was one of nine Americans who had been able to escape the embassy on the day of the attack.

Though these stories surprisingly didn't take hold in the United States, rumors began circulating in the Iranian press about the possibility that some Americans were hiding out in Tehran.

In addition, there was a strong chance that the Iranians at the foreign ministry had been monitoring the calls Laingen and Tomseth were making and so knew that the Americans had gotten out and were on the loose. Beyond that, there were all the employees at the Iran-America Society who had seen the Lijeks and Staffords and easily could have told someone. There were also their colleagues from the consulate. Had the Iranians been able to get to them?

Not five days after the houseguests had left Koob's house, Sam was accosted there by a group of militants who threatened him with a gun. They asked him about the house and he explained that the occupant was already down at the embassy, being held hostage. They eventually let him go, but he was badly shaken. He immediately went into hiding and would remain so for the duration of the hostage crisis.

6

LESSONS FROM THE PAST

After I'd received the memorandum, the issue of the houseguests had never completely gone from my mind. The State Department was taking a wait-and-see approach, but I wasn't convinced that this was the best course of action. As I often tend to do when I have a difficult problem that needs to be worked out, I'd gone into my studio one Saturday afternoon to paint. And it was during that session, while I was working on "Wolf Rain," that I realized we couldn't afford to wait and let the urgency of the situation overtake us. Sure, the houseguests were safe for now, but they'd already been in hiding in Tehran for nearly two months. How much longer could they hold out? I'd always told my team that, whenever possible, it was better to perform an exfiltration before the bad guys knew you were there. If the houseguests were discovered for some reason before we could get to them, then it would be nearly impossible to get them out.

One of the reasons I was so concerned about the exfiltration of the houseguests was that I'd recently been to Iran. In my capacity as chief of disguise, in April of 1979, seven months before I'd even heard of the houseguests, I had volunteered to infiltrate the country to help rescue a high-priority agent, and in many ways the case was a good benchmark for what awaited the six Americans.

It was an open secret that during the reign of the shah there was a close relationship between the CIA and the shah's government. In fact, one of the more recent U.S. ambassadors to Iran, Richard Helms, had formerly been the director of the CIA. But unknown to the Iranians, the CIA had also recruited a sensitive source who was a trusted member of the shah's inner circle. He was known within the CIA by his operational cryptonym. I have chosen to call him "RAPTOR."

RAPTOR was able to provide invaluable insights for U.S. policy makers concerned with the shah's intentions. The intelligence he provided was passed clandestinely to his handler, who in turn prepared it as a raw intel report in a staff cable and sent it to headquarters from Tehran. Typically this information was so good that it was hand-carried by a CIA officer directly to the president in the Oval Office.

The manila envelopes used to hold the flimsy cables were marked with bold blue borders and the words TOP SECRET—RESTRICTED HANDLING—EYES ONLY printed in bold red letters in the center of the envelope. Because of these markings, these reports were known as "blue stripers." All copies were numbered and carefully controlled in this way. The restricted-handling, blue-striped envelope was double wrapped, then zipped and locked in a heavy blue canvas portfolio that was never out of the control of the courier.

All intelligence reports are given a grade from one to ten. The most valuable of these sometimes receive the grade "double-ten." RAPTOR's reports were typically double-tens.

RAPTOR had known for some time that the shah was losing his grip and had repeatedly warned his CIA handlers, but as can happen when raw intelligence doesn't match up to the preferred scenario held by policy makers in Washington, RAPTOR's warnings tended to be overlooked. Intelligence is only as good as the consumer's ability to believe and utilize it.

When the shah left the country in January, RAPTOR had immediately gone underground. With the tentacles of the Revolutionary Guard spreading deeper and deeper into all facets of Iranian society, he knew he wouldn't be able to hide for very long.

At that point, he began surreptitiously meeting with "Don," a local CIA officer in Tehran who tried to organize his exfiltration. The two, however, didn't see eye to eye. Don, a young hothead who thought he could do everything on his own, had proposed disguising the Iranian as a Gulf Arab, something that RAPTOR knew he wouldn't be able to pull off. Unfortunately, rather than trying to work with the asset to see what else he could come up with, Don had simply said, "Take it or leave it," which only made the problem worse. It was then that Hal, the CIA station chief in Tehran, had sent out an urgent cable requesting my help.

The case was challenging right from the beginning. A born warrior, RAPTOR longed to go out in a blaze of glory, an ivory-handled Colt in each hand. The prospect of being grabbed at the airport while wearing a disguise was too much for his traditional sense of honor to bear. To complicate things, he'd trained most of the security staff who worked at the airport, so they all knew his face. He was sure they would see through any disguise and spot him instantly. Since the success of the operation would hinge on his confidence and ability to carry it off, nothing was going to happen unless we could convince him to trust us. I knew from past experience working as a technical officer on numerous exfiltrations that some are more dependent on disguise than others. In RAPTOR's case, I realized that the disguise was paramount. With the Revolutionary Guards right on his heels, it would be important to impress him with our professionalism right away. It wasn't courage that he lacked, but confidence.

My first stop upon entering the country was the library on the second floor of the chancery of the U.S. embassy in Tehran. The city had the feel of a war zone. Armed gangs roved the streets and it wasn't uncommon to hear an explosion in some distant neighborhood. Though perhaps the most striking feature was the people themselves—browbeaten and scared. Everywhere you looked the sidewalks were full of women dressed head to toe in their black chadors. It was as if the whole city was in mourning.

As we pulled onto Takht-e Jamshid Avenue, I noticed that the walls of the U.S. embassy were covered with graffiti—a vivid reminder that anti-American sentiment in the country was strong, and growing.

At headquarters we had gone through our entire holdings of Middle Eastern and Mediterranean travel documents, finding three different nationalities that could work. But since we didn't know what RAPTOR's skin tone looked like, we decided I should make the final decision when I got face-to-face with him in Tehran. In the meantime, I had gone to the library to look for something in particular.

The library was a quiet, musty, dimly lit room. Despite this, however, I could see that it was well used, with a stack of returned books waiting to be reshelved. There was no librarian at the desk, probably as a result of the drawdown, and so I proceeded on my own. I scanned the shelves and after a few minutes found what I was looking for. The book was bound in green and tan Moroccan leather and the title on the spine was stamped in gold-embossed capital letters: STEWART—THROUGH PERSIA IN DISGUISE.

I pulled the volume down and turned it over in my hands. It was the collected memoirs of a British officer, Colonel Charles E. Stewart. In 1880, roughly one hundred years before my trip, he had donned the disguise of an Armenian horse trader and spent nearly two years traveling on horseback with his small party, surveying the region. He'd covered a remarkable amount of distance over that time and never once was he suspected of being a European.

The operation to exfiltrate RAPTOR was not unlike the journey of Colonel Stewart. I knew that the book, which had many pictures of the people Stewart had encountered in the region, would come in handy when I went to see RAPTOR later that night. Of course, first I would have to get to him, no easy task in a city teeming with mistrust for all things foreign, especially American spies.

Any good surveillance detection run, or SDR, always begins with the assumption that the hostiles, whoever they may be, are everywhere, and watching. This maxim had been drilled into my head in my OPS FAM (operations familiarization) course at "the Farm," a ten-thousand-acre facility where novice CIA officers go to learn their tradecraft before heading overseas. Later, when I visited Moscow in the mid-1970s and ran up against the state-sponsored paranoia of the KGB, I would come to see how true that statement was, when just about everyone—even the ticket puncher at the zoo—was an informer.

Now, on the streets of Tehran, my colleagues and I would use these skills to throw off any potential pursuers who might try to use us to get to RAPTOR. Hal and I were joined by Andrew, a local documents officer. Weaving through the narrow streets, the three of us quickly backtracked and then ducked into a bustling department store on Abbasabad Avenue. It was a favorite technique used by Agency officers, because the large stores usually had multiple exits and it was almost impossible to cover them all. Emerging from the store, we then strode through the middle of the street, dodging the suicidal traffic of Tehran—many of the cars driving without headlights—in order to throw off any vehicle surveillance that may have been following us. Such a move would probably be considered provocative by Moscow standards, where the operatives were all highly trained professionals, but here in Iran, where the opposition was basically composed of revolutionary zealots, it got the job done.

The nondescript apartment building was located just off Motahari Boulevard, right next to a hotel that housed a popular restaurant.

RAPTOR was hiding in the shadows of the second-floor landing, and as we approached, he stepped out into the light and embraced me, his eyes brimming with tears. I studied him with an artist's attention to detail—the gaunt, sickly man in the ill-fitting sweater bore little resemblance to photos I'd been shown of a confident-looking colonel in his mid-thirties.

RAPTOR led us up to a fourth-floor apartment, which was bare except for a soiled couch and a partially dismantled TV set.

The kitchen counter was stacked with worn magazines that had been flipped through too many times, and Farsi newspapers, along with a bag of rice, a sack of lentils, and some canned food. It was obvious he'd been camping out here for several weeks. In lieu of curtains, old newspapers covered the windows.

Moving purposefully, Andrew and I walked RAPTOR through the dark apartment and toward the bathroom. I knew it was important to put him at ease. "This won't take long," I said, telling him not to worry.

As we entered the bathroom, Hal pulled open a narrow window at the back of the apartment and tossed out a coiled rope. This was to be our "escape route" in the event that Revolutionary Guards came charging up the stairwell. The window opened up onto a light shaft ending forty feet below, which adjoined the nearby hotel. After climbing down the rope, we could then enter through a laundry window and leave the hotel through a service entrance. All of this had been figured out the previous day, when the three of us had taken turns casing the service entrance from the hotel restaurant. During Hal's turn, he'd gone into the restaurant's washroom, which had a window that opened up onto the shaft. While he was leaning out, the band on his expensive wristwatch broke and the watch tumbled out onto the windowsill below. When he got back to the table, he explained what had happened. While he was lamenting his loss, I'd gone to see what I could do. Descending two flights of stairs, I entered the laundry and quickly put on a dirty waiter's coat to blend in. I then made my way through the large tumbling machines to the washroom and retrieved the watch from the light shaft. Hal was speechless when I returned and dropped it onto the table in front of him.

Inside the apartment's bathroom, RAPTOR improvised a light-bulb by attaching the twisted copper ends of a flat television antenna wire to a bulb with his right hand, while using his left to jam the opposite ends of the wire into the electrical socket next to the sink. I set down my kit and quickly got to work.

"I've done this hundreds of times," I told him, as I applied the special disguise materials I'd brought with me. Half his face, from his hairline down to his upper lip, was soon covered by a stretchy material that obscured his vision and forced him to breathe through his mouth.

As I did this, Andrew assisted me by preparing a special adhesive, stirring it under a stream of water from the tap. Hal, meanwhile, sat on the sofa in the bedroom and monitored a small two-way Motorola radio he held to his ear. The radio connected him to a team of CIA officers who were outside, watching the street below. We were leaving nothing to chance.

"Just a few more minutes," I said as I tested the disguise with my fingertips. Suddenly, we heard a knock on the door and everyone froze.

RAPTOR pulled the wires out of the socket and we emerged from the bathroom. We made our way through the living room toward the front door. Blinded by the disguise materials, RAPTOR was forced to grope his way along, as I led him by the hand. I showed him by feel where the doorknob was and he, in turn, put his mouth up to the crack between the door and the molding.

"Who's there?" he whispered, his mouth just inches from the door.

"It's me, Uncle," responded the hushed voice of a young boy.

We all relaxed. One of RAPTOR's relatives owned many flats in the building and the voice belonged to the man's son.

The child asked if RAPTOR needed anything from the bazaar. "No," he responded. "Come back and see me later."

We listened to the boy's light footsteps as they faded down the stairs. Then we returned to the bathroom, where I was finally able to remove the disguise materials.

After this episode, RAPTOR was moved to a CIA safe site near the U.S. embassy. The two of us continued to meet repeatedly over the next three days as I finalized his disguise. We had decided to take him out through Mehrabad Airport right under the noses of the Revolutionary Guards. It was a risky move, but I was confident the plan could work. I had transformed the middle-aged Iranian colonel into a sixty-five-year-old Jordanian businessman, complete with a receding hairline and lumpy woolen suit. RAPTOR spoke decent Arabic and could affect a British accent when he spoke English, which would help him pull off the disguise.

On the day before departure, we all met with RAPTOR for a final dress rehearsal. Wearing his disguise, he sat at the dining room table flipping through the well-worn travel documents that Andrew had provided for him. When he looked up, a smile spread across his face and I could see that he was pleased with our efforts. To the untrained eye, he was a dead ringer for a distinguished Arab salesman who had traveled the Gulf states for decades. I had even coached him on how to walk and talk and fumble for his documents when presenting his papers to the immigration officers. In addition, he'd spent hours with Andrew going over his alias documentation, travel plans, and cover story. He'd also memorized a list of phone numbers for "affiliate" offices in the Middle East, which were really CIA fronts prepared to vouch for him should Iranian officials call.

Everything seemed ready. RAPTOR had proved to be a quick study and was motivated, and yet I was worried. I'd noticed over the past few days how he would periodically slip into a deep depression.

His biggest fear was being caught and tortured. "You have no idea what they would do to me," he said. Normally I would just chalk this kind of talk up to nerves, but when he asked if he could have a cyanide capsule, I became genuinely concerned.

"I'm not sure he's going to be able to pull this off," I told Hal the night before the exfiltration.

"What do you have in mind?" he asked me.

"I'll wake him up early tomorrow and make my final assessment then," I said. "If I don't think he can make it through on his own, I'll personally see him past the controls."

It was going way beyond headquarters' mandate, but I didn't see any other option.

The following day my fears were confirmed when I woke RAPTOR, now known as "Mr. Kassim," at three in the morning only to be confronted by a wreck of a man with a greenish pallor and a haunted look in his eyes. It was clear that he hadn't slept at all and was certainly in no condition to attempt getting through security on his own.

While Andrew prepared a light breakfast for RAPTOR, I took Hal aside. "I'm going to take him into the airport," I said. Hal seemed to know this was coming, and nodded his agreement. "I'll go ahead with Andrew and check out the terminal one last time and then confirm the flight," I said. No doubt headquarters would think I was taking an unnecessary risk, but I wasn't about to be second-guessed by someone in an office thousands of miles away. We were the operational officers on the scene and nobody knew better than us what was required.

The predawn streets of Tehran were eerily quiet as Andrew and I drove toward Mehrabad Airport. Anti-American slogans and posters covered every wall of the deserted city, giving us an almost overwhelming sensation that in order to succeed we would somehow have to overpower the entire country itself. Passing beneath an ornate archway, we stopped the car near the drab concrete main terminal, right on schedule.

I waited for Andrew to park the car and then the two of us did a quick sweep through the terminal, which was empty except for a few komiteh slouched on some benches, while a group of temporary revolutionary officials stood around their counters sipping tea. No one seemed to care as we walked up to the Swissair check-in counter to confirm that the flight was on time.

Andrew then passed through immigration controls, while I walked outside to wait for Hal and RAPTOR. Since Andrew had always worn a disguise when he'd met with RAPTOR, the plan was to use Andrew as our "spotter" in the airport. This meant that his job would be to make a call from a public phone in the departure lounge and pass a "go" or "no go" signal, depending on whether or not RAPTOR had made it onto the flight. At that point Andrew would then board the plane, introduce himself to RAPTOR, and proceed to escort him to freedom.

I waited outside, deciding to take a walk in order to avoid looking suspicious. It was still dark and I headed to the far end of the parking lot to watch the sunrise. It also helped to calm my nerves. By the time I returned to the terminal, taxis and vans were beginning to arrive, disgorging their passengers onto the sidewalk. I spotted RAPTOR and Hal getting out of a cab and casually walked over. I shook RAPTOR's hand and flashed a warm smile, hoping the act would help to put him at ease. His hand was cool and moist and his grip lifeless. He forced a smile from behind the disguise. He looked to me like a man on his way to the gallows, and I began to worry he might fold before he even got to the check-in counter. I grabbed his bag and said good-bye to Hal, whose job would be to return to the safe site and wait for the call from Andrew.

We entered the terminal and approached customs, and I was pleased to see that RAPTOR's disguise aroused not even the slightest bit of suspicion among the amateurish revolutionary customs agents who'd been told to look for wealthy Iranians trying to smuggle goods out of the country.

After the check-in counter, I stayed with RAPTOR as far as the immigration controls, where the Revolutionary Guard clerk stamped his passport and handed it back to him. It was now time to say good-bye, but as I once more shook his hand, I sensed that something was wrong. I saw that the haunted look had returned to his eyes, and so rather than leave, I decided to stick around the airport and wait until his flight had departed.

I was sitting in the waiting area twenty minutes later when I caught sight of Andrew through the glass partition. He was clearly agitated by something and he motioned me over. He explained that the Swissair flight had been called but there was no sign of RAPTOR anywhere. "I saw him enter the departure lounge," Andrew said, "but after that he disappeared."

My mind raced. Where could he be? I told Andrew to go back and board the flight; then I returned to the Swissair desk. I explained to the agent that I had a serious problem. "My uncle is boarding your flight to Zurich but I'm afraid that I forgot to give him his heart medication. Can you escort me through immigration so I can find him and make sure he knows how to take it? You see, he's a very old man."

The Swissair clerk nodded sympathetically and quickly escorted me through security and into the departure lounge, where he turned me loose.

I scanned the wide hall, looking for any sign of RAPTOR. He had to be here somewhere. My eyes fell on the door to the men's bathroom.

My shoes echoed on the tile floor as I entered. The bathroom appeared to be empty, but I noticed that one of the stall doors was closed. I walked over.

"Mr. Kassim?" I whispered.

The stall door opened a crack and I saw one anxious eyeball glaring back at me.

"Come on, Mr. Kassim. You'll miss your flight."

The door opened further and I could see that RAPTOR was shocked to see me—both his eyes were now wide open like a startled animal's.

"How did you get in here?" he stammered.

Without replying, I grabbed him by the elbow and hustled him out of the bathroom. As we hurried across the departure lounge and toward the gate, a few Revolutionary Guards gave us sideways glances but otherwise didn't seem to care. RAPTOR had been paralyzed with fear but my sudden appearance had snapped him back.

Five minutes later I learned from the Swissair clerk that the flight was on its way to Zurich, and it was up to me to call Hal and let him know that RAPTOR had gotten out. That afternoon we received a return cable from Andrew stating that RAPTOR was safe. He also relayed a funny story. While they had been on the flight, RAPTOR had removed his fake mole and handed it to Andrew as a souvenir.

The RAPTOR operation was on my mind as I headed over to the State Department to find out about the status of the exfiltration plan to rescue the houseguests. The State Department memo had said they were planning on taking the lead, but I was concerned about their ability to pull it off. I knew there were several challenges to this case that might not seem important to the uninitiated. Infiltrating and exfiltrating people into and out of hostile areas is one of the most dangerous jobs in the spy business. It's also one of the full-time concerns of OTS, which has worked on these kinds of operations since the OSS days. The "authentication" of operations officers and their agents by providing them with personal documentation and disguise, cover legends and supporting data, "pocket litter" and so forth, is a fundamental element in any clandestine operation. At OTS, personal documentation and disguise specialists, graphic artists, and other specialists spend hundreds of hours preparing materials, tailoring the cover legends, and coordinating the plan. If valuable human assets can no longer remain in place, then it is the official policy of the CIA to bring them in from the cold.

When it came to the houseguests, I could see that this was

going to be a tough nut to crack. RAPTOR had been a highly trained operative and still he had wilted under the pressure. With the six Americans we were basically dealing with untrained amateurs who were hiding out in a city seething with hatred for westerners. It would take all the resources we had to figure this one out.

The Department of State building at Twenty-third and C Street in downtown Washington, D.C., is massive. It was located just across the street from our own Foggy Bottom offices, so close in fact that sometimes we would eat lunch in their huge cafeteria.

The architecture of the State Department headquarters, both inside and out, was designed to be modern and sleek but had faded rather quickly into a series of bland rectangles with no character.

We were meeting with an undersecretary of state, a dignified woman who was very much in charge. She had a spacious office on the seventh floor. Present at the meeting, in addition to a young documents officer and myself, were two of her assistants, a member of CIA's cover staff, and a CIA Near East Division case officer who thought he was running the meeting. The case officer began by describing how he would plan and execute the exfiltration of the six State Department diplomats.

The undersecretary brought him up short. "Excuse me," she said, "but we haven't yet assigned the responsibility to you. We understand you're here to give advice, not to take charge. I assure you that since these are our diplomats, the department has the utmost concern with how we should comport ourselves in effecting their rescue."

Our man sat down and one of the undersecretary's aides took the floor. He described what they thought was the way to go about mounting such an operation. They seemed to favor a plan to bring out the six incrementally, effectively running three or more operations in tandem, not necessarily coming out through Tehran's Mehrabad Airport. At this point I interrupted.

"Excuse me," I began, "but my experience tells me that when we are managing a complex operation for more than one or two people, it's best to consolidate your risk, put everyone together under an appropriate cover, and take the shortest and quickest route out. It's one of the principles of guerrilla warfare: choose the time and place for action and overwhelm their senses."

I looked around the room and saw that I had everybody's attention.

"Exfiltrations are like abortions," I said. "You don't need one unless something's gone wrong. If you need one, don't try to do it yourself. We can give you a nice, clean job."

The undersecretary looked at me, startled, obviously appalled. Then, with a wry smile, she said, "Well, you do have a way with words, Mr. Mendez. I think maybe we can get on with it, and with you, after all."

I had begun honing my skills in exfiltration in the early 1970s. At the time, the Soviets were moving out into the third world and as a result we were getting more and more "walk-ins." A walk-in is just that: a defector who shows up at a U.S. embassy or otherwise presents himself to an official American entity and either asks for asylum or has valuable information that he wants to share. Any good case officer needs to know how to handle a walk-in, as it's the bread and butter of the spy business. Screw up a walk-in and you're done—simple as that.

So many Soviet personnel were going missing without a trace during this period that the KGB thought we must have been kidnapping them. In retaliation, there was even talk at the highest levels of the KGB about a program to kidnap American officials, but ultimately Yuri Andropov, the head of the KGB, nixed the idea.

My first exfiltration involved a high-level KGB officer codenamed NESTOR, who was posted to a Soviet embassy in a densely populated capital of the Asian subcontinent. At the time, I was stationed in Okinawa and running the twenty-five-man graphics branch when a cable arrived marked IMMEDIATE, asking for an artist-validator. The cable had been sent by a CIA officer I'll call "Jacob Jordan." He and I had first worked together on a job in Hong Kong in 1968, when I'd been asked to help forge the travel documents for a top Chinese asset.

Jacob, a senior OTS disguise and documents officer for Asia, was already a legend when I started working with him. Despite being from the Midwest, Jacob had an appearance and demeanor more Savile Row than Sears Roebuck. He wore custom-made shoes and expensive suits and in every way affected the air of a British gentleman. In all the time I spent with him, I never once saw him break character. A gifted linguist, he spoke fluent Mandarin Chinese, Korean, and Japanese. After joining the CIA's Technical Services Division (the precursor to OTS), Jacob's first posting was to Shanghai in 1949. By the time China had fallen into the hands of the communist Red Army, he was considered the leading American expert on the region.

Less than twenty-four hours after receiving Jacob's cable, I found myself, along with a documents officer, "David," holed up in a tiny vaultlike room in a Southwest Asian seaport. The two of us had flown into the country posing as tourists, and after checking into our hotel, had been picked up at a prearranged site by a local CIA officer, "Mac," and driven through back alleys to this secure location. The site was in a commercial office building that was a front for nonofficial contacts. The building stood amid a sea of similar office buildings, so it was no problem for us to blend in with the myriad British and American businessmen who plied their trade in this busy port.

Once we were inside, Mac introduced us to two more local CIA officers, "Raymond" and "Jane," who had been working around the clock for the past few days.

The whole reason for our being there had been set off twelve days earlier when NESTOR had walked out of the Soviet embassy and contacted a local CIA officer, telling him that he wished to defect. After confirming that NESTOR was indeed who he said he was, the CIA officer had given him instructions on how to get in touch, then promised to help organize his escape. NESTOR, meanwhile, had gone underground for several days before arriving at the prearranged rendezvous where Jacob was waiting.

If we could get him out of the country, NESTOR would be considered a huge catch. Not only was he an officer in the KGB's First Chief Directorate, the part concerned with foreign espionage, but he was also a member of a group that the CIA had dubbed the "Junior KGB." Under an alias, NESTOR had spent several years attending schools in England and the United States while posing as the son of Soviet officials legitimately stationed there—so he spoke fluent English with both a British and an American accent. After that, he had attended several KGB institutes in preparation for being stationed in Asia. As a result, not only could he provide invaluable intelligence on the KGB's operations in Central and Southeast Asia, but as an added bonus he could also help identify other "juniors" who were being trained overseas.

As expected, NESTOR's disappearance had triggered an avalanche of activity on the part of the KGB and the local Special Branch (SB). Surveillance around Western embassies and border crossings increased dramatically, while the KGB and SB flooded the airport, bus depots, and railway stations with agents. In addition, newspapers across the country ran notices about a missing Soviet attaché, and included a good photo of NESTOR to help anyone identify him. Being a Moscow-trained case officer, NESTOR had been able to avoid pursuit by shaving his head and disguising himself as one of the locals. But in order to get him past the thick security network arrayed against us, we would have to be at the top of our game.

We were especially worried about the security controls at the airport. Because of the manhunt going on, the airlines were requiring that all passengers reconfirm their flight in person before leaving the country. Somehow we'd have to come up with a way to overcome this final obstacle. But we'd need to move fast. We had only three days until it was time to launch.

When it comes to exfiltrations, the uninitiated almost always think about "black options," usually involving a nighttime helicopter pickup or a desperate border crossing in a car involving hidden compartments and an American spy smooth talking his way out of danger. The problem inherent in most of these scenarios is that if anything goes wrong, then there is no chance for plausible deniability. The American flag is going to be draped all over that helicopter or car if the plan falls apart. In certain situations, you have no choice—the only options available are black and you take your chances.

In most situations, however, a quasi-legal departure on a commercial flight is usually the simplest and most effective means of getting an asset out of the country. Jacob would provide the disguise for NESTOR, while David and I would create two sets of alias documents for him to use.

As I sat down to look at the operational plan for NESTOR, I could see immediately that there was no shortage of ideas about what to do back at headquarters. Raymond had brought over a thick stack of cables, each offering a different opinion. It seemed that everyone was piling on, something I would come to call the "committee effect."

Later, after a few days of twisting in the wind, Jacob came to a decision. He had been sleeping out at the safe site with NESTOR, prepping him for his disguise, and he knew the situation better than anyone. NESTOR was getting anxious, and as Jacob read through the cable traffic he shook his head in amazement. "Okay," he said when he was finished. "Here is what we are going to do." As I listened to Jacob lay it out, I realized I was learning a valuable lesson, one that I would take with me for the rest of my career: never preempt the man in the field. In this case Jacob knew that NESTOR spoke fluent German and could easily carry off the persona of a German businessman, headquarters reservations be damned. More important, since NESTOR was beginning to lose his nerve, Jacob informed us that he was going to take him through the airport "trunk to tail," meaning that he was going to be physically present in the airport to run interference in case anything went wrong. It was a risky move as NESTOR might compromise Jacob, but it would also allow him to address the problem of NESTOR's having to physically reconfirm his reservation, since Jacob could do it for him.

Once the cover had been chosen, Jacob got to work on NESTOR's disguise, transforming the short and stocky Russian into a distinguished German businessman. Using a camera that I had provided, he snapped a few photos in various poses and lighting setups, allowing David and me to put together a full complement of alias documents that would give the impression of a man at different stages of his life.

On the night of the exfiltration, my job was to watch from the rooftop departure lounge to see if Jacob and NESTOR had made it onto the plane. We had chosen a TWA flight that was set to depart at one in the morning. The flight was an hour late, however, and when it did finally arrive, the "smit"—a thick haze that hugs the ground composed of equal parts smoke and burning shit—was so dense that I could barely make out the silhouettes of the passengers as they made their way out onto the tarmac. When I didn't see Jacob or NESTOR among the embarking passengers, I became nervous. I was to learn later that everything inside had gone according to plan until NESTOR had arrived at the customs counter, where a turbaned official had promptly taken his passport and disappeared into a small room. A few minutes later the official returned followed by a European who was actually one of NESTOR's KGB colleagues. The two men stared at each other for a few long seconds before NESTOR, caught up in his persona, lit a Cuban cigar that Jacob had furnished him and exhaled a thick cloud of smoke in the direction of the KGB officer. The man continued to study NESTOR, but finally waved him through. The cigar had been the final piece that had fooled his ex-colleague.

A few minutes later I was able to see Jacob and NESTOR boarding the plane along with the remaining passengers.

When the plane finally took off for Athens a little before three in the morning, it fell to me to call Raymond and let him know that the operation had been a success. As I fumbled for a coin at the public pay phone, my body sagged from the heat and stress of the last three days. I had a sudden flash of panic that the phone wouldn't work, something that would haunt me for many years. But after dialing I heard it ring and then the unmistakable click as Raymond picked up the other line. As per our prearranged code to indicate that NESTOR had gotten out, I asked, "Is Suzy there?"

Playing along, Raymond shouted, "No!" and slammed down the phone.

When I finally made it back to my hotel, I was exhausted but couldn't sleep as the gravity of what we had accomplished sank in. Not only had we just pulled off one of the most important exfiltrations in the history of the Agency, but in my mind, we had also established a sort of framework by which all other exfiltrations would be run.

Every intelligence agency is ultimately judged on its ability to successfully rescue people and bring them out of harm's way, which is essentially what an exfiltration is. The key to doing this is readiness, and in the wake of NESTOR, the CIA began looking at ways we could improve our capabilities. One of the main lessons I had learned is that exfiltrations are almost ninety percent logistics—just making sure everything is lined up as it needs to be. Anticipating each one of those logistical problems can really mean the difference between success and failure. This need for readiness had already been highlighted in an earlier exfiltration involving Stalin's daughter, Svetlana, who had decided to defect while on a trip to India in 1967. She had been married to a man from India, and when he died, she had brought his ashes back to the country. Normally when Soviet citizens traveled, they were required to leave their passports at the local embassy. But she had convinced the Russian official that she was going to be leaving early the following morning and asked to have her passport so she could go without having to wait. After he handed it over, similar to NESTOR, Svetlana then left the Soviet embassy and walked straight over to ours. This was at midnight and the case officer sent an immediate cable to Washington asking for guidance. The response from headquarters was something to the effect that if Stalin had had a daughter, she would never have married an Indian. The case officer was now on the spot. Here was the one walk-in that could define the rest of his career. If it really was Stalin's daughter, then by morning the embassy was going to be surrounded and there'd be little chance of getting her out. Luckily, she had brought her documents along with her, which made things easier. Deciding that he couldn't take the chance, the officer put her on a plane and flew her out of the country in the early hours of the morning, before a proper search could be organized. She eventually made it into the refugee channels in Europe. As it turned out, she was telling the truth.

This operation as well as NESTOR's taught us that it would be in the best interest of the Agency to forward-deploy materials that would enhance our readiness. We began looking at probes and establishing prearranged routes for certain areas. One such route even included a border crossing on elephant back.

In order to tackle this concept of readiness, I came up with the idea of cross-training a select group of technical officers in various disciplines such as disguise and documents. It seems like a no-brainer now, but at the time it wasn't the way we did things. Dubbed the "generalist program," the idea was to create technical officers who could do things that were critical in the field and needed to be done quickly. Ideally, one officer could do the work of two specialists. In addition, a new position at headquarters would eventually be created, known as the special assistant to exfiltration, whose job it would be to keep tabs on all the CIA's exfiltration cases active worldwide. This would give us the ability to marshal resources at a moment's notice. When it came time for the next walk-in or exfiltration, we would be ready.

7

ASSEMBLING THE TEAM

Walking back to Foggy Bottom from our meeting with State, I realized that, much like the NESTOR case, there was no shortage of opinions when it came to the houseguests. Headquarters, Ottawa, and the State Department were all piling on. With the houseguests settled, however, it appeared as if we had some time to weigh our options. And then, just when I thought it couldn't get any more complicated, I learned that a Canadian journalist in Washington was onto the story and was about to go public.

In mid-December, the Canadian embassy in Washington, D.C., got a call from a journalist asking for confirmation on a story he was writing. Was it true, he wanted to know, that the Canadian embassy in Tehran was housing a group of fugitive American diplomats? The reporter was Jean Pelletier, and he was the Washington correspondent for the Montreal-based newspaper *La Presse*. Early in the hostage crisis, Pelletier had begun to question the logic behind why the State Department was being so secretive about how many Americans had been working at the embassy the day it was captured. The White House had yet to release an official list of names, or discuss details, which struck him as odd. He put himself in their shoes: *Why?* Then it hit him—had some Americans gotten out? Working his contacts at the U.S. State Department as well as at the Canadian embassy in Washington, he was able to eventually get confirmation to support his theory. For Pelletier it was the scoop of a lifetime, but he also had reservations. If the story were to be published prematurely, he realized, it could do more harm that good. Later in the afternoon his suspicions were confirmed when he got a call from the Canadian ambassador to the United States, Peter Towe, who asked him to sit on the story until the Americans had gotten out.

Pelletier agreed, but the fact that the story was beginning to leak made the Canadian government extremely apprehensive. What was to stop another journalist, one not as sympathetic, from writing a similar story? The last thing Canada needed was an international scandal involving its embassy in Tehran. The fact that the six Americans had gotten away did not bode well for them, as it might help to convince the militants that they had clandestine training—more "proof" that they were spies and not diplomats.

As word spread through Canadian diplomatic circles that a journalist was on to the secret of the houseguests, Ottawa began scrambling. In several cables back and forth to Iran, Ambassador Taylor was asked to give his opinion on possible scenarios to get the six out of Iran. Being that it was a small embassy, he often conferred with Roger Lucy, as he'd been a big help to Taylor during the evacuation of Canadian nationals from Iran the previous year. Most of the Canadians had been located in the Caspian region, so

Lucy had taken a driver and scouted along the Turkish and Russian borders, seeing if it was feasible to try to get them out overland. Ultimately they had decided to use a nearby airfield to fly them out instead.

The various ideas being floated for the houseguests ranged from driving them down to the Persian Gulf and getting them out on a ship to smuggling them out through a ratline and into Turkey. Both Taylor and Lucy felt that any scenario that involved driving overland was probably not going to work, as it would just increase the chances of getting caught if something went wrong.

When Canadian foreign minister Flora MacDonald heard the news, she was particularly alarmed. Something had to be done about the houseguests, and fast. At a meeting of NATO foreign ministers in Brussels on December 13, she cornered U.S. secretary of state Cyrus Vance and expressed her frustration that the United States was not doing enough. She then told him about Pelletier and the potential damage that could happen if the story of the houseguests ever became public. She was blunt and to the point, telling him that if nothing was done about the houseguests, she would put them on bicycles and have them ride for the Turkish border.

Informed by a colleague of the various catastrophes afoot, I realized we had to move fast. In the lead-up to the embassy takeover, gangs of komiteh had executed countless members of the shah's former government as well as any perceived collaborators. There was little doubt in my mind what would happen to the six Americans if captured. I spread the word that there was going to be a meeting in my office. I knew each member of my team was hard at work on other projects and that what I was about to tell them was only going to add to their already busy workload, but they were professionals and would give me everything they had no matter how much I asked from them.

The authentication branch had its offices on the third floor of Central Building at Foggy Bottom. As chief of the branch, I had an office suite located midway down the building's main corridor. Stepping through the open doorway, you were in a spacious outer office with a desk for the branch secretary, a reception area, and a registry area where members of the branch would come to collect or send out the classified mail. More urgent or highly sensitive communications would be moved around by hand-carry.

If you stood in the entrance of the branch offices and looked left, you would see the doorway to the deputy branch chief's office. Tim Small had been at one time my boss. Now I was his. Tim was older, in his fifties, an austere, humorless man from Eastern Europe whose office reflected his personality perfectly. There was no personal decor. Everything was in order; the desk was clean, the in-box empty. Tim dotted his I's and crossed his T's before anything else. "It pays to check" was his mantra. In fact, he was right. Nevertheless, we called him "the old fart," a nice balance to some of our younger officers.

Looking to the right, you would see the doorway to my office. Front and center on my desk was a sign about a foot long and six inches high. WORK STINKS, it read. On the walls were some paintings I had recently completed; my art rotated through the office as I completed fresh pieces and sold older ones.

The tall windows behind my secretary, Elaine Younger, looked down onto the interior courtyard of the compound. Elaine had a voice like a foghorn, partly due to her long history of smoking. Callers who had not personally met her would call her "sir" on the phone. She had been in the U.S. Marine Corps during World War II and was a no-nonsense woman. She typed with a cigarette hanging from her mouth. She guarded the door to our offices with true vigor and was as loyal to me, her new boss, as she was to her country, and God help anybody who crossed either one of us. Elaine had been there long before any of us arrived and would be there after most of us had gone. We were just passing through, as far as she was concerned.

The group entered my office one by one. In addition to Tim Small, there was Truman Smith, chief of production from graphics. Truman was a consummate graphics guardhouse lawyer-bureaucrat. He knew how to please his boss and how to commit mayhem on a guy's morale. Tall, blond, and with bad posture, the fiftysomething had the physique of an aging former football player—a lineman perhaps. Not particularly well liked, he was effective. "Deadlines R Us" might have been his motto. He and Tim Small had reached a cosmic balance of dislike. While there was room for only one of them, the jury was still out on which was worse.

Next came Joe Missouri and Dan Varga, two bright, young, energetic analysts from documents.

Joe had been in the CIA only about two years. He was a prime example of a "young fart," the kind that would balance out Tim Small's sometimes closed mind. I liked to put young and old in the same room because they would certainly have different takes on the same problem. Joe would eventually become our man in Canada on this operation, but that's getting ahead.

Joe was only about twenty-four years old. He was talented, not so much in languages as so many in Docs were, but in creating cover stories that were enormously credible. He was audacious. He also had a fierce sense of humor that served him, and us, well. Piercing dark brown eyes, a Mediterranean complexion, and a not-too-tall stature: Joe was a good "inside man."

Dan, meanwhile, came from the analytical portion of the CIA, the Deputy Directorate for Intelligence (DDI). He held an advanced degree in Chinese and was the picture of a young professor: receding hairline, trimmed beard, longish hair, plastic-rimmed glasses that looked like the standard GI issue. He had quite a sense of humor and was extremely smart. I was anxious to see what he would bring to this endeavor.

Next there was Doris Grange, our chief of disguise. Doris was a petite woman, but with a demeanor that prevented her from being overlooked when she spoke. She was both stylish and businesslike in her professional appearance, and one of the most capable disguise officers we had—she was the chief of her division, after all. Doris was charming but ambitious. She was considered a role model by many of our junior female officers. But underneath the aggressive facade, she had a soft nature and was a natural mentor.

The last member of our team was Jack Kerry, our resident PhD chemist. Jack was new to the CIA and to OTS. His assignment would be to support us in any research, development, and engineering (RD&E) requirement we might have—for instance, supplying us with a piece of technical equipment, or building one if it was needed. He was a gentle soul, extremely intelligent, intellectually curious, and very much an outdoorsman. His thinning hair, sparse beard, and prematurely gray hair belied the fact that he was only thirty-five years old.

I closed the door after Jack entered. Elaine didn't even look up, just flicked her cigarette ash into the wastepaper basket next to her desk.

"Everyone remember that memo from State we received a little while ago?" I asked. They all nodded. "Well, it appears things just became a whole lot more urgent." I explained the situation with Pelletier, which got everyone's attention.

"Okay," I said. "Let's start with the basics."

Since the epiphany in my studio, I had been informally tasking team members with preliminary planning for the exfiltration, and now it was time to examine the results. Our first priority would be to establish the route by which we could get the houseguests out of the country. We always knew our best option was on a commerical flight out of Mehrabad Airport.

This meant our major area of concern would be how to get the houseguests through the airport's draconian immigration controls. Every country's airport procedures were different, and the best way to understand them was to send a probe in and out to collect data. Iran's controls had been put in place under the shah, but thanks to the revolution, there was no telling what to expect. Protocol could shift from one day to the next. We were fortunate in one sense, however, since we already had a large collection of data on the customs and immigration controls at the airport thanks to the RAPTOR operation seven months before. In addition, we could augment our data collection by continuing to support the insertion of the advance team or running our own probes. Eventually a team of intelligence officers would need to make the final probe into Iran and meet up with the houseguests to assess their state of mind and ability to carry off the operation. Near East Division, meanwhile, would look into a potential black route for getting them out overland as a fallback, much like the one that Ross Perot had used to exfiltrate two of his employees a year earlier. At this stage, it was important not to rule anything out, and to have a fallback plan if necessary.

With that out of the way, we then turned to the problem of the cover, which posed a unique challenge. We had six American diplomats, male and female, varying in age from fifty-four to twenty-five. As far as we knew, none of them could speak a foreign language and none of them had any clandestine training. To make matters worse, because they worked in the consulate, which was heavily trafficked by Iranians, we suspected that their faces were probably pretty well known and that they might be on a watch list.

"We don't yet know what we are going to use for documents or what their cover is going to be, but we are going to have to come up with some of those answers quickly," I said. "I'm going to have to interface with NE/Iran on this and get them on board with anything we're going to do."

I turned to Dan and Joe. "So what do you think, guys? What have you got?" It would be the job of the documents branch to fabricate a realistic cover story for the houseguests to accompany their alias documents. For this reason they often kept backstopped alias documents on the shelf ready to use in a moment's notice. But depending on the subject, there are really only a few nationalities that would work at any given time, and until they started inventing new countries, we had to be incredibly careful about wasting them.

This problem had been highlighted when the militants at the embassy had ferreted out two altered documents issued to two

CIA officers captured at the embassy. Both of the documents corresponded with friendly Western powers, and had almost created a diplomatic scandal. The defense minister for one of the countries in question just happened to be touring Langley when the news broke, and he asked pointedly how many more of these items the CIA had fabricated. "Just the one," he was told. "Like hell," the minister had muttered. As a result we had to be incredibly selective about what kinds of documents we used.

"How about one of the Nordic countries?" Dan responded.

"Okay," I said. "What are six people from northern Europe doing in Tehran?"

Joe piped in. "Do they all have to be from the same place? We could issue each of them a travel document from a different country and then have them line up at the airport as if they just happened to arrive all together."

"The real problem," I said, "is that no one in headquarters believes that these people are going to be able to carry any foreign cover. They're not even sure they could carry false U.S. passports."

In an earlier call with Hal, who after the RAPTOR operation had been promoted to the Near East Division's chief for Iran, the two of us had discussed the possibility of the houseguests' using foreign documents for their cover story. Since none of the houseguests had even basic training in the tradecraft needed to carry off a foreign cover, he doubted it would work. "Besides," he had said, "almost everyone in Iran speaks a foreign language, and we can't risk that they might stumble upon somebody who could question them in their 'native' tongue."

"What is State saying?" asked Tim.

"Their idea is to have them be unemployed U.S. schoolteachers who had come to Iran looking for work," I said. "They could give us any of the documentation we would need, but that would still make them U.S. citizens, which doesn't seem like the best idea to me."

"What about Canadian passports?" Doris asked.

"That would make the most sense, but I don't know if they'll go for it. I'd like to pose the question while I am in Ottawa and see if they jump."

"When are you going?" Joe asked.

"I am scheduling it now," I said. "I want to get up there as soon as possible, and if we are going to ask them for Canadian documents, we need to have done it yesterday." I had already decided that it would be Joe's job to come up with a cover legend for the six. Working in documents did not mean that Joe was a forger. The forgers were the artist-validators who worked in the bullpen, a position I had held myself in the earliest days of my career. Documents people were in charge of maintaining travel documents and understanding the controls related to those documents. They often traveled on probes to update their portfolios and knew what kinds of documents would be needed by a person in order to carry off a certain cover.

"Joe, I want you with me. This may not be legal, and they may say no, but if they say yes, I want to be ready to move on it."

"What do we need to take with us?" Joe asked. Joe had already gone across the street to the State Department and requested current passport photographs of the six houseguests. He had also collected current samples of their handwriting and had assigned them alias names in advance. He had done all of this background work without knowing in which direction we were going to go with their documentation. *Be prepared*. It was not just a Baden-Powell Boy Scout motto. It was the motto of the intelligence officer as well.

"Bring everything you've got," I replied. "We might be able to use it all."

There was a knock at the door. I looked up to see Elaine poking her head around the corner. "They're here," she said. When she saw the puzzled look on my face, she took a drag off her cigarette and blew the smoke out into the vestibule. "The Christmas Door Decorating Committee from the art shop," she explained. I looked at her without speaking. "I'll just close the door and they can do this without any fuss," she said, closing the door with a small clatter. I shook my head.

I turned to Doris. "In the meantime, Doris, we don't know yet what the disguise requirement will be, but I want to make sure that you and the disguise section are ready in case you are needed."

"Got it," she said.

"Okay," I said, "this has just become the highest priority. So get your heads together and see what you can come up with."

8

COVER STORY

As the end of December neared, the houseguests' initial calm was beginning to wane. They spent hours on end trying to combat the boredom, drinking too much, sleeping too much, and fantasizing about escape. After reading so many le Carré novels, Schatz had a good idea of how he could pull it off. In one scenario he wore "native dress" to blend in while he hiked over the border into Pakistan. In another he drove a car he'd stashed somewhere in the city up to the Turkish border. In a third, he was at the controls of a small speedboat racing across the Persian Gulf, the chaos of Iran disappearing behind him in a haze. The more he read, the more he fantasized.

The others were getting antsy as well. By this time they had played Scrabble so much that they could recognize the individual tiles just by the wood grain on the backs of the pieces. After nearly two months they began to feel forgotten and wondered if anything was being done to rescue them.

Their only source for news was to listen to the BBC in the morning. Mark had gotten into the habit of sleeping late and often missed the broadcast, so Anders would give him a recap. In an attempt to deflect anger away from the United States, on December 15 the shah, who was well enough to travel, had left the United States and gone to Panama. The militants, however, seemed not to care. In their minds it was the United States that was pulling the strings, not Panama. To make matters worse, on December 26 the Soviets had invaded Afghanistan, which only heightened tensions in the region. With the Soviet army fighting on Iran's doorstep, the military options for attacking Iran became even more limited. In a strange twist, the White House suddenly found itself in the awkward position of having to do all it could to bring the hostages home while at the same time trying to counter Soviet aggressions in the region. In many ways, the invasion of Afghanistan became the initial spark that would eventually lead Iran and the United States back to the table. No one could foresee this, though. Iran had gone through a series of new foreign ministers, each more ineffective than the last. The will of the Revolutionary Council could not be questioned for any reason, and anyone seen to be negotiating with the United States was labeled a traitor. On top of this, the militants at the embassy continued to stoke the revolutionary hysteria sweeping the nation with their rhetoric and public displays of blindfolded Americans, all of them liars, all of them spies, all of them out to destroy the revolution.

It's no wonder, then, that on December 31, when the UN secretary-general, Kurt Waldheim, traveled to Iran in an attempt to ameliorate the crisis, he was nearly assaulted at the airport by angry crowds. And as if that wasn't humiliating enough, later that afternoon he was rebuffed by the Revolutionary Council and unceremoniously sent home like a dog with its tail between its legs. A few days later he would meet with White House officials and recount what had happened. As President Carter wrote in *Keeping Faith*, Waldheim had tears in his eyes as he spoke about his visit, and believed that "he was lucky to be alive."

Christmas helped to break up the monotony for the houseguests, if only for a few days. To get in the spirit, Cora decided to bake Christmas cookies. The Sheardowns had a massive countertop and soon it was covered by all manner of iced cookies. Mark and Lee were helping to decorate when suddenly an Iranian secretary from the Canadian embassy showed up at the door, and they were forced to abandon their work. Taylor of course hadn't told any of the Iranian staffers, and so none of them knew about the houseguests. When the secretary walked into the kitchen, Zena had to pretend that the cookies had been one of her projects. The secretary was impressed, saying she had always been curious about what Zena did while she was at home.

One evening, when Roger Lucy was bringing the houseguests back from the Taylors', Lee, Mark, and Bob stopped outside the garage. It had recently snowed and they couldn't resist scooping some of the snow up in their hands and launching snowballs at a nearby streetlamp. They laughed like kids until it occurred to them what might happen if the streetlamp was damaged. No doubt it would result in a visit from the local komiteh. They immediately stopped horsing around and went back inside.

For Christmas, John had somehow managed to buy a huge turkey from a farm outside of Tehran, and everyone pitched in to do their part. Lee took the lead in preparing the bird, along with a security guard from the Canadian embassy who was a former military cook. In true *Galloping Gourmet* fashion, they started drinking early. The turkey was so large that the roasting pan required two people to lift it out of the oven, one person on each side. Near the end of the roasting, as they took the bird out to see if it was done, one of them stumbled. The turkey slid out of the tipped pan and shot across the floor. The two of them looked at each other, then at the doors to the kitchen, then quickly picked it up and popped it back into the pan. When they were finished cleaning up, the two chefs raised a toast to having saved the meal. Later, Ambassador Taylor brought the Staffords over and everyone sat down to enjoy the meal, none the wiser.

For presents, Schatz bought everybody some worry beads and a Khomeini prayer rug. "I'm going to use mine as a doormat," he said. Others suggested using it to train a puppy. In an ironic twist, the Iranian government had given the Sheardowns a tin of caviar as a Christmas gift, and everyone happily devoured it. Looking back, the houseguests remember the Christmas of '79 with fondness, realizing correctly that they were incredibly lucky to be celebrating it at the Sheardowns' and not trapped along with their colleagues at the U.S. embassy.

The militants had promised the hostages at the embassy that they would be able to participate in some kind of Christmas celebration, complete with a service and a chance to go to confession. Instead what they got was a charade. In groups of threes and fours they were brought into a room filled with decorations. A Christmas tree with twinkling lights sat in the corner while tables had been stacked with Christmas goodies, some of them sent by Americans in care packages. Three American clergymen had been invited, and the hostages were filmed sitting on couches and singing "Silent Night" to the accompaniment of one of the clergymen on the piano. Of course, while this seemingly innocuous scene was playing itself out, a row of militants stood just off camera, twirling pistols and fondling rifles. Before entering the room, the hostages had been told that they were not allowed to talk.

Recognizing the event for what it was, many of the hostages refused to speak to the ministers, whom they felt were traitors for helping the militants. A few were annoyed when one of the ministers, William Sloane Coffin of the United Church of Christ, suggested that the hostages should sing and hold hands with the Iranians as a sign of solidarity. For most of the hostages, the ceremony only reminded them of what they were missing: home. One hostage later described it as the moment he hit rock bottom.

Still, the one positive thing to come out of the whole experience was that the clergy were able to convey to the hostages that the people back home cared, and cared a lot. All over America, special Christmas services were being held in honor of the hostages, while schoolchildren wrote Christmas cards and sent candy and cookies. For most of the hostages, who were not allowed to receive mail, it was the first time they had ever heard about the public reaction back in the United States. And it lifted their spirits to know that there was a whole nation hoping and praying that they all made it home safe.

By early January, I felt we were sufficiently ready to travel to Ottawa and present our case to the Canadians. Before going, however, I would need to head over to the Near East

Division at headquarters and confer with them. The deputy chief, Eric Neff, had recently been to Ottawa, and I wanted to find out the best way to proceed with the Canadian government.

Eric's office, on the sixth floor of the headquarters building, was spacious by headquarters standards, with plenty of light coming in through tall windows that gave a panoramic view of the tops of the trees. These were the very same trees that had caused Allen Dulles to remark that our Langley compound was more like a "campus" than a government facility.

As always, Eric was dressed in his somewhat excessively refined manner, with a polka dot tie, French cuffs, and custom-made boots. He stood in sharp contrast to the rest of the male CIA population, who sported Harris tweeds, button-down shirts, club ties, and cordovan wing tips, almost like a uniform. To Eric the dress code was always formal. The other guys in Eric's division often complained about it, noting that if they were ever invited over to dinner at Eric's house they would be required to wear their patent leather slippers. Eric and I had worked together on a project in South Asia when he was a CIA chief there, and I had nothing but admiration for his abilities. Sitting in on the meeting were Joe Missouri and Hal, the chief for Near East/Iran.

Once the houseguests had become a top priority, Eric had traveled to Canada to make the CIA's initial representation. While in Ottawa he'd been able to establish a unique back-channel method whereby we would be able to communicate through Ottawa to Ken Taylor in Tehran. It was very effective and in the coming month would become almost like our own private compartmented line. In my communications with Ken Taylor I would find a kindred spirit. He had performed admirably in sheltering the hostages and had been a valuable go-between for the State Department and the diplomats trapped at the foreign ministry. He appeared to be a quick study and had a knack for being able to keep a secret, qualities that would make him an asset on the ground for us in Tehran. One of the first things I would do would be to ask him what he thought about cover options for the houseguests.

At this point, however, the key issue was documentation.

"Can we ask the Canadians for the use of their passports?" I asked Eric, cutting to the chase.

Eric said, somewhat defensively, that he had already raised the issue. "But you can do it again, if you wish," he continued.

I nodded and told him that I would. I indicated Joe, and mentioned that I would be taking him with me, then introduced the young officer to Eric and Hal. Joe was dressed more like a seedy professor than one of Eric's officers in full dress mode, and he seemed hesitant, almost apologetic, when he shook Eric's hand.

Joe's role in Ottawa would be to establish the continuity between the CIA and the Canadians, essentially setting up partnerships between his OTS colleagues and their mirror images in Ottawa. This would free me up to handle the more strategic negotiations with the Canadians, Tehran, and the U.S. government. Dealing with the State Department, the White House, and the senior levels of the CIA, working through Eric, was a daunting task. I would soon discover that the simplicity with which the Canadian government operated would make it a dream to work with by comparison.

Eric, by his very nature, was overbearing. He wasn't really sure how I would proceed, but he did try to exercise some of the privilege of his office. His instructions were a little stilted, but he meant well. For instance, when in response to my question about the passports he said he'd already raised the issue, he was a little miffed that I would bring it up, as though I was stepping on his toes. Eric was trying to figure out how to run an exfiltration, something he had never done before, and represent himself to Canada as an expert on the subject. He was also the channel between President Carter and Stansfield Turner, the director of central intelligence. It was like a tripod: the president, the DCI, and the Canadians. Eric's job was to maintain a delicate balance between the policy makers and the clandestine elements in the field. I didn't envy him.

The winter sky was gray and there were traces of snow on the ground as our plane touched down in Ottawa. The city itself struck me as being a little dingy, but the parliament buildings gave a certain air of elegance to what was essentially a small town.

We checked into the Lord Elgin Hotel, a stately, gothic pile of stones in the middle of Ottawa close to most government offices. It was decorated with photographs, paintings, and flower arrangements full of tulips, an incongruous contrast in the middle of the dark winter days of Canada.

Just in case he needed a reminder that the life of a real spy was nothing like what we see in the movies, the airline had lost Joe's luggage. And with only the clothes on his back, he was forced to borrow one of my ski sweaters, which he would wear for the next ten days while he remained in the Canadian capital. Strangely, it would not be the only article of clothing that I would lose on this operation.

The following day, Joe and I headed over to the U.S. embassy for our first meeting with members of the CIA's Canadian offices. The CIA chief in Ottawa, a tall, slim, middle-aged man, cheerfully went over the meetings they had set up for us that day.

At the first meeting later that morning, Joe and I got right to the point. We sat down across the table from a slight but impeccably dressed middle-aged man. I'll call him "Lon Delgado." He clasped his hands together and looked me straight in the eye.

"What can I do for you?" he asked.

"We're here, first of all, to thank you for all that Canada has done for America on this matter," I replied. "Second, as you might guess, we're here with our hat in hand, asking for more favors. And so we apologize for that. We feel fortunate that our relations, government to government, are so beneficial."

I paused, measuring my words. "What do you think the prospects would be for allowing us to use Canadian passports to provide cover for our six diplomats?" There it was, out in the open. The thing we wanted most and thought would be the hardest to negotiate. I realized that we were asking for the Canadians to make an exception to their own passport law. My research had told me that the only way to do this was by a special "order-in-council," requiring the consent of Parliament.

Mr. Delgado opened a file in front of him and extracted a piece of paper with a large red wax seal on it. He set it aside and softened his demeanor while he responded. "I think we've already done that," he said.

We were stunned. I tried to imagine what it would take for a representative of a foreign government to come to Washington and ask the U.S. Congress to pass an exception to our own passport law. It was no minor matter.

What I didn't know was that the Canadians had been working on the problem of the passports for quite some time. From the day that the houseguests had come under their care, I think the Canadians realized the logic of allowing them to use Canadian documentation. I would later learn that the order-in-council had been passed during a rump session of Parliament, when Flora MacDonald, working in concert with Prime Minister Joe Clark, had maneuvered the issue in such a way that it could be passed without debate. This was because only a few cabinet ministers knew anything about the houseguests to begin with and the need for secrecy was paramount.

At that point I decided to press our luck, asking Delgado if we could have six spares for the six houseguests to give us a redundant capability for the operation, as well as two additional passports for use by CIA "escorts." Lon agreed to get us an extra set for the houseguests, but rebuffed our latter request. The exception to the passport law had been made for refugees, not professional intelligence officers. "Sorry," he said, "but you'll have to get your own."

There is an understanding among intelligence services that there is no such thing as a "friendly" service. At this time in history Canada did not admit to even having a secret intelligence service. But this man was probably very close to representing that capability. And it certainly felt friendly. Mr. Delgado continued, "Do you have a list of names to be used for the passports?" he asked. "And by the way, we are going to need photographs as well."

Without hesitation Joe reached into his briefcase and brought out an envelope, the contents of which were the list of names that he had already prepared as aliases for the six. Accompanying each name was a passport-sized photograph. Along the vertical margin on each photo we had forged the alias names in the handwriting of each of the six houseguests. This was the way it should be in the Canadian passport.

Mr. Delgado reviewed the material very quickly. He commented that the photographs looked good but that one of the names we'd chosen had a slightly Semitic sound to it—not a good idea in a Muslim nation. He thought we should fix it and Joe suggested a new name. Delgado nodded in the affirmative and Joe produced another clean photograph of Kathy Stafford, handing it to me. "You're an artist-validator, Tony," he said.

Using a technique I'd learned from my early days in the bullpen, I positioned the photo on the corner of Delgado's desk and signed Kathy's new name in her handwriting.

J oe and I left the meeting encouraged. The first phase of our plan was coming together with much less effort than we had ever imagined. We had a commitment for six Canadian passports for our subjects plus a set of duplicates, which would give us an option for a fallback plan if we needed it.

After breaking for lunch at the Lord Elgin, we were picked up by an official car and taken to the ministry of defense.

Prior to coming to Canada, we had learned that Ambassador Taylor was in the process of drawing down his embassy, which could help us with our intelligence-gathering operation. Of special interest to us were the military police who had been working at the embassy. Many of the military police were well traveled and familiar with border procedures around the world. We wanted to set up a system in which if any more of them traveled in or out of Mehrabad Airport, they would have a standard debriefing on the controls.

With that done, I returned to Washington the next morning, leaving Joe behind to follow up on the passports and to meet with the national security forces who would help in rounding out the documentation packages that would complement the passports. They would also arrange for the collection of an Iranian visa issued in Canada. Joe would spend the following ten days in Canada tending to these chores.

I boarded my flight home feeling a sense of accomplishment accompanied by relief that we had been able to move this project forward in a major way. I also felt gratitude that we were working with a neighbor who was truly supportive of America's dilemma.

On my way home, I reflected on Canada and its government. The "Small Is Beautiful" mantra kept playing in my mind. The Canadian government appeared ready and able to turn on a dime if necessary, and our government seemed bloated and sluggish in comparison. The fact that the Canadians had anticipated our needs and had taken the extraordinary steps required to reach out to us was a little overwhelming and certainly unprecedented. They were redefining what it meant to be a good neighbor.

With the issue of documents behind us, we could now focus on the question of which cover story to use. The importance of having a good cover story and accompanying documentation can sometimes be the difference between life and death. One of the most famous cases in the history of the CIA happened in Cuba in 1960. A group of three audio techs,

Thornton Anderson, Walter Szuminski, and David Christ, all from the Technical Services Division, had traveled to Cuba on a bugging mission. Ostensibly they were posing as three American tourists out to have a good time. All of them carried forged documents saying that they were electrical engineers, and in their wallets they carried credit cards and driver's licenses, all of it faked by the capable TSD techs who had furnished them with their aliases. Their real purpose for traveling to Cuba was to install clandestine listening devices in a building that was slated to become the embassy of a very important hard-target third country. In the middle of installing the devices, however, they were captured and thrown into the local prison. If just one of them broke, or a flaw was detected in their documentation, then they would all be labeled spies and most likely executed. In total the men would spend nearly a month undergoing harsh interrogations during the night, but they never once cracked. Eventually they were transferred to a notorious prison outside Havana. They would finally be released three years later, when the U.S. government arranged to swap them for some tractors. In all that time, their cover held and they were never found guilty of spying. For their courage all three would be awarded the Agency's highest medal for bravery, the Distinguished Intelligence Cross.

When I got back to Foggy Bottom, my team and I began an all-source quest for information on the types of groups traveling in and out of Mehrabad Airport. We soon discovered that groups traveling legally to Iran included oil field technicians from European-based companies, news teams of all nationalities covering the hostage situation, and all sorts of curiosity seekers and aid workers from around the world. Many of these people were U.S. citizens.

None fit our purposes, given the profiles and patterns of these groups, and the careful scrutiny and control applied to them by the Iranian security and immigration services.

Unlike in the movies, cover stories are normally designed to be boring so as not to attract attention. They are also chosen based on the experience of the person. There are several factors that go into the process of choosing a cover. Does the person speak a foreign language, and can they pass for another nationality? Do they have any clandestine training? We had made both NESTOR and RAPTOR businessmen. In the past I had traveled as a tourist or a midlevel diplomat, both situations I could easily manage. Just as important as who the person might be is his or her ability to carry off a new persona and make it believable. This was why it had been so important for Jacob Jordan to meet with NESTOR, and why I was now proposing to headquarters that we send in a team to assess the houseguests. Whatever reason we came up with for them to be in Iran, it had to be something that they could wear as comfortably as a suit, something that became them and was almost second nature to them. No easy task when you are dealing with six amateurs.

The State Department had proposed that the six use U.S. documentation and be disguised as unemployed English teachers who had traveled to Iran presumably to find work, while Ottawa's idea was to turn the houseguests into nutritionists who had traveled to Iran to inspect crops. A third option had them posing as petroleum workers. None of these options was really clicking for me. Most of the English schools in Tehran had closed months earlier and it would seem odd to have such a large group of out-of-work teachers show up all together. As far as the Canadian plans, I didn't think it would take long for a Revolutionary Guard to figure out that these people knew nothing about agriculture or petroleum. Iran was completely snowbound in the winter and it just didn't seem believable that a group of nutritionists would be inspecting crops at that time of year.

We needed a cover that could help to engage them, get them to believe in us and to become willing participants. Pretending to be someone you are not isn't as easy as it sounds, especially if your life depends on it. I had seen trained operatives like RAPTOR nearly break under the pressure.

My team and I discussed the pros and cons of each option. Everybody seemed to agree with my assessment, but no one had any better ideas.

With several other things on our plate, I broke up the meeting and we decided to reconvene later.

We spent the remainder of the week working out the problem but still weren't able to come up with anything. Then, as I was standing in my studio getting ready to head back to Ottawa to check in on Joe, an idea suddenly occurred to me. While it was true that normally cover stories were designed to be mundane, we weren't dealing with a normal situation here. So instead of boring, what if we went in the opposite direction? What if we designed a cover story so fantastic that nobody would believe it was being used for operational purposes?

By the time I had landed in Ottawa, I had formulated a plan. If we could pull it off, it would be one of the most audacious rescue operations in the history of the CIA. But before moving forward I would have to call the one person who could make that plan a reality. I picked up the phone and dialed.

9

HOLLYWOOD

I met Jerome Calloway for the first time during the early 1970s, on the set of a spy-themed TV show. The show was popular in the late 1960s and early 1970s, known for pushing the limits of visual effects and makeup. Calloway had been brought in by the production specifically to devise each episode's signature shot—the crafty spy finally revealing his true identity. The show, along with a film that Calloway had worked on around that time, had caught the eye of Lou Terno, then the CIA's chief of disguise. Much like in the TV show, during the film a succession of well-known actors magically revealed their movie star good looks after taking off a series of outlandish, but entirely believable, disguises. For instance, a famous male singer with one of the most recognizable faces in the world was disguised as an old woman, but you would have never known it. For Terno, the wonder he experienced as he watched the star emerge from his vulcanized chrysalis was akin to that of a remote Amazonian tribe suddenly witnessing a Fourth of July fireworks display. It was miraculous. "How come we can't do that?" he exclaimed.

Terno had then flown out to Los Angeles to meet with Calloway. This was right after NESTOR, when the CIA was beginning to think about forward-deploying "kits" to improve our readiness in case we might need to carry out an exfiltration within a moment's notice. Terno wasn't sure what Calloway could do, but hoped he'd be open to advising us in some way.

Calloway, who had served in the army in World War II, was only too happy to help. He was a patriot through and through, and loved the idea that he could again do something for his country. Before getting involved with Hollywood, he had worked for many years creating false noses and glass eyes for wounded soldiers. In fact, even after he had become a lion in the entertainment industry, this aspect of his early professional life was always the one that had most gratified him. To him, producers were just a bunch of barracudas out to take your lunch.

A few months after Terno's trip, I had flown back to Washington from Okinawa to receive some training as part of authentication's new generalist program. This was the very same program that I had proposed after the NESTOR operation as a way to deploy cross-trained technical officers closer to the action. Jacob and I were given the opportunity to test out the theory by forming the first team. We were to be stationed in the Far East, but first I would need to get trained in disguise.

Back then the disguise techniques used by the CIA really weren't anything to write home about—mostly utilizing off-the-rack department store wigs, glasses, and hats. It's no wonder, I thought, that most officers in the field refused to wear this stuff. In all, the training lasted about ten days, at which point I was certified an "expert." It was while I was on my way back to Asia that Terno asked me to stop off in LA and visit with Calloway.

From its inception, the CIA has relied on the ingenuity of outside contractors to help American spies keep pace with their adversaries. Unlike our Soviet counterparts, who enjoyed strong government support, in the wake of World War II America's spies found themselves out of a job when President Truman disbanded the OSS in 1945. It wouldn't be until 1947 that the United States would have a functioning intelligence agency again, but even then it was grossly underfunded when compared to its rivals. In addition, America's spymasters found it hard to compete with the private sector, which could not only pay more, but also offer its scientists the prospect of accolades and recognition, something a spy agency could not. As a result, the CIA found itself at a technological disadvantage for nearly the first two decades of its existence. Even by the early 1960s, for example, the CIA had yet to create a small and reliable spy camera that agents could use to copy documents. This disadvantage became painfully obvious when one of America's most important Russian agents, Colonel Oleg Vladimirovich Penkovsky, was rolled up in the fall of 1962 and executed in 1963.

To overcome this technology deficit, the Agency began hiring more techs right out of college, while farming out various projects to the private sector. For instance, in looking for help to design a new miniature camera known as the T100 in the early 1970s, OTS techs turned to a precision optical contractor that was able to design the camera's 4mm-diameter lens. When it was finished, the camera was so small it could fit into a fountain pen. Another example saw OTS techs working with a leading hearing aid manufacturer to create a microphone that was small enough to fit into a .45 caliber bullet. The techs were looking for a way to plant a listening device inside a tree that was in the courtyard of a foreign embassy. The trick, of course, was that the microphone had to work even after the bullet had embedded itself into the tree. It took some time, but ultimately the company was successful.

In addition to Calloway, I would work with many outside contractors throughout my career. In the mid-1970s I worked with a magic builder who had designed magic tricks for illusionists and Hollywood productions to help perfect a device known as the JIB. The idea behind the JIB was to allow an officer riding in the passenger seat of a car to evade surveillance by having a dummy pop up in his place just as he exited the car. In order to succeed, however, the exchange had to be done so quickly that the KGB surveillance car trailing behind didn't see it happen. The device went through several iterations, from an initial slightly modified inflatable sex doll to a space-age contraption that weighed nearly fifty pounds. Thinking of how we could simplify it, I had contacted the magic builder, who was a friend of Calloway's (the two had actually worked together on a James Bond film, of all things). The magic builder's solution was an elegant device that could be hidden inside a variety of objects and worked on the same principle as an umbrella. When it was finally finished, the driver of the car could even animate the device by using a small controller to make its head turn.

During our first meeting, Calloway took me around the set of the spy-themed TV show, introducing me as his "friend from the army," a phrase he always accompanied with a wink. In later years this would become a big inside joke with him. "This is my friend— he does special effects for the army."

By the time I met him, he was already considered one of the most innovative makeup artists in the movie business. He had won top industry awards for his work on a science fiction film.

As he took me around, someone came up behind us and said, "Jerome Calloway is a sissy." We turned to see one of the stars of the TV show walking up behind us. The joke was funny if you knew Jerome. A first-generation American who had grown up in Chicago, Calloway had a larger-than-life quality to him. His big, expressive face sat framed by a pair of thick-rimmed fifties-style glasses, while his hair was often slicked back with a thick sheen of pomade. He was a large man who looked more like a bouncer than a makeup artist, and he wore white short-sleeved shirts and black ties almost as if they were his uniform. Here and there, however, he would exhibit a certain kind of panache. He wore a little pinky ring with a precious stone in it and drove a pastel yellow Pontiac, the biggest one they made.

Despite having grown up far away from the movie business, Calloway had been drawn to the limelight from the very beginning. He told me that when he was just a kid in Chicago, he had heard about a warehouse fire in his neighborhood. He'd rushed down in the hopes that by volunteering he might get his picture in the newspaper. When a photographer had snapped a photo of him and another person lugging a stretcher, he thought for sure he would see himself on the front page. The following morning, however, he was disheartened to see that the photographer had cut him out of the picture with the exception of his hands. He used to relate this story as a cautionary tale on the emptiness of fame. "You go to all that trouble and in the end, the only thing they might remember you for are your hands!"

Going anywhere with Calloway was an adventure, whether it

was to a local hamburger dive for lunch or into one of the many worlds that inhabited his stories. An inveterate storyteller, Calloway had a flair for the dramatic. And when his arms would get working and that toothy grin would flash, his enthusiasm was contagious. Several well-known movie stars refused to work unless he did their makeup. One of his favorite clients was Bob Hope. A born joke teller, he and Hope would trade one-liners the whole time Calloway would work on him.

After taking me around the set, Jerome and I went back to his studio in Burbank, which was essentially the garage of his suburban bungalow. His house was small but neat. He was married to a nice woman in the cookie-cutter mold of the 1950s and lived with his ninety-year-old father, an ex-plumber for the city of Chicago whom he aptly called "Pop."

Walking through his garage was like walking through a museum of sorts. Calloway had modified the space by adding a little office and studio. He had tables and workstations all lined with materials in various stages of completion. There were two storage sheds behind the garage that were filled with just about everything he had ever done—rubber noses, ears, monster parts. He was always getting calls from other makeup artists asking for help, some even as far away as Australia. If you told him you were looking for a particular kind of nose, nine times out of ten he would find it in a shoe box in one of his storage sheds. Though perhaps the most striking artifacts he had stored in his garage were the busts of several famous actresses. Back before the days of plastic surgery, Calloway had been hired to take molds of the chests of certain actresses to then be able to make natural foam rubber "falsies" to put in a bra and make the women look more endowed. He kept these busts covered by towels, but occasionally he would unveil them when a friend would drop by. One of the many stories that he told involved a famous English actor walking in and seeing the mold of his wife's chest. "Do you recognize it?" Calloway had asked him. "She looks familiar," the actor said hesitantly. Calloway then informed him that it belonged to the man's wife, who was a young up-and-coming actress at the time.

Joking aside, Calloway was truly gifted at his job. He was innovative and intellectually curious, always pushing new technologies. Ahead of his time, he was constantly reaching out to chemical manufacturers, looking for products, developing products, doing whatever he had to do to get the results he wanted. And nothing but the best would do. He was a master and a blast to collaborate with. If you had a job that needed to be done, or even just a loose sketch, then Jerome either had the solution or would work it out in a very short time. Oftentimes he had already done it and had it hidden away somewhere in his studio. "That sounds like the piece I made for Robert Mitchum."

Needless to say, the two of us hit it off right away. The process of creating a good disguise was very similar to that of creating a work of art, and I think the two us realized we were kindred spirits. After our first meeting, it wouldn't be long before I would be asking for his help.

Returning to Asia from Los Angeles, I soon found myself in Vientiane, the capital of Laos. With the war winding down in neighboring Vietnam, Vientiane had become a hub for clandestine activity. It was like Dodge City on the Mekong. As soon as night fell, intelligence services from all over the world would descend upon the city's principal roundabout to perform their rolling car pickups. A rolling car pickup is just that: an officer driving the car slows just enough so that a person can quickly dive into the backseat without being seen. There were so many rolling car pickups going on at this roundabout in Vientiane that people were getting into the wrong cars. At one point I was responsible for running twenty-six different disguises. It was all I could do to keep track.

Then one day I was approached by one of the local CIA senior case officers with a real problem. He was one of the few—if not the only—African Americans in town, which made him an easy target for surveillance. By a strange set of events, he had found himself stationed in the country when the new U.S. ambassador to Laos, who had known the officer in Congo, had requested him. The officer had been meeting with an important Laotian minister who had vital inside information on the communist side of the Indochina peace talks. The two had been meeting in secret for many weeks, but with the Pathet Lao closing in on the city, the local militia had instituted a curfew and had begun throwing up random roadblocks. The case officer knew that if the Laotian minister was caught with him it would be a disaster.

After he explained his predicament, I sat there for a few seconds wondering what I was going to do. Coming up blank, I explained to the case officer that we would accompany him on his next pickup to meet with the minister and get him programmed for a disguise. In the meantime, I sent a cable back to headquarters right away asking for their instructions. Almost immediately I got a reply saying they didn't know what to do either. The thing that worried them the most, they said, were the ears. In other words, the only thing they could think of was a device we were working on for our officers heading to the Soviet Union, which sat on the face but didn't cover up the ears.

I then thought about some of the appliances I had seen in Calloway's garage and wondered if he might have something that could help. First, however, I would have to meet with the Laotian minister to get his measurements, which I was able to do after being subjected to my own rolling car pickup. After I had all his information, I sat down and wrote a long cable outlining my plan. In the cable, I specified my idea, then asked headquarters to forward the information I was including to Calloway.

As I was later to learn, Calloway had gotten the measurements and had gone right out to his storage sheds. He had made masks of most of the stars in Hollywood for their stunt doubles to wear, and it just so happened that the specs I'd sent him fit those for Victor Mature and Rex Harrison.

After an interval of a few weeks, I received a package from headquarters. Inside were two masks, along with the other materials I had requested, including a pair of flesh-colored gloves. The disguise techniques that Jacob and I were eventually able to put together for this operation are still classified. When we were finished, Jacob and I were able to transform the African American case officer and the Laotian minister into two Caucasians who loosely resembled Rex Harrison and Victor Mature. As it turned out, after we had disguised them, they were on their way back from the safe house when our worst fears were realized. A random roadblock had been set up and the two were forced to stop. Rather than panicking, however, they flipped out their brand-new diplomatic ID cards. The soldiers looked at the ID cards, peeked inside the car, and waved them through without incident.

The success of this operation was reported to headquarters in the highest channels. It was really the beginning of what we would call advanced disguise.

Over the years, as Calloway and I became good friends, I would come to spend a lot of time out in Los Angeles. On some of those trips, I would work alongside his team at whichever studio they were working for, just as if I was another member of his crew. On one of these outings I was sculpting a new prototype head to be used for the JIB while he and his team worked on the masks for a science fiction monster film. Another time, he and I were walking on the lot of a film studio when a tour bus came by and the driver announced, "Ladies and gentlemen, award-winning makeup artist Jerome Calloway." Calloway, of course, pointed at me.

After I had become the chief of disguise, we would rotate disguise officers into Hollywood apprenticeships. And, like me, they often worked on the sets of the films he was making. He taught a generation of CIA officers the rudiments of how to make an effective disguise. Beyond that, he also became an invaluable sounding board for future scenarios, many of which are still being used by the CIA today.

Calloway became an asset for the disguise branch in other ways as well. On one of his many trips to Washington, I set up a lunch meeting between him and our chief of operations. At the time I was looking to expand the disguise section. Calloway knew this, and the topic came up at lunch when the chief asked how my branch was doing. "Fine," Calloway had responded, "but they'd be doing even better if they had more office space." Sure enough, we got it.

When Jerome was visiting Washington a couple of years later, I decided to include him in a training exercise. "Flick," a chemist from a chemical company that also collaborated with the CIA, just happened to be visiting, and I thought it might be good for the two of them to see how we operated in the field.

After the generalist program took off, we were continually training three to four officers at a time, getting them ready for their assignments overseas. In order to cross-train them in the various disciplines, we would immerse them for several weeks in one subject to teach them a particular craft, such as making dental facades. Then, for their final exam, we would put it all together in one complex operation that would require them to use all of their newly acquired skills. In one such exercise, a team of three trainees had to surreptitiously infiltrate a fictitious country, establish a headquarters in a hotel room at the Key Bridge Marriott in Rosslyn, Virginia, and then go out and pick up a terrorist who was on the run. At that point, they were to bring him back to the hotel, where he would be disguised for an exfiltration out of the country.

In order to have some fun, we decided to let Calloway and Flick play the border guards for the fictitious country. The two were thrilled, and went to our costume closet to make it more realistic. The border crossing was set up in Crystal City near the Pentagon. When our team showed up in a van, they found Calloway and Flick sitting at a card table in a vacant lot, wearing fur hats and Polish uniforms. The trainees were unfazed and walked up to the table. "Hello," they said. "We'd like permission to enter your country."

"Why do you want to come in?" Calloway asked.

Using the cover they had prepared, they responded, "We're flea enthusiasts and we're planning on attending your flea festival."

Ever the quick study, Calloway said, "Okay, but our fleas are restricted, so we're going to have to do an inspection. Drop your drawers."

The trainees must have had an idea what was going to happen, because when they dropped their pants they were all wearing American flag underwear.

After a quick examination, Calloway and Flick cleared them through and they hopped back into the van and drove to the Key Bridge Marriott. After checking in, they disguised themselves, then headed down to the bar to meet their local contact, played by another trainee. This person would respond using a sign/counter-sign, which the team had worked out beforehand. In this case, however, rather than using a word or phrase, the team had come up with something a little more creative.

Calloway, who was always telling jokes, had a favorite that had made its way into our office. It was a knock-knock joke involving a drunk at a bar. "Knock-knock," Calloway would say. "Who's there?" the person would respond. "Argo," he'd say. "Argo who?" the person would dutifully answer. "Argo fuck yourself!" he'd exclaim, drawling out the words as if he'd just finished off a bottle of bourbon. It wasn't long before the punch line had become a battle cry of sorts when the workload was heavy and we had a lot on our minds. Whenever that happened, Calloway would cut the tension by shouting out "Argo!" at which point everyone would respond in kind.

The trainees had decided to use ARGO as their countersign. Though, rather than say it, one of the officers had etched the word across a dental facade that he had created. So the exchange went something like: "The moon is blue," followed by a big smile with ARGO written across the person's front teeth in red.

The third part of the operation involved picking up the terrorist, who had decided to bring along his girlfriend, played by Doris Grange. The girlfriend was the twist, as the team hadn't prepared documents for a woman and so had to disguise her as a man.

When the exercise was over, we got a private room in the hotel and celebrated. It had been a fun day. Calloway enjoyed himself immensely and I think appreciated the complexity of the tasks required of an officer on an exfiltration.

After our operation to create the body double for the shah had fallen through, before flying back to Los Angeles Calloway had reiterated that he would be willing to do anything to help out. By the first week of January 1980, the crisis was still front-page news and I knew that Jerome would be feeling as frustrated as the rest of us.

When I'd been getting ready for my follow-up trip to Ottawa, I kept thinking about the problem of the cover story for the houseguests, going over and over in my mind the types of people traveling into and out of Iran. As I was standing in my studio, Calloway's final words rang in my ears. Was there a way that Calloway could help out with the houseguests? I thought of all the stories he'd told me, all my experiences out in LA. Then, by the time I'd landed in Ottawa and had checked into the Lord Elgin once again, I'd hit upon an idea for a cover story that I thought just might work. Rather than pretending to be petroleum workers or nutritionists or teachers, the six Americans would pose as part of a Hollywood production company that was scouting locations in Iran for an upcoming film. The plan, which would normally be out of the question for most clandestine operations, had several attractive features. For one, Hollywood film crews were typically made up of people from all over the world. And of all the groups heading into Iran, it wasn't implausible to imagine a group of self-absorbed Hollywood eccentrics traveling there in the middle of a revolution to find the perfect locations for their movie. Beyond that, it had the one quality that I felt the other stories lacked. It was fun, which I knew would help the houseguests to connect with it in a way the other stories couldn't. With their lives on the line, it would help to make their performances that much more believable. While some people might not know the first thing about agriculture, everybody had some idea of what Hollywood was like. The prime criterion for any cover was always, Would I be willing to use it? In my gut, I felt it was our best option.

But before I could present the idea to the Canadians, I needed to call Calloway to see what he thought. He had no idea what I was working on at the time, and since it was an open line I had to be circumspect about what I could say.

"Hi, Jerome. It's your friend from the army," I said.

"Hey, Tone," he said, using a favorite nickname for me. "What's up?"

"How many people in a Hollywood location scouting party?" I asked him.

"I read you," he said. "About eight." He listed them off one by one: director, cinematographer, production manager, art director, transportation manager, script consultant, associate producer, and business manager.

He then explained that the group's purpose would be to examine the potential locations for the film from an artistic and business standpoint. The associate producer represented the financial backers. The business manager concerned himself mainly with banking arrangements; even a ten-day shoot could require millions of dollars spent on the local economy. The transportation manager rented a variety of vehicles, ranging from limousines to transport the stars to heavy equipment required for constructing a set. The production manager made it all come together. The other team members were technicians who created the film footage from the words in the script.

When he was finished, I thought it sounded perfect. "Thanks," I said. "That's a big help."

The following morning, I met with Delgado bright and early to run my new idea by him. He sat patiently as I outlined my past involvement with Calloway and explained the cover story for the Hollywood location scouting party. He was immediately intrigued, and said he thought it could work. He agreed with me that the eccentricities of the people working in the film business were well known, probably even among Iranians. Even better, he said, Canada had a fairly robust film industry, so the cover would fit perfectly with the Canadian documentation.

I then began thinking of how I was going to create a crack in which to drive a wedge and get my idea through headquarters. I thought back to something I had learned from the NESTOR operation, when Jacob had been forced to deal with everybody at headquarters piling on. In that situation, Jacob had basically handed headquarters a *fait accompli*: essentially, he was already doing the thing that he was proposing to do. The tactic had also been used during the exfiltration of Svetlana Stalin, when the local case officer had sent a cable to headquarters telling them basically that they were going to put her on a plane to Athens, because if they didn't, then by morning her absence would have been discovered. So by the time headquarters got the cable, the operation was already under way. In essence, this is what I had in mind to do now. Delgado and I would work out the details of the operations plan, solve the problems, make a schedule, and then tell headquarters that he and I had an agreement and that we both wanted to move on this plan by the end of the week.

With Delgado on board, I then briefed the chief of station in Ottawa, who nodded his agreement. "Sounds great," he said. At that point, I sat down at the chief of station's desk and wrote out a sixteen-page operations plan in longhand on a yellow legal pad. The operations plan is the comprehensive plan that you hope headquarters will sign off on, so you try to be as detailed as you can and answer any question you can think of. I remember that while I was writing the cable, the chief of station and the U.S. ambassador were standing in the doorway of the office watching me. "He's writing the solution right now," I heard the COS whisper to the ambassador. When I was done, I handed it straight to the communicator, who typed it up and sent it off to headquarters, compartmentalized handling FLASH.

The following morning I was back in Washington, sitting in my office trying to catch up on some cables, when the phone rang. I had a good idea who was on the other end even before I picked up. "Hello?" I said.

Sure enough, it was Hal from the Near East Division. "Eric wants to see you," he said. "You think you can find some time this morning to come over?" The cable I'd sent from Canada had, as expected, already made the rounds, and while Hal didn't tell me, I could tell that Eric was not very happy about it. I told my secretary where I was going, then headed out into the parking lot. In my early days in the graphics bullpen I used to ride a bike to work. Having a car seemed almost like a luxury. When I got to Eric's office he looked up from a folder on his desk and told me to sit down. "I have some issues with you," he said. He went on to explain that in his opinion I'd made an error by sending the cable based on the approval of the chief of station, who was only a liaison. His main point, of course, was that I should have coordinated with him, rather than try to go around his back with the COS, whose job in Canada was more representational than anything. "You know that, Mendez," he told me. With that out of the way, the tension seemed to leave the room and he told me that the plan was a damn fine piece of work, recognizing that it could have advantages even beyond the problem of rescuing the six house-guests. He explained his thinking:

The Pentagon was still in the process of ironing out the plan for Eagle Claw, and given Tehran's geographical location, hadn't yet come up with a feasible way to insert a force of army commandos to rescue the hostages. The movie cover could be an elegant solution that might actually be welcomed by the Iranian Ministry of National Guidance. The ministry had been charged with countering negative publicity on Iran by—outrageously enough—promoting tourism. Tehran was also looking for ways to alleviate some of the cash-flow problems caused when President Carter froze Iran's assets in the United States. A motion picture production on

Iranian soil could be an economic shot in the arm and would provide an ideal public relations tool to help counteract the adverse publicity stemming from the hostage situation.

A relative "moderate," Abulhassan Bani-Sadr, was about to be elected president of Iran, and we judged it possible that he could be sold on these economic points and then might be able to gain agreement from the radical factions of the regime. If so, the cover for infiltrating the Delta Force commandos (in preparation for a hostage rescue attempt) as a team of movie set construction workers and camera operators to prepare the location was a natural. We imagined it might be possible to even conceal weapons and other material in the motion picture equipment.

It was a scenario that could work on many levels. However, as I was driving back to Foggy Bottom, I was momentarily consumed by doubt. The Hollywood option had been so readily embraced that I wondered if it might just be wishful thinking on everyone's part. On the surface, the idea was so preposterous that I had expected some pushback, and when I hadn't gotten any, it was only natural that I began to wonder: Had we overlooked something? Were we creating an unnecessarily convoluted plan that was going to get somebody killed? Since I was the plan's architect, I had to be certain. For some reason, despite the plan's implausibility, it was the only option I felt comfortable using myself.

The rest of my day was spent meeting with my team and getting them up to speed on the Hollywood option as well as the other covers. Joe Missouri was still in Canada working out the problem of the secondary documents, such as credit cards and Canadian driver's licenses, which were turning out to be difficult to obtain. Much like our own government, the Canadians had certain restrictions in place on the use of their security documents. In an attempt to get the driver's licenses, Joe had eventually met with the head of the national security forces, who had told him it wasn't going to happen without some kind of special approval from on high. At that point, they had called in the solicitor general (a post similar to the attorney general in the United States). Joe later recounted how the solicitor general had come in and looked at the head of the national security forces, then at Joe, then back to the head of the national security forces, and said: "Get the fucking things." In addition, the Canadians had finished a set of six passports and some OTS artists in Canada had quickly inserted the proper cachets, including a visa that originated from a country in Europe. These were to be emergency documents in case the houseguests needed to escape immediately, and so they were assembled rather quickly and sent off through the diplomatic bag. The next set would be sent much later, along with the secondary documents that Joe was working on.

was in my office later that day when Matt, deputy chief of OTS operations, came in. He was dropping by to check on our progress. Matt had seen my cable and so knew about the idea for the Hollywood location scouting party, but now it was time to make it a reality. "If anyone checks, we need the foundation to be there," I said.

"How are you going to make it happen?"

The best kind of backstopped stories are those where you could go into the city or town where the person's alias documents say he or she is from, then to the street and finally the house, where inside on the mantelpiece you would see a photo of the person alongside his or her supposed spouse or family. That was the level of back-stopping I was proposing now.

"Hollywood is a town that runs on image," I said. "I want to get an office, get it staffed, do as much as we can." Since the house-guests were going to be pretending to be members of a location scouting party, we would need to create a production company and a film for them to be working on. Since I knew the lay of the land, it only made sense that I would be the one to fly out there and get it done. I told him I planned to ask for an advance of funds from the budget and finance office for ten thousand dollars to cover our expenses.

Matt thought about it for a second. He knew we were taking a chance because we hadn't yet gotten consensus approval for the Hollywood option, but the risk was minimal compared to the pay-off. If we ended up also using this cover to rescue the hostages down at the embassy, then laying the groundwork now seemed like the smart thing to do.

His face brightened and he shook his head. "Only you could think of something like that," he said. "I like it."

We then began discussing the logistics of the exfiltration. Up until this point I had yet to assign the team of officers who would be infiltrating Iran to link up with the houseguests. "Who'd you have in mind?" he asked.

I think it's safe to say that from the beginning I was con-vinced that I should lead the team. Technically, as the chief of the authentication branch, I was a manager and too senior to be out in the field. Further, by the nature of my job I knew too much about the inner workings of the CIA's clandestine operations. If I was to be compromised, then that would be a huge security risk. Still, thanks to the fact that I had recently been in Iran, and due to the high-profile nature of this exfiltration, I think everyone was willing to accept the risks. With the lives of six Americans on the line, the direct involvement of the Canadian government, as well as pressure mounting on President Carter from every quarter, all of us knew that failure wouldn't be an option.

"Me, and somebody from documents," I replied. "Maybe Julio."

"Julio" was a thirty-one-year-old documents officer stationed in Europe. In my mind, Julio was one of the most capable documents guys we had. He was a true "gray man" and could carry just about any persona you asked of him. When people think of spies, most think of Hollywood films in which the spy is always flamboyant and larger than life. In the real world of espionage, however, a spy has to be able to blend in. One thing I always say when it comes to the types of people the CIA looks for is that it's not the guy who gets all the stares, but the one who, after you see him in line at the bank or after he passes through the checkout counter at the supermarket, you cannot remember what he looks like. Le Carré got that right. He could be tall, short, European, American, South American—whatever is required to get the job done, which is what Julio was like. Originally from the Midwest, Julio had studied at the Sorbonne and was a gifted linguist who spoke German, Spanish, Farsi, and French. It seemed that if you gave him the weekend to learn a new language he'd come back on Monday completely fluent. Besides this, Julio had participated in numerous exfiltrations, in which he had proven himself more than capable. During one such operation in the Middle East, he had picked up a high-profile terrorist who wanted to come over to our side. Julio had met him at a safe site and gotten him out onto a ferry, only to have the ferry turn around and return to the harbor. The boat's propellers had gotten fouled on some trash, and Julio was forced to improvise. It's easy to imagine how spooked the terrorist must have been as the ferry made its slow turn back to the docks. In those types of situations it can be incredibly difficult to get a person to go back through the whole process of trying to escape a second time, but Julio proved to be unflappable and got the terrorist out of the country the next day.

Equally as important as this sort of unflappability, with this operation, was the great need to talk the talk. Inspiring confidence on the part of the houseguests was paramount; the whole thing would fall apart if even one of them didn't believe in it. These were bright people, but many of those concerned with approving the operations plan did not believe that a group of six novices could organize and act cohesively. I believed I could convince them that our plan would work.

"I think that's a good choice," Matt said.

The following morning, on Thursday, January 10, I called Elaine in and told her to go over to budget and finance to ask for an advance of funds for ten thousand dollars in cash. Our B&F people were world-class bean counters who invented bureaucracy for fun. Ten thousand dollars was the maximum allowed. Anything more required the right hand of God. When Elaine came back with the money, I put it inside one of our concealment briefcases. I knew I would catch flak from B&F, but the money was going to be well spent. It was time to head out to Hollywood and create our production company.

10

STUDIO SIX

I arrived in Los Angeles on Thursday evening, and after grabbing the rental car, headed off into the flickering circuit boards of the city streets. Normally when I came to LA I stayed at a small Hawaiian-themed motel in the Valley, near Calloway's house in Burbank. I wouldn't be meeting Jerome until the following morning, and with an evening to kill, I decided to take my time and enjoy the drive.

Los Angeles held many mixed emotions for me. For one, I had a little bit of family history connected to the place. My parents had honeymooned in LA and my mom would always talk about their visit to Olvera Street. In addition, my grandfather Frank Gomez was one of the masons who'd built Grauman's Chinese Theatre. He'd even carved his name into one of the theater's cornerstones. This was before he'd changed his name to Mendez and moved with my father and uncle to Nevada.

Beyond that, there was the allure of the cinema, which had

meant so much to me as a kid growing up in a small dirt-poor town. Back then movies were more important to me than real life. In a pre-television environment and isolated as we were, the only escape mechanism I knew was to enter the Rex Theater on Saturday afternoons and watch a movie. The theater was located in tiny Caliente, Nevada, a town that had grown up around the railroad. In fact the tracks ran right down the town's main street. Full of dime-a-dozen stores and bars, Caliente was dull in every way except for the Rex. The marquee was almost as large as the theater itself. In the dusty monochromatic high desert it looked like a palace to me. I was a huge fan of John Wayne and Alan Ladd and films like *Rio Grande, Fort Apache, Red River,* and *The Blue Dahlia.* I wondered why life couldn't be more like the adventures on the screen. I marveled at the makeup and sets that Hollywood used. I watched the actors closely, mimicking them in the mirror when I returned home. I was hopelessly addicted to this visual world, and have remained so all my life.

Then there was the feel of Los Angeles itself. The town had an undeniable energy about it—it was a place where time seemed to stand still in the vortex of rapturous imagination. If you looked closely, you could spot the signs of it all around you. In the landmarks along Sunset Strip and Hollywood Boulevard. In dive bars and back-alley clubs where the stars of the moment collided with those of the past. In the faces of the newly arrived, whose lives were full of earnest hope and promise, and in those whose dreams had come crashing down. I had traveled all over the world, but the city was like no other I had known. It was a place that twirled around you like a Russian ballerina, that caught you up in its spin and pulled you along until you found yourself wrapped in its spell.

The decade of the 1970s had been a particularly important one for Hollywood. It was a time when an influx of youth was pushing the limits of realism and fantasy and breaking down the barriers that had been established in the early 1960s. Leading the way were a group of directors who made up what came to be known as New Hollywood: Francis Ford Coppola, Martin Scorsese, Stanley Kubrick, Steven Spielberg, George Lucas, William Friedkin, Brian De Palma, and Roman Polanski, to name a few. These filmmakers didn't just play with convention—they smashed it, making gritty, realistic films and science fiction opuses that starred then relatively unknown actors like Al Pacino, Robert De Niro, Harvey Keitel, and Harrison Ford. *The Godfather, Taxi Driver, Badlands, A Clockwork Orange, Chinatown, The Exorcist, Apocalypse Now, Star Wars, Jaws, Mean Streets, Close Encounters of the Third Kind,* and *American Graffiti*—these were just a few of the films that defined the decade.

These directors and their works not only changed the culture of Hollywood, they also ushered in a whole new phenomenon: the blockbuster. Coppola's *The Godfather*, Spielberg's *Jaws*, and Lucas's *Star Wars* would smash records at the box office and change the way movies were made for decades to come.

It was a period in which anything seemed possible. In addition to spawning some of the most influential writers, directors, and producers to come along in a generation, it also ushered in an unprecedented wave of technological and artistic advancements, such as the creation of Industrial Light and Magic, which would push visual effects into the realm of the impossible.

As I drove north from Hollywood Boulevard, I hoped we'd be able to tap into a little bit of this magic ourselves.

arrived at Calloway's house at nine o'clock the following morning. Jerome answered the door and took me into the kitchen, where one of his associates was already waiting for us. I had called Calloway from Washington before coming out and asked him to bring in somebody who could help set up a company. "He needs to be someone you trust, and someone who is known around town," I'd said. The person Calloway had chosen was veteran makeup artist Bob Sidell. A character in his own right, Sidell looked like a slightly smaller and less intense version of John Milius, the screenwriter for *Apocalypse Now*. Forty-two years old, balding, and with a bright, expressive smile, Sidell wore a neatly combed beard and thick gold-framed glasses. Calloway had known Sidell for nearly twenty years, the two having worked on several movies together, including the science fiction film for which Calloway had won an award. That morning Calloway had called Sidell and simply told him to come over for a cup of coffee. "I've got someone I want you to meet," he'd said. Sidell was between jobs and happy for an excuse to see his old friend.

Born in 1937 in Philadelphia, Sidell spent his early childhood in Detroit, before moving to Encino, California, where he joined the U.S. Navy right out of high school, being stationed on an antisubmarine destroyer based out of Hawaii.

Eventually Bob made it into the hair and makeup union thanks to some help from his wife's uncle, who was a makeup artist. Back then, it was essentially the union that controlled the makeup artists and then farmed them out to the various productions around town. After a ten-week training program in which journeymen, including

Calloway, volunteered their time to help with his training, he was certified and his name was put on the list. His first job was working on the movie *Nevada Smith*, starring Steve McQueen. Eventually he found a home at NBC working on several variety shows, including *Laugh-In*, and alongside stars like Dean Martin and Sammy Davis, Jr.

Sidell was a talented makeup artist, but where he really excelled was logistics. He had a real gift for dealing with the minutiae of a task; Jerome knew his man well.

"What's up, Jerome?" Sidell asked as I took a seat. I could tell he had no idea who I was. Later I would find out that while a few of Calloway's friends knew he had done some work for the CIA, Jerome had never discussed specifics with any of them.

"Tony wants to talk with you about a project," Calloway said. "But before we get into it you're going to need to sign something."

I had brought along a confidentiality agreement, which I slid across the table in his direction. Sidell did a double take and looked at Calloway, who nodded.

"Have you been watching the news?" I asked him, as he slid the signed form back to me.

"Yeah, sure," he said.

"Then you know what's going on in Iran?" I asked.

He went on for a minute or two about how angry and frustrated he was by the situation over there, describing how wrong it was for the Iranians to be holding innocent Americans hostage inside the embassy.

"What if I was to tell you that not all of our diplomats are being held at the embassy?" I said. That got his attention. I explained the situation of the houseguests, then finished, "And it's my job to get them out."

I gave him a second to digest what I'd just said. Then I explained the problems we were having with the cover story, and the idea for having the houseguests be part of a movie crew. "We did all the research about what kinds of groups are moving into and out of the country, looking for the type of group we are dealing with. In my opinion, this option seems the most believable," I explained.

Sidell was immediately on board. "It's a fantastic idea," he said, "but what do you need me for?"

"Bob, here's what we are doing," I said as I spread out some of the photos of the houseguests and their aliases. "Let's say that somebody decides to check on one of the houseguests—say, Teresa Harris." I held up a photocopy of Cora Lijek's Canadian passport. "They have a variety of ways to do it—they can use the telephone, they can fax, they can actually come walking in through the door. And they may do all of that. What they have to find on this end of the question is Teresa Harris's office. If anybody is checking on her, they need to know that she has an office."

Sidell nodded, picking up the photocopy of "Teresa Harris's" Canadian passport and examining it closely.

"What I need is someone here to tell them that she is away, on location, scouting a site for the movie. Filming is going to begin in March, so time is precious. She'll be back in a week or so—whatever. Got it?"

Sidell nodded again. He was going through the pile of copies of the rest of the houseguests' passports.

"It'll work," he said. "We'll make sure that it works."

As we were talking, Dave from our contracts department showed up. Dave worked out of the CIA's West Coast procurement office and was basically there to monitor the funds and make sure that Calloway and Sidell got whatever they needed. I'd had my secretary cable him before I left Washington to let him know that we'd be meeting at Calloway's.

"And Dave here is going to make sure you get everything you need," I said. With that I handed Dave the briefcase with the ten thousand dollars, and he flipped it open and looked inside. After sitting across the room carefully counting out the hundred-dollar bills, he quickly signed a receipt for the briefcase and then handed it over to Sidell, who went through the same meticulous routine. This would save me the trouble of having to worry about the accounting side of things and also help me out with the B&F people. With that out of the way, Dave sat back and enjoyed the show while Calloway, Sidell, and I began discussing what we would need to do to set up our production company, which I had decided to call "Studio Six Productions," after the six houseguests trapped in Iran.

Our first priority was to get office space. Sidell explained that it shouldn't be too hard because film companies were often created and disbanded overnight, and so the film business catered toward short-term leases. Calloway had told me on more than one occasion that there was a long history of the mafia laundering money in Hollywood by opening up and closing production companies overnight. It was a common pattern and a convenient way to wash funds. It was a very itinerant business; all you needed to do was get a story and some funds and you could always find somebody to make a movie for you. The success of the movie or TV show was never a consideration, but occasionally the mafia would find themselves with a hit on their hands. Urban legend has it there was a wildly popular TV show that ran during the 1970s that came about this way. Calloway swore that the show was funded initially by the mob and nobody ever proved to me that he was wrong.

They took turns making calls to see what they could find, and we'd hit pay dirt after only an hour or so.

"Got it," Sidell said, turning to us. "Sunset Gower Studios has some space opening up tomorrow." Apparently, Michael Douglas had just finished producing *The China Syndrome* and we could have his offices. Sunset Gower was an independent studio located on the old Columbia Pictures lot, the home to such classics as Frank Capra's *Mr. Smith Goes to Washington*. It seemed like prime Hollywood real estate, and the fact that Michael Douglas had been connected to it would only give our production company that much more cachet.

"We'd get three offices and a reception room," Sidell said.

"If it worked for Michael Douglas, it will certainly work for us," I said.

With that out of the way, we began looking at the various roles the houseguests might play. I would have Joe work out the details later, but in the meantime I thought it couldn't hurt to ask Sidell and Calloway what they thought. Along with copies of the passports, I had brought a list of the houseguests and their various ages and names. Both agreed that any credible person in the film business would need a long list of previous credits. The trick, said Calloway, was finding those kinds of jobs that give a person clout—art director, cinematographer, transportation coordinator—without necessitating that they have a name to go along with it, like a director or a producer. These would be easier for the Iranians to check.

In addition to this, since the Hollywood personas the house-guests would be playing would most likely be members of one of Hollywood's ubiquitous unions, Sidell reminded us that they would all need to have guild cards in their wallets. We made a note of these things and we agreed to look into it over the course of the following days.

I had already decided that I would take on the role of the production manager, which would give me a logical reason to carry the production portfolio, as well as to keep track of everyone on the scout. My partner, Julio, meanwhile, would play an associate producer, representing our production company's ostensible South American backers.

On Saturday morning we went down to Sunset Gower Studios to look at our office space. They put the name of our production company on a little placard that was slid into a slot on the front door. It was all coming together, and rather quickly, I thought. We spent the rest of the day scrounging up office furniture and typewriters and calling in every favor that Calloway and Sidell had in order to get the phone lines connected. We installed several working lines, including a few that were listed. Earlier when we had discussed the idea of the production company, Sidell had agreed to man the office for the duration of the operation. This role would be absolutely necessary to complete the ruse that Studio Six was indeed a working production company and not just an address.

One of the offices became mine and another Sidell's. Since Calloway was so well known, we were trying to keep his involvement a secret.

At that point, Sidell asked if it would be okay to bring in his wife, Andi, to act as production secretary. I told him yes, but that they couldn't tell anybody about what they were doing, not even their kids.

Later that night, Sidell asked his wife to take a walk with him outside their house and filled her in on what we had been doing. He told me later how she'd gone almost comatose just taking it all in. And as if that wasn't shocking enough for her, he told her, "Oh, and by the way, congratulations—you now have a new job. You're going to be the production secretary. You start work on Monday."

On Sunday, we reconvened back at Calloway's house. Now that we had our production company up and running, we needed a script. We began by asking ourselves what kind of production would travel to Iran. Because *Star Wars* had recently been such a huge success (and was filmed in Tunisia), we immediately thought the genre would be perfect for us. Sci-fi stories often incorporated mythological elements and it would be a bonus if we could find something with a Middle Eastern flavor to it. It was then that Calloway told me about a script he'd been pitched several months back. Based on Roger Zelazny's science fiction novel *Lord of Light*, the project had eventually fallen through when a member of the production team was arrested for embezzlement, but not before initial preproduction had begun. Even better, the producers had hired Jack Kirby, a famous comic book artist, to do concept drawings. At some point, the producer had envisioned a theme park connected to the project called Science Fiction Land, complete with a "Thunder Chariot-Launching Complex," "Jet Tube Transporter," even a three-hundred-foot-tall Ferris wheel, all of it set against the backdrop of the Rocky Mountains in Colorado.

Calloway still had the script and the concept drawings, so he went to get them.

"Brahma's Pavilions of Joy," I read as I examined an artist's sketch of a road flanked by thousand-foot statues. In another sketch, a man wore robotic-looking "electronic battle armor" and a massive helmet with six horns. "What's it about?" I asked.

"Who knows!" he said. "Some space opera set on a colonized planet where men become Hindu gods or something like that."

I flipped open the script and read at random: " . . . Vishnu the Preserver and Yama-Dharma, Lord of Death, have covered the whole of Heaven . . . with what is said to be an impenetrable dome."

"This is perfect," I said. "The Iranians won't be able to understand this stuff." I was thinking that, for operational purposes, the more confusing the better. If someone were to stop us, then it would be easy for us to overwhelm them with confusing conceptual jargon. In addition, I could add the sketches along with the script to the portfolio, which would give our production another layer of authenticity.

Tehran had a famous underground bazaar that even matched one of the locations in the script, which would give us something to pitch to Iran's Ministry of National Guidance, if it ever came to that.

"What are we going to call it?" I asked. We all agreed that we needed something catchy from Eastern culture or mythology. After several tries, we hit on it.

"Let's call it Argo," Calloway said with a wry smile. He then went on to explain how "Argo" also had major mythological connotations. "It's the name of the ship that Jason and the Argonauts sailed in to rescue the Golden Fleece."

"That sounds just like our operation," I said.

At that point I grabbed a yellow legal pad and sketched out a logo for our film. Sidell and Calloway recommended that we place an ad in the trades. Since Hollywood is an industry that thrives on image, it would be a good idea, they said, to toot our own horn to create a bit of recognition for the project. If the industry *knew* it was going to happen, then that meant it *was* going to happen. Calloway had some of the trades lying around, so I quickly flipped through a few of them to see the kinds of ads they ran. The more dramatic and eye-catching, I realized, the better. In the end I settled on a full black page to signify the blackness of outer space, in the center of which a planet was exploding as a group of asteroids, shaped in the letters ARGO, were hurtling toward it. In thinking about a way we could pump up our film even more, I came up with the tagline "A Cosmic Conflagration," which had a kind of genteel shabbiness to it. When I was finished, the ad read

ROBERT SIDELL AND ASSOCIATES
PRESENT
A STUDIO SIX PRODUCTION

ARGO

A COSMIC CONFLAGRATION
FROM A STORY BY TERESA HARRIS
COMMENCING PRINCIPAL PHOTOGRAPHY
MARCH 1980

The following day, Calloway and I went down to the *Hollywood Reporter* and *Daily Variety* to place the full-page ad, which was scheduled to run on Wednesday, January 16.

While this was going on, Sidell went out to get us some props, heading to an industry-backed retail establishment that provided various tools and equipment for the motion picture industry. There, Sidell picked up a shooting schedule board with the day-by-day divisions to make it look like the production board for the film, as well as a viewfinder for the cameraman to wear around his neck.

When that was finished, I made the first business call from our studio offices to the Iranian consulate in San Francisco, using my alias as the production manager. I said I required a visa and instructions on procedures for obtaining permission to scout a shooting location in Tehran. My party of eight would be made up of six Canadians, a European, and a Latin American.

The call to the Iranian consulate was a washout. Officials there suggested that we contact the Iranian embassy in Washington, D.C. This was not surprising, because many Iranian diplomats had been carried over from the shah's regime, and most were unsure of their current status and their visa-granting authorities.

Tuesday morning was spent collecting whatever "pocket litter" we could get our hands on, including the guild cards, as well as receipts and anything else that would bolster the appearance that our houseguests indeed lived and worked in Los Angeles.

Later that afternoon, Calloway and I had a "launch" party down at the Brown Derby, the iconic industry hot spot where Clark Gable once proposed to Carole Lombard. I was scheduled to leave first thing the following morning, and Calloway wanted to send me off in style with our own little version of the Hollywood tradition of celebrating a production's launch.

Being a professional Irishman, Calloway knew how to have a good time. His drink of choice was a margarita, and there was only one problem that kept it from being absolutely perfect: it was always served in a tiny glass. Initially he fixed this by ordering a pitcher for himself. However, it wasn't long before his favorite haunt began serving us "JC's"—margaritas in big bucket-sized glasses.

Calloway and I hoisted several of them that evening before launching into an Argo battle cry.

Afterward, as we talked about some of the personalities that Jerome had met over the years in the film business, I brought up my cover legend. The alias I would be using was "Kevin Costa Harkins," a persona I had first created to handle all the exfiltrations we were doing on the Asian subcontinent in the early 1970s. A CIA operations officer might have, at any given time, multiple active alias identities issued to him. Central Cover staff dispensed these as situations arose. One alias identity was not enough. You might want to conceal travel to certain destinations, or break up your travel pattern so that it didn't look interesting to a foreign immigration officer. The names were registered and controlled by Central Cover so that there would be no overlapping or duplication.

Kevin Costa Harkins was a backstopped alias that I used from time to time over the years. He was ostensibly a northern European who had a California connection. He had an apartment off Ghirardelli Square in San Francisco. He was an artist and a world traveler. He was obviously well-off and could pick up and go somewhere on a whim. It was an ideal cover for an intelligence officer who might have to show up at an odd place at an odd hour.

The fact that I would be coming from California was an advantage if I was going to be involved in scouting a movie location. I could show close ties between my artist persona and the Hollywood cover we were creating for our operation. No question I could show residence in California—interested parties would assume that I could be connected with the Hollywood crowd. However, for obvious reasons, the best part about Kevin was that he was a foreigner, which meant I wouldn't be traveling on a U.S. passport.

As I told Calloway about Kevin, he immediately grasped the northern European connection. Ever the professional Irishman, he set out to give me a more complex understanding of the name Costa Harkins as it related to places he had been and people he knew. The origin of the name "Costa Harkins," as it turned out, went back to the time of the Roman Empire, as they pillaged, conquered, and colonized farther into northern Europe. Certain counties in Ireland assimilated many of the Romans, particularly those who were seagoing and had wrecked their ships on the shoals of County Cork; these became the so-called Black Irish.

As I listened to him, I was inspired. I was going to have a decent cover story for once. A tale I would love to tell. Jerome was delighted. He and I practiced our ancestral accents and lifted our glasses in a toast to our mutual roots.

When it was time to say good-bye, Jerome got quite serious all of a sudden, as if it had just occurred to him that this might be the last time he was ever going to see me. "Take care of yourself over there," he said to me. Never an overly affectionate man, he gave me a great big bear hug.

T he following morning, as I flew back to Washington, the trades were coming out with our Argo ads in them, announcing that principal photography was set to commence in March.

As I landed in the capital, I was thrilled with the way things had come together. We now had an actual working office at one of the movie studios staffed with Hollywood insiders who could back up our story if anyone checked from Tehran. As far as backstopped alias docs go, it didn't get any better. Now I only hoped that headquarters and the Canadians would be as pleased as I was.

11

A COSMIC CONFLAGRATION

No sooner were my feet on the ground in Washington than I learned that the situation with the houseguests in Tehran was becoming critical. Beyond the danger of the press leaking information, it seemed there was the direct threat that the houseguests could be discovered at any moment.

On one occasion, Ken Taylor's wife, Pat, had received a mysterious phone call from an unidentified person who asked in perfect English to speak with Joe and Kathy Stafford, then hung up. Ken Taylor, of course, knew that there were journalists who had been piecing the story together and because the caller had spoken English he hoped it was just a Western journalist fishing for information. But in a calculated move, he decided not to tell the six Americans about the call for fear of alarming them.

After nearly three months, there were people in Iran who knew that the six Americans were on the loose. By this time the militants had a good handle on the various employees working at the embassy

199

the day it was taken. Many documents had been shredded in a commercial shredder, the kind that cut the paper into long strips, but the Iranians had employed child carpet weavers to splice the strips back together. In addition, several boxes of documents had inexplicably been left behind on the first floor of the embassy as the staff had fled. Even more damaging, however, the entire contents of Bruce Laingen's safe had been captured, revealing not only secret communications between Washington and Tehran, but also the identities of several of the employees, including the three CIA officers.

Cora would later find out that the militants had eventually taken a consulate employee around to the various offices and asked who worked in each one. It was clear that the numbers of those who had been captured didn't add up, and when the militants had pointed this out, their colleague had covered for the missing Americans by saying that they had been out of the country when the embassy fell. The militants had apparently bought it, but there was no telling for how long.

Another time, Anders and Schatz were sunning in the courtyard when they'd been forced to duck into the house as a helicopter hovered directly overhead. The four houseguests then huddled inside and waited for what they assumed was the coming assault. Earlier they'd come up with a two-part escape plan in case something like this happened. The first part envisioned their hurrying up to the roof and then out onto the road that ran above Sheardown's house. The second part was—well, that was the part they hadn't worked out yet. With a helicopter hovering overhead, it wouldn't be but a matter of seconds before they were spotted. They hunkered down and eventually the helicopter flew off. Zena called John at the Canadian embassy to find out if he knew anything. As it turned out, a mullah had been assassinated at a nearby mosque, and the Revolutionary Guard were combing the neighborhood looking for the assailant.

S uch close calls, coupled with the monotony of their confinement, tested the houseguests' fortitude. Zena withdrew into herself more and more, while the others tried to cope with the uncertainty as best they could. Cora, it seems, decided to sleep late into the morning, and then most of the day. Mark remembers climbing under his bed one night as the Sheardowns gave a curious Iranian visitor a tour of the house. Every one of them felt they had overstayed their welcome with the Canadians and wanted desperately to find a solution. Another issue that occurred to them was the possibility that one of them would become seriously ill and need medical attention. The odds that they could be captured, killed, or suffer some freak accident increased with every second they remained in the country.

Early on, the houseguests had been told that when the other hostages were released, they would be escorted down to the airport by a group of Western ambassadors who would then try to put them on the same plane. As the weeks dragged on, however, this scenario seemed less and less likely. The fact that they had managed to escape, in their mind, would no doubt make them prime suspects in the eyes of the militants. What if the militants demanded to interrogate them? Or accused them of being spies simply because they had avoided capture? They saw themselves as being a separate entity from the embassy takeover altogether and felt that the State Department wasn't doing enough to help them.

Fed up with what they saw as inaction, they met one night in the den to draft a letter in which they expressed their frustration and fear of being left behind in the event that the hostages were freed. And even though they knew that Ambassador Taylor probably wouldn't send the letter, they were certain that the intent of their message would get out.

Meanwhile, the mood in Ottawa was also growing tense. Knowledge of the fugitive Americans was becoming an open secret. Flora MacDonald, for one, was getting increasingly nervous, as several people approached her to ask about the houseguests. The Canadians began making discreet arrangements to close down their embassy. It was anybody's guess as to how much longer the secret of the houseguests could remain safe.

Back in Washington, the various efforts being mounted against Iran were still running at full tilt, and I immediately sat down with my team to go over the final technical preparations for the Argo cover story. In addition, since headquarters had yet to sign off on any one particular operations plan, that meant we had to finalize materials for Argo as well as the other two cover stories—the Canadian nutritionists and the American English teachers. Despite our backstopping, apparently there were still some people within the State Department and National Security Council who were skeptical of the Hollywood option. It was too ambitious, too ballsy, too complex. In my mind, these were the very characteristics that would make it work.

Everyone in the office had been impressed with the *Variety* ad, but I reminded them we still had a lot of work to do.

Now that we had Studio Six up and running, the next step would be to build up the portfolio, assign the houseguests their roles, and work on their secondary documentation. I knew we had a very small window in which to get this done, so we had to move fast.

Joe Missouri had recently returned from Canada and I put him on the task of fleshing out the backstories for each of the houseguests. I had nothing but confidence in Joe. He could invent any story for any situation. I had shared with him some of the notes that Calloway and Sidell had given me about the various roles that each houseguest would most likely play as well as their credits. It would be Joe's task to look at the personalities and ages of the houseguests and come up with the plausible jobs for each. For instance, we learned that Kathy Stafford had had an art background, so he made her the art director.

I can remember seeing Joe at his desk, a cigarette dangling from his lips as he plucked away at his manual typewriter. Joe was as bright as they come and fit the mold of a new breed that was immersed in the world around him. He was having fun, and would occasionally come to show me what he'd done. In order to make it easier for the houseguests to remember who they were, Joe had come up with the ingenious trick of using details from their real lives. For example, in coming up with the name for Mark Lijek's alias, "Joseph Earl Harris," Joe had used the first and middle names of Cora's father. Likewise, for the birth date of Mark's alias, he'd used Cora's father's birthday.

Trying to memorize an alias can be a daunting task, especially if your life depends on it. Sometimes you can't help but get confused, especially when you're traveling on multiple documents. I remember one instance when I traveled to Moscow on an alias and was checking in at a hotel when the clerk said, "Okay, Mr. Mendez, we have you staying two nights." Without breaking stride, I slid across my alias passport and said, "Oh, Mendez couldn't make it. I came instead." Inadvertently, somehow the reservation had been made in my real name. In fact, sometimes when you sign into an embassy you can spot the people who have momentarily forgotten who they are supposed to be because they have signed in under one name, then scratched it out to write a different one in its place.

When he was finished, Joe had taken the roles of various members of the production party and rewritten them in the form of résumés. Not only would this help the houseguests to learn their aliases, but it could also be carried out in the open in the production manager's portfolio, which would lend credibility to my own cover.

While this was going on, I met with Truman, our chief of production, to talk about the Studio Six business cards. Each houseguest would be given his or her own card, which contained the individual's title and the phone number of our LA office. I had thought of an idea while on the trip back from LA and ran it by him. "How about a big red number six on them," I said, "made out of film strips." He nodded his agreement. I also handed him the exemplars for the guild cards that Calloway and Sidell had "borrowed" from their friends, as well as the script and Jack Kirby's sketches. For the script we would need to take out any reference to the previous title and insert "Argo." For the sketches, I wanted some of the illustrators from the bullpen to create their own versions of outer space creatures and far-out drawings, as if our art director had been working on her own ideas. I realized this was a strange request, but I had nothing but confidence in our artist-validators, who were hired because of their ability to do it all. No task seemed out of their reach, including fine technical schematics and forged writing. Most were blue-collar "tradesmen" who prided themselves on their quirkiness. They were a unique breed of cat in the midst of our bureaucratic organization. They were difficult to manage. More than once they threatened to go on strike. But they were highly competent at what they did.

Truman, who was originally a typesetter, fit right into the mold of these blue-collar types. As chief of production, Truman oversaw anything we might need in the graphics department. He would assign a number to each of the jobs that came into the graphics branch and attach that number to a large manila envelope known as a job jacket. This was how the progress of the job was traced and the hours tracked from section to section. This was, of course, because almost every graphics job required multiple departments. OTS had ink experts, paper experts, photo experts, even a printing press at its disposal.

Once I had given them the guild cards, the artists would pore over them from every angle. It's not enough for a document to look right. It also has to feel right. For instance, how does it sound when you crinkle it? So you examine the paper and go down to your paper stock and get the one that fits. The same goes for laminated IDs. If someone is going to stop you in the middle of the night to examine your ID, he may not even be able to see it, but he can certainly feel it. Maybe one of the traps is that the laminate is sticky. All of these things are factored into how the graphics branch reproduces documents.

Allen Dulles said it best: *"Any intelligence service worth its salt can make the other fellow's currency."* In other words, every nation needs to have its own airtight security measures, while at the same time be actively working in secret to reverse engineer those of the enemy faster then they can invent them.

After we had fleshed out the portfolio, the next job would be to work on the houseguests' travel documentation. Now that we knew who they were, we had to show how they'd gotten into Iran in order to get them out.

This is not as easy as it sounds, as it entailed not only booking tickets but also inserting the various cachets and border stamps into the houseguests' passports to show that they had indeed followed the particular itinerary we were saying they did. The process is always complex and involves dozens of highly skilled technical officers working in tandem. In this case we had decided on an around-the-world itinerary, with the houseguests making their final flight into Iran from Hong Kong. What this meant was that Joe needed to go to our archives and look up the particular cachet that was used by the immigration officer at Hong Kong the day the houseguests were said to have departed. This is why it is so important to continually update the travel records and why the CIA is constantly launching probes, sending officers or agents through areas to update our database. After finding the right cachet, Joe would then send it to the chief of production, whose job it was to see it through the various phases involving numerous departments within OTS. When the process was complete, Joe would be handed a travel document with an appropriate cachet stamped into it. But that would be for just one country. Imagine having to insert dozens of stamps into one travel document. Further, imagine hundreds of operations going on simultaneously, and you get an idea of the complex nature of the work going on in the graphics department.

To complete our scenario, Doris was busy putting together some disguise materials. These would be included in the bag that would eventually be sent by Ottawa to the Canadian embassy in Tehran. Since I was going to be heading into Iran, I was a little bit more hands-on than normal, and she would come to me from time to time with a progress report. Because of the houseguests' inexperience in wearing sophisticated disguises, we chose to emphasize basic behavioral and visual clues for them to masquerade behind. Diplomats are traditionally conservative in their appearance; we would encourage them to become more flamboyant, edgier, sexier. Lots of perfume and aftershave, shirts unbuttoned, tight pants, gold chains, loud jewelry, hair blow-dried—outfits that they never would have chosen. Their behavior would have to change too: they would need to be louder, more aggressive, more histrionic, arrogant even. In short, all the stereotypes that an outsider would associate as characteristics of a person who worked in Hollywood.

We also didn't know how much space we were going to have, since the disguise materials would have to fit in the same bag along with all the documents. Doris came back with a small do-it-yourself kit for each of the houseguests, which included products such as styling gel, makeup, mod-style glasses, eyeliner, etc., as well as a typed sheet of detailed instructions on how the houseguests could alter their appearance. The props kit also included the viewfinder that Sidell had picked up for the cameraman to wear around his neck, as well as the materials I would be bringing with me in the portfolio, such as the script and sketch pad.

With headquarters and the State Department still vacillating about the various cover options, I wrote an updated version of the operations plan in which I laid out my idea of taking all three options with me into Iran. I would then present them to the houseguests and let them decide whether they wanted to leave individually or as a group and choose which cover they preferred. It wasn't an ideal scenario, but with so many different governmental organizations involved, I felt it was the only way we could get there in time. I also knew that since I was going to be the one to present the options to the houseguests, I could help steer them in the direction I thought we should go. Anything was better than just sitting around and waiting for the bureaucrats to make up their minds. I knew the Canadians were getting nervous as well. It was time to get our diplomats out before it was too late.

About a week after my return from California, everything was ready. Joe and I hopped on a plane and flew to Ottawa to load the pouch.

As soon as we were in Canada, Joe and I set about finalizing the documents and collecting yet more pocket litter, such as maple leaf pins, matchbooks, business cards, receipts—this time, things that would give the houseguests the appearance of being Canadian citizens.

The Canadian pouch turned out to be the size of a pillowcase, barely big enough for our exfiltration kit of documents and disguise materials. The Canadian couriers apparently had a much easier time than the typical U.S. State Department courier, who usually accompanies several mailbag-sized pouches. The Canadian courier is allowed only one bag, and he keeps it with him at all times. So here was a final setback: some of our extra disguise materials would have to be left behind.

Before flying to Canada, I had done a review of all the materials we had collected for the scenario of U.S. English teachers and I realized that it could possibly lead to an embarrassing situation. The Canadians had succeeded in getting backstopped Canadian documents for their proposed scenario—driver's licenses, Canadian health cards, business cards for nutritionists—while permission from the various agencies for the CIA to obtain similar backstopped alias documents for the schoolteacher scenario had been too slow in coming. I remember going to the chief of graphics at seven p.m. the day before leaving to ask what he had on file. The only thing he could find was a credit card for a major department store. I thought it was better than nothing, but when I called Fred Graves, the chief of OTS operations, to ask if we could use the credit card, his response was essentially "Nope." As a result, the U.S. alias document packages were going to be terribly outclassed by the Canadians'. In fact, the only reason for sending these U.S. alias documents was to appease one of the policy-making levels in the operations planning. But I was experienced enough to know that this comes with the territory. Besides, I didn't bear them any ill will. I knew they were only doing what they thought was best for their people.

If our Canadian counterparts took inventory of the documents when we loaded the pouch, we knew we would look fairly silly. This bothered us. As soon as we arrived at the U.S. embassy in Ottawa the next morning, we made the rounds collecting business cards and other wallet stuffers to fill out our package.

As it turned out, the Canadians didn't examine the contents of the bag. Embarrassment avoided.

We had six Canadian passports and twelve U.S. passports. Of course, we had already forwarded a set of six Canadian passports, so this meant we had a redundant capability for both nationalities. For the first set, OTS techs in Canada had already forged the visas, which had come from a country in Europe. But for the second set, the operational visas had been left blank. Julio and I would complete the visas and entry cachets on the ground in Tehran, giving us some last-minute on-site flexibility.

Lastly, a highly detailed set of instructions on the use of the documents and on the final briefing of the subjects had also been prepared for easy reference—written by nonexperts—while airline tickets were enclosed showing around-the-world itineraries. I felt good as I left Canada, knowing that we were a few steps closer to getting the houseguests out.

Back home in Washington, I began preparing for the next phase of the operation, which would be to travel to our OTS office in Europe. There, I planned to link up with Julio, prepare my alias documents, and get my visa.

Before leaving, however, I paid a final visit to OTS. As I was walking down the hallway, I happened to pass Fred Graves's office. "Mendez!" he called after me as I walked by, sounding a lot like a marine corps drill instructor. "You are not out there in the field anymore having fun!" he shouted. "You've got to come back here and manage—you are no longer an operator!" I knew it was just Graves's way of keeping me on my toes, but it was also a good reminder that if anything went wrong my ass was on the line.

The following evening I drove with Karen to Dulles International Airport. With my kids, I had tried not to make a big deal of the departure. They were teenagers by this point and had more important things to worry about. Karen was different. As we pulled up to the curb at the airport, I could tell she was worried. I also knew that she understood the importance of what I had to do.

We had said good-bye numerous times before. It almost had a rhythm to it. It wasn't like looking down the barrel of a gun and your life flashing by. It was more of a tradition, knowing there was danger ahead but that it could probably be managed. Of course, we all think we can manage it until we can't. There was always a heavy sadness when I left on one of these jobs. I had last been overseas on the exfiltration operation in April, nine months before, when I had rescued RAPTOR. Karen had known then, as she knew now, that I would be in danger, but she never knew the details. Not before, not even after. It was better that way.

I took the key out of the ignition and turned to face Karen. Pulling her toward me, I kissed her and held her close for a long moment. I could feel her heartbeat. There was a pause—we just sat there not saying anything. She finally broke the silence. "You need to get a real job," she said.

"This is a real job," I said. "It's a good job."

"You need to get another job," she said.

I got out of the car and swung my bags out of the trunk. Karen got out too and walked around the car to where I was holding the driver's door open. I handed her my wedding ring—officers always use cover legends of single people. I could have left the ring at the office. Or on my dresser. But the handing of my ring to Karen was part of our tradition. "Here," it said, "keep this for me and I'll be back to get it." We never said those words. But they were the words. "I'll be back."

As she drove away and left me at the curb, a momentary wave of sadness passed over me. I hoped I would be able to keep my promise.

12

GETTING READY TO LAUNCH

I arrived in Europe on the morning of January 22. I planned to meet up with Julio before my final launch into Tehran, which was tentatively set for January 23. Julio would follow one day later, which would give us redundancy in case one of us didn't make it. Julio and I had been in communication for some time as I finalized the details of my documents package with the OTS office in Europe. The plan was for the two of us to apply for Iranian visas separately in different European cities, and then to link back up in Frankfurt before finally infiltrating Iran. In case neither of us had any luck, I had already arranged a fallback position. One of our colleagues in Europe had an OTS-issued alias passport he used from time to time. Early on, I had instructed him to obtain an Iranian visa in this passport so we would have an exemplar, an original and up-to-date version of the actual visa. He had no problem getting the visa, and if necessary, I would piggyback on his alias if I wasn't able to get one of my own.

We had about ten people working on the Argo operation in Frankfurt: a document analyst, a disguise officer, and a half dozen people from graphics. The chief of our local office was in the middle of things with his cigar fired up at all times, but was not what we would call hands-on. His deputy, Al, on the other hand, was very much involved. A lawyer by training who had also taken a degree in engineering, Al was a high-energy, insightful, meticulous man who understood the nuances of what we were about to undertake. He was a good man to have on our team, grounded and careful.

On the morning of January 21, the same day I left Washington, Julio had traveled to Geneva on his alias passport to apply for his Iranian visa there. The reason it is so important to get a legal visa is because it's very easy to check to see if the person you are claiming issued you your visa was actually on duty that day. It was also important to have an exemplar to compare to the OTS forgeries we had prepared for the houseguests and sent along to Tehran. As a part of their security measures, countries were constantly changing their stamps, or inserting traps or other such devices that would signal the document had been forged. During my first assignment at the Agency as an artist-validator, it had been my job to study these stamps to look for irregularities and traps. They could be anything from a slightly faded letter to the color of the ink. I remember one country specifically used cheap staples that rusted easily. If they examined the visa and didn't see this rust on the staple, then they would know that something was not right.

By the time I had arrived in Frankfurt, Julio had already returned from Geneva with his visa. "No problem," he said, holding up his freshly stamped passport. "They seemed eager to have me visit their country." Despite being almost milky white, he'd had no trouble convincing the clerk that he was an associate producer from South America. Of course, I'd never doubted him for a second. The genius of spies like Julio is that they could be almost anybody. There was nothing remarkable about his appearance in any way. He was of average height, weight, and build; his hair was thinning and he wore glasses. He was an everyman. When coupled with his. talent for mastering foreign languages, he was a chameleon.

My plan was to get my visa the following morning, on the twenty-third, before flying into Iran later the same evening. In the meantime, I had a lot to do and only a short amount of time to get it done.

I spent the morning of the twenty-second finalizing my alias documents package. OTS techs had been hard at work preparing my Kevin Costa Harkins alias even before I had arrived, but there were still a few details to work out, such as getting my photo taken. Since my cover was that of a European, I had to look the part. Back in the late seventies especially, there were several identifying traits that could peg you as an American just based on the style of clothes you wore. European shoes, for one, were very different. The importance of these subtle details could not be overstated. I had seen numerous case officers get tripped up despite having perfect documents because they were wearing obvious American brands. As any experienced covert officer knows, success is about paying attention to the little things. An OSS officer once told me that he'd kept alive in Italy behind enemy lines because he'd put a pebble in his shoe, which reminded him to limp since he needed an excuse for not being in the army.

For this reason, one of the first things I'd done in Frankfurt was go shopping. The city had a large department store called Kaufhof, which was like a German version of Macy's. It may seem humorous to picture a spy trying on outfits in the men's section of a department store, but that is exactly what I did. At the time, trench coats were in vogue, so I picked one up, along with a change of clothes and, of course, shoes. Beyond the style, I made sure that anything I bought was as drab as possible. Anything flashy would just draw attention to myself. Buying the clothes would also give me pocket litter, which would help to lend credibility to my disguise.

Later that afternoon, we received a FLASH cable from Ottawa. Our first batch of six Canadian passports had arrived in Tehran, but Roger Lucy had discovered a problem. Lucy had gone down to the airport to retrieve the pouch, which had been flown into the country on an Iraqi Airways flight. The Revolutionary Guards would sometimes intercept the pouches of Western embassies and as a result the courier carrying it had been instructed to physically hand it to Lucy. Lucy had been collecting the diplomatic mail for nearly ten months by this point and was well known at the airport. The pouch was handed off to him without incident; however, after he'd returned to the embassy and examined the passports he found a flaw. Somehow the handwritten Farsi fill-in on the Iranian visas showed a date of issue sometime in the future. Lucy had taught himself Farsi and realized immediately that the problem lay in the fact that the Persian calendar begins on March 21. This meant that the visas would have been issued to the houseguests after they supposedly had already entered the country. As to how this had happened, I could only think that the Farsi linguist assisting our team in Ottawa had misinterpreted the Farsi calendar. Taylor and Lucy were both concerned that the mistake would set back our departure by several days, something that would cause them a considerable headache, since they were planning on closing down their embassy almost immediately after we'd extracted the houseguests.

We fired a message back through Ottawa assuring Taylor that this was not a problem, since we could easily alter the mistake once we arrived in Tehran. In addition, these were the contingency passports, only to be used in the event that Julio and I couldn't get into Iran. If that happened, then we would forward instructions to Taylor and Lucy so that they could correct the mistake themselves. However, if our insertion was successful, we would use the second set, which had yet to be imprinted with the operational visa.

By this time the Canadians were hastily closing up shop in Tehran and readying for the exfiltration of the houseguests, which was scheduled for Monday, January 28, the day of the Iranian national election. In preparation, Taylor had asked John and Zena Sheardown to return to Canada. For John Sheardown, who had really been the first person to welcome in the Americans, it was a very emotional farewell. The group gathered around the living room and John broke the news. As some of the houseguests would later explain, John wanted to tough it out until the end and felt like he was abandoning the houseguests, whom he had come to feel responsible for. The Sheardowns complained about having to leave, but in the end they had little choice. "I want to stay and finish the job," he told them. The houseguests, for their part, encouraged the Canadians to go. They knew how much danger the Sheardowns had been in for harboring them and in some strange way they felt a sense of relief not to have to carry that burden anymore. Still, it was hard to say good-bye. As Bob Anders would later tell me, they felt as if their base of support and strength was being taken away.

After the Sheardowns had gone, the houseguests were on their own for a day or so, but felt nervous about what they might do if a person came to the door or the phone rang. At that point, Taylor gave Lucy the task of taking care of the six, and he left his place to move in with them. However, since Lucy was busy during the day helping Taylor at the embassy, a Canadian MP, known as Junior, was sent over to watch the house while Lucy was away.

The six Americans were a bit surprised by the Sheardowns' hasty departure. But it also raised their suspicions that a plan might be in the works to get them out. Mark reasoned that since Zena didn't have diplomatic immunity, it only made sense that she would leave before any sort of rescue operation was attempted. Earlier clues as to the possibility of their escape had come when Taylor had discussed the issue of whether they wanted to use Canadian or U.S. documentation. The mere fact that the question had been asked had indicated to the houseguests that a plan of some sort was being put together. However, since neither Sheardown nor Taylor had given them confirmation that someone was coming to get them out, they tried not to get their hopes up.

Back in Frankfurt, Julio and I spent the afternoon of January 22 going over our operations plan. For weeks OTS had been debriefing travelers and collecting up-to-the-minute intelligence on Iranian document controls at Mehrabad Airport.

When you have worked in this business as long as I have, you come to realize that every airport, departure lounge, and gate has its own feel. Depending on what part of the world you are in, there are certain cultural and professional mores that come into play concerning how an airport runs. How organized is the staff? Are they literate, or well trained? Do they respond to threats or is it better to flatter them? Are bribes permissible? Is there a watch list? What are the things that customs agents might be looking for? What is the layout of the airport like? Over time it's possible to develop a sixth sense on how to deal with certain situations. In India, for instance, if confronted by a customs agent about a missing document, you might act indignant and blame the other guy: "How should I know where that document is? It's your form! The guy in New Delhi didn't give it to me, so it's your problem—not mine." Such a ploy would never have worked, though, in the former Czechoslovakia, where border agents were feared for their iron efficiency during the Cold War.

Nine times out of ten, the immigration officers would be illiterate or poorly trained, while the customs agents were top-notch. In that case it would be wise to know the types of items that the customs agents were keying in on. Once, when I had flown into another city on the subcontinent for an exfiltration, I had placed copies of *Playboy* and *Time* in my suitcase where they were easily accessible, knowing that these would be obvious distractions. Sure enough, I was stopped, as I knew I would be, and when the first customs agent saw the *Playboy* magazine his eyebrows shot up. "Take it," I said. The next agent frowned when he saw the *Time* magazine. That particular issue had a very negative article in it about the official religion of the country I was traveling to. "This is forbidden," the second agent said. "It's yours!" I responded. Then, without waiting for them to continue their search, I quickly closed my suitcase and moved on. I had several visa stamps and nearly ten thousand dollars in cash hidden in a secret compartment.

When it came to the controls at Tehran's Mehrabad Airport, the biggest concern we had was with a two-sheet disembarkation/embarkation form that went back to the repressive days of SAVAK. The form was printed on "no carbon required" (NCR) paper. Upon arrival, each person had to fill one out, at which point the immigration official would keep the white top sheet while the traveler retained the yellow copy. In theory, when the traveler then left the country, he or she would have to hand over the yellow sheet so the immigration official could then match it to the saved white one to see if there were any irregularities. Since we were planning on forging this yellow form, we would essentially be taking a risk. Due to the capricious nature of the komiteh men at the airport, there was no telling whether the immigration officials would take the time to compare our yellow forms with their nonexistent white counterparts.

In order to minimize this risk, we had been collecting as much intelligence as was humanly possible on the controls at Mehrabad to see if they were matching these forms.

There are basically two ways to collect information on airports. One is passive and the other is to send in a probe. An example of passive collection would be a traveler noting things he or she might see while just passing through; then, upon returning, he or she would fill out a detailed report. This act of collecting intelligence is fairly low risk, since the traveler is not really going beyond the usual procedures of travel. Early on in the hostage crisis we had sent an all-points cable asking for anyone transiting through Mehrabad to monitor the controls.

Once we had identified the gaps in our intelligence—the "known unknowns," as you might say—we would move on to the second method, which is to send in a probe. In this case you are usually trying to test out a specific theory or concept.

By mid-January, the CIA had been able to place several officers into Tehran who were collecting intelligence on a variety of things, including Mehrabad. The most prominent of these officers was Bob, the old OSS operative who had been brought out of retirement to run the intelligence support for Eagle Claw. Bob was essentially one of our nonofficial cover men, or NOCs, and he had been tasked with reconnoitering the embassy and setting up a trucking company as part of Eagle Claw. The trucks were to be used to transport the Delta Force commandos to the U.S. embassy in Tehran as part of the final assault. Bob was a true professional who could speak several foreign languages and adopt just about any cover he needed. For this mission he was traveling on real documents from an Eastern European country, and so in no way could he be traced back to the CIA. For the purposes of our operation, Bob had become a huge asset as well. His job required that he frequently come and go, and he was often passing through our OTS office in Europe, reporting on what he had seen at the airport. Bob also had individuals working under him in Iran, who were busy collecting intelligence.

Beyond this, of course, the Canadians had also been a great help. Early on in the crisis, I had asked Ambassador Taylor to inform any of his personnel transiting through the airport to assist in our intelligence-gathering capabilities. On my trips to Ottawa, I had been able to debrief several of the Canadian MPs who had come through the airport, and the information the Canadians provided proved to be invaluable.

All of this intelligence painted a picture of the challenges that we would face in trying to get the houseguests out through

Mehrabad. The first time I had gone through the airport to rescue RAPTOR, I had noted that the regular customs official had been replaced by a komiteh thug. By late January it appeared as though the Iranians were slowly getting their act together. Still, our best information was telling us that the Iranians were not matching up the white and yellow immigration forms at the airport. I hoped we would be able to get in and out with the houseguests before that changed.

On the morning of January 23, I drove with one of our female disguise officers to Bonn, to obtain my visa. I was in alias as Kevin and had brought with me the Argo portfolio, which I planned to use to wow the Iranian immigration officials. I had altered my appearance with a simple disguise and wore a green turtleneck and tweed blazer, which I would continue to wear throughout the operation.

As we approached the Iranian embassy in Bonn, I was a little concerned to see that the embassy of my ostensible country of origin was right across the street. If the Iranians chose to do so, it would be perfectly proper for them to send me back to my own embassy to get a letter of introduction before they would grant me a visa. If such a thing happened, it would be a real test of my ability to pull off my cover. I was dropped off down the block, then walked back to the entrance of the Iranian consular section.

The reception area was a large, dull room that contained a few straight wooden-backed chairs along with some Persian carpets strewn about on the floor. A row of clerestory windows ran along the upper portion of one of the walls but offered little in the way of natural light. Instead, the space was lit by a series of dim fluorescent bulbs that gave it a gloomy, almost foreboding quality, like something you might see in a Hitchcock movie. A half-dozen visa applicants were sitting in the chairs filling out applications, while a handful of young Revolutionary Guards in civilian clothes were standing around scrutinizing everyone with hard looks. It was only then that I realized that, stupidly, I had left the portfolio in the car when I was dropped off. I still had my alias passport and other personal identity documents, but I was furious with myself. Fuming, I sat down to fill out the forms and went to the clerk's window to give them to the consular official. The disheveled clerk scrutinized me in the cocksure manner of a zealot convinced of his own superiority. I could tell he was eager to show me that he belonged to a komiteh and was suspicious of all westerners.

When people ask me what it is like to play an alias, I always tell them that it's very similar to being a good liar. The trick is that you have to believe the lie and believe it so much that the lie becomes the truth. In other words, as I walked into the consulate as Kevin, I wasn't pretending to be Kevin. I *was* Kevin, and he was me.

For me, there are two basic approaches to role playing: doing it by feel and doing it in a controlled manner. Normally I'm a bit of a control freak, but when it comes to role playing, I tend to be a wing-it kind of guy. But if you are not on edge when you are standing in front of an immigration officer and putting down your alias documents, then you're not really ready. When you can fool a person into thinking you are someone else, it feels very powerful being the only one who is in the know.

"What's the purpose of your visit?" the clerk asked me, scratching his beard.

"A business meeting with my associates at the Sheraton Hotel in Tehran," I said in my best northern European accent. "They are flying in from Hong Kong tomorrow and are expecting me."

"Why didn't you get your visa in your home country?" he asked me, now seeming to be bored with the transaction and just going through the motions.

I explained how I'd been traveling through Germany when my boss had sent me a telex informing me of the meeting. I shrugged. "I didn't have time to head home."

The clerk thought about it and nodded twice. Twenty minutes later I was on my way out the door with a one-month Iranian visa stamped into my alias passport. I hadn't even needed the Argo portfolio, but I had gotten lucky and I knew it.

Back in Frankfurt, Julio and I made final additions to the ops plan, the details of the visa acquisition, the plan for infiltration by Julio and me, and the escape and evasion (E&E) portion of the plan. This last part was a necessary component, although we all knew that if anything went wrong, the chances of executing an escape and evasion were practically nonexistent. The security at Mehrabad was overwhelming, and armed. There would be no chance to second-guess ourselves once we had committed to the departure. At that point the only way out of the airport would be on a flight.

We chose to fly out of Zurich because we wanted to arrive in Tehran on an early morning flight when the terminal at Mehrabad was quiet. We also wanted to fly on Swissair because of its reliable record. In addition, the Air France flight that we would document the houseguests as having arrived on landed at Mehrabad at almost the same time as our own flight. This meant that the houseguests would have ostensibly gone through immigration on the same day as us. The signatures and ink colors of the immigration entries would be identical to those in our own passports, which would provide genuine exemplars for us to copy later.

When everything was set, we filed a FLASH cable that included our final operations plan, requesting permission to launch. It was standard procedure to request headquarters' approval before proceeding.

While Julio and I waited, we were given a cryptic message by one of the local case officers that somebody wanted to meet with us. We took a walk down the hallway and into an empty office, where our contact Bob stood waiting. Having just returned from Tehran, he gave us some last-minute intelligence on the controls at Mehrabad. He then looked us up and down to make sure we were appropriately attired. Satisfied, he nodded and said, "You'll do fine." It may not seem like much, but this was high praise coming from a legend in the spy world who had once parachuted behind enemy lines during World War II to work with resistance groups. I took it as a good sign that our operation had just been given a blessing from one of the masters of our craft.

Within half an hour of sending our cable, a response had arrived from the director of central intelligence, saying: "Your mission is approved. Good Luck." Spies are not ones to get overly dramatic, especially among their colleagues. I turned to Julio and the two of us locked eyes. There was nothing to be said. We were both professionals and knew the risks. He reached out his hand to shake mine.

This was a bit out of character for him, and I smiled thinly. "See you in Tehran," I said.

As per our plan, I would be the first to depart. As I headed out the door for the Frankfurt *flughafen*, Al, the deputy chief, came sprinting down the hall. "Hold up," he said. "The president is making a finding." He turned to me, looking slightly perplexed. "What does it mean?"

"I think it means he's making a decision," I replied.

The chief of the office joined Al, Julio, and me in one of their offices. The chief paced back and forth, chewing on his cigar, running his fingers through his thinning hair, obviously nervous. Al, on the other hand, was very composed. I had a pretty good feeling about this operation and thought the president would be happy with it. The U.S. government didn't have much else—not that we knew of, at least. I was calm, like the lull in the eye of a storm.

The communicator walked the next message down the hall to us. We were in a knot in the middle of the office when he burst through the door. "It's a go!" he exclaimed with a grin before even reaching us, a breach of operational etiquette that we were only too happy to forgive. A commo guy should never verbalize the contents of a message.

The message had two lines: "The President of the United States approves your mission. Good luck." I stared at it for a second taking that in. It's not often that you get a personal message from the president on one of your missions. If there was ever a sign that we were about to embark on a high-stakes operation, here it was. The president—and if it went bad, the world—would be watching.

Then I was out the door, driven to the Frankfurt airport by a colleague from graphics to catch my Lufthansa flight to Zurich.

The president had thrown a slight monkey wrench into my tight schedule, but it looked like I would just make it.

I arrived in Zurich around ten o'clock that night, and my connecting Swissair flight to Tehran was set to leave at one o'clock in the morning. The flight to Tehran was fairly full, as indicated by the number of people in the transit lounge. As it turned out, the Swissair flight was going to be the last one out of Zurich that evening.

While I waited, I had a moment to reflect. Despite all the planning we had done, there was no way to be certain about a single thing in Iran. Many of the country's official positions had been taken over by untrained thugs. In some ways this was a huge advantage for us, because they often didn't know what they were supposed to be doing—in fact, you could sometimes even show them what needed to be done. On the other hand, this meant that we couldn't expect the opposition to be acting rationally. In Moscow, for instance, if an officer was ever captured, he would usually be PNG'd. The Soviets would take a picture of the offending officer and publish it in the national newspaper, *Izvestia,* declaring him persona non grata, then kick him out of the country. I knew, however, that in Iran such civilities would be nonexistent. When I'd exfiltrated RAPTOR, the country had been dangerous but the mood different. Back then the U.S. embassy was still in one piece and Americans could come and go freely. Now, however, the entire country seemed united behind one purpose: directly engaging in revenge on America and the CIA. I was under no illusions as to what would happen to me or Julio if they found us out.

I walked over to a large set of windows that looked out onto the tarmac. I stood there for a few seconds watching a 747 taxi past, when suddenly I became aware of my reflection in the glass. I was dressed in my Kevin Costa Harkins disguise and I noticed the absence of my wedding ring. Instinctively I felt for it, remembering my promise to Karen. *Is this something I really want to do?* I asked myself. *Do I want to go back to Iran and risk the possibility that the revolutionaries are "expecting" me?* I could feel my body trembling as I went through what we always called the "gut check." The idea is that you make your operational plan as good as it can get, and when you get to the ninetieth percentile of confidence, you know you are ready. So the question was: Am I there? Am I at or above the ninetieth percentile? Lives were at stake—not just the houseguests' but also Julio's and my own. Beyond that, who knew what kind of retribution the militants would take against the hostages, or the Canadians, for that matter. Even though espionage operations always try to balance the use of clandestine resources against the risk of human lives, President Carter and his national security advisers had already made those calculations at the White House. For the moment, however, I would have to block out all that. My concerns were relatively simple. Could I get in and rescue the Americans safely?

There was an unwritten rule at the CIA that gave the officer on the ground the option of aborting an operation when he or she believed it would fail. There was no shame in backing out. It was just another way of encouraging risk assessment at the last moment, and it had saved many lives.

I stood there weighing my options. I opened the Argo portfolio and flipped through the résumés of the houseguests. One of the questions that had been put to me as a part of the interview process way back in 1965 when I had joined the CIA was: "What if you got in a situation where you just disappeared and nobody knew where you were?" My response was immediate: "Try to find me." Even though I had never met these six Americans, I knew that, because it was in my power, I had to do whatever I could to help them, regardless of any reservations I had about my own safety. It was the same thing I would expect someone to do for me, and one of the reasons I had the confidence to put myself in harm's way.

And just like that, the momentary uncertainty I had been feeling about the mission passed, replaced by a kind of euphoria as the stress left my body. This was a good ops plan and we were ready, I thought. At that point I was committed to doing whatever I had to do to make it work.

Just then, an announcement over the public address system said that the Swissair flight I was about to board had been canceled due to weather at Mehrabad Airport. Murphy's law had struck.

I made a sterile phone call—a call to a European number not registered with any phone company—to Julio to let him know. "I'm languishing in Zurich," I said. We agreed to stick to Julio's schedule the following day and enter Iran together—again, not perfect, though it'd have to do.

After that I went out and hailed a taxi and went to a hotel, where I slept like a baby.

The following afternoon, Julio arrived from Frankfurt and the two of us joined up in the departure lounge. Both of us had our game faces on, and together we boarded the flight to Tehran.

13

ON LOCATION IN IRAN

Our plane touched down in Mehrabad at five o'clock in the morning on Friday, January 25. As we taxied on the tarmac, I could see that piles of ash-colored snow had been shoved to either side of the runway. Even at this early hour, the air hung heavy with the smoke from the wood fires burning throughout the city. As the engines shut down and the stairs were wheeled up to the aircraft, I could see a few of the passengers shifting nervously in their seats. I noticed that some of the women who were previously uncovered had donned black chadors, a reminder that we were about to enter into a world with its own rules. Other passengers stared straight ahead. I was certain the revolution had touched all their lives in some way. I watched an anxious man gnaw at his fingernails. What was he worried about? As we sat there the cabin was oddly quiet, so much so that when the door was finally opened I could hear the loud click of the lock. Then one by one, we all got to our feet.

Julio and I disembarked in the frigid morning air and made our way into the terminal. There was not much to distinguish Mehrabad from a hundred other Middle Eastern airports, except, perhaps, for a hint of art deco in the balustrades mounted around its exterior. It was a low, sprawling, concrete box, and typically packed during the morning and afternoon hours.

We quickly filled out our yellow and white disembarkation/embarkation forms, which were lying in stacks on nearby tables inside the arrivals lounge. Since it would be Julio's job to fill out these forms for the houseguests later, he surreptitiously grabbed a few extra copies using a little sleight of hand. Walking up to the table, he set his newspaper, the *Frankfurter Allgemeine*, down on top of a stack of the forms. He then filled out one for himself, rearranged his hand luggage, and in one motion picked up his newspaper with the forms underneath. Folding the newspaper in half, he then stuffed it into his attaché case and was done.

The airport was peppered with all manner of tourist images of smiling Iranians enjoying a winter vacation at one of the country's mountain resorts. The Ministry of National Guidance had a tourist branch, which was doing its best to promote the country as a destination in order to bring in some money. The ads had sayings in English, French, German, and Farsi, all of them variations on typical tourist catchphrases such as "Enjoy Iran!" In one of the posters there was an Iranian movie star posing with his family with their ski outfits on. I thought about how incongruous the image was with the hostage crisis going on in the heart of Tehran. Julio seemed to have reached the same conclusion. "This place has gotten a bum rap," he said with a wolfish grin.

I shook my head in amazement. "Yeah, next time I'll bring the family."

After filling out our forms, we took our place in the immigration line. I could see that there were several plainclothes Revolutionary Guards and komiteh members milling about the arrivals lounge, but they seemed more interested in hassling the returning Iranians, rather than bothering foreigners. The economic situation in the country had only gotten worse since I'd been there nine months earlier, and the Iranian authorities were concerned about people smuggling goods into and out of the country. This would probably mean that we could expect tougher exit controls as well. The immigration desk was no longer being manned by an untrained civilian irregular but by an official immigration officer in uniform. I hoped that my operation to rescue RAPTOR hadn't left a paper trail down at the U.S. embassy. By this time the militants had probably been able to put together most of the secret documents that had been shredded during the assault. If anything had been left over from the RAPTOR operation, or if there was something linking it to me, then there was a chance they might have put my name on a watch list. As we approached the counter, however, the immigration official couldn't have cared less about us. After tearing apart our white and yellow forms, he stamped our passports and waved us through without even giving us so much as a second glance. (As it turned out, I would learn later that the militants did find a secret document in Bruce Laingen's safe that mentioned the exfiltration of RAPTOR. Luckily my name was not on the sheet, but Tom Ahern, the chief of station in Iran who had been captured during the assault, caught hell for it. Later he would tell me that the militants had been extremely pissed off when they learned that RAPTOR had escaped.)

Breezing past customs, we hopped in a sputtering Opel Kadett taxi and headed over to the Sheraton, which was located on one of the main thoroughfares linking Mehrabad to downtown Tehran. Our taxi driver was a thin old man who wore a sweater vest under his jacket against the cold. He seemed happy to see us, and launched into a lengthy soliloquy, in English, on the beauties of Tehran. He assumed we were from America and asked if we were hungry. Without waiting for a reply, he broke off a large piece of unleavened bread he had with him up in the front seat and passed it back. It was still warm and actually quite good.

The route our taxi was navigating was lined with a multitude of handmade signs espousing revolutionary slogans and anti-American propaganda—a reality that belied the innocence portrayed in the tourism posters. Moscow this wasn't, but Julio and I would still have to stay on our toes. During the shah's reign, SAVAK had maintained a massive network of informers and domestic spies, and there was no telling who or what the Revolutionary Guard had co-opted.

The Sheraton in Tehran looked like it had been transplanted from Detroit. It was a typical modern high-rise monolith surrounded by a parking lot—just like every other Sheraton in the world.

The hotel was popular with foreign businesspeople and travelers, so Julio and I fit right in as we entered the large lobby. A quick scan revealed no overt surveillance, but I assumed it was present. Years of undercover work in Moscow had taught me that it's best to assume the other side is always watching, even when you can't see them.

After checking in, Julio and I went down to the Swissair office to reconfirm our airline reservations for our departure the following Monday. We were scheduled to depart for Zurich at seven thirty in the morning and I wanted to make sure there would be no surprises. If something was to go wrong and we were forced to abort, it would be nearly impossible to get the houseguests to go through the whole process of psyching themselves up to go back through the airport again. Making sure we had a seat on the plane was just basic tradecraft.

When we arrived at the Swissair office, however, it was still closed. I knew from my previous trip that the U.S. embassy was right around the corner, and with some time to kill we decided to take a walk.

The walls of the embassy were completely covered with signs and graffiti, all of them denouncing America, President Carter, and the shah. Here and there, the grim visage of Khomeini glared back at us from a placard or poster like some cartoon villain. At this hour, the streets were eerily quiet and as I stood there staring at the embassy it gave me a feeling of deep and yawning helplessness. I was so close and yet at the same time unable to do anything to free my fellow countrymen trapped inside. At the minimum, I could take note of what I'd seen and report back to the Eagle Claw planners, but it was little consolation.

We continued down Roosevelt Avenue and onto a little side street nearby, where our tourist map told us we should be able to find the Canadian embassy. Instead of the red and white maple leaf banner of Canada, however, we found ourselves staring at the blue and yellow flag of Sweden. In fact we had arrived at the building where Lee Schatz had been working on the day of the embassy takeover.

We huddled for a second, consulting our map. A solitary Iranian policeman stood on guard near the building's entrance, his hands thrust into his pockets.

"Why don't we ask him," I said with some volume, indicating the policeman. I was in character, going with the flow. Of course, the Department of Defense or OTS could have provided us with the most detailed and up-to-date map of Tehran available on the planet, but being caught with such an obvious piece of tradecraft would have immediately blown our cover. We were supposed to be from Hollywood, not Langley.

Julio and I approached the guard, and after several attempts at communicating in German, Arabic, and even Spanish, Julio threw up his hands (even though Julio spoke Farsi, to do so could have aroused unnecessary suspicion). I held out our tourist map and jabbed at the maze of streets. "Canada," I said. Then, even slower, "Can-ah-duh." The guard only stared at me and blinked.

While this was going on, a young Iranian wearing a faded green army jacket and jeans stood watching us from across the street. I had seen him out of the corner of my eye but tried not to let on that I knew he was there. To me he looked just like one of the "students" who had attacked the U.S. embassy. As we stood there figuring out what to do next, the young man crossed the street and approached. Ignoring us, he went straight up to the guard and the two had a heated exchange in Farsi. The man kept looking at us, then back to the guard, and I assumed he was asking the guard what we were doing there. He then turned to Julio and addressed him in crisp, unaccented German. Julio perked up and it wasn't long before the two had fallen into a lively discussion. Julio snatched the map out of my hand and they pored over it. The Iranian pointed to a street north of the U.S. embassy.

Julio thanked the Iranian, but the young man wasn't finished. He borrowed a piece of paper from my notebook and wrote down the address. Then he flagged down a passing Mercedes taxi and handed the slip of paper to the driver. For a moment I wondered if it was some kind of trap. Had he just given the taxi driver the address to a local komiteh headquarters instead of to the Canadian embassy?

He held the passenger door open for us to get in. Before doing so Julio attempted to hand him a few rumpled rial bills, but the man shook his head and made a little gesture as if to say, "Please, it was all my pleasure." He put his hand on his heart and flashed a wide grin, revealing several gold teeth. I thought about the irony of this whole exchange. Here was a man going out of his way to illustrate to two undercover CIA officers that Iranians were hospitable, caring people. It was hard to reconcile this with the notion that less than a block away innocent American diplomats were being tortured and held against their will.

The taxi then took us across town to the Canadian embassy, where we arrived a little before noon. Ambassador Taylor had been expecting us, and a burly Canadian MP, Claude Gauthier, took us up to meet with him in his outer office on the second floor. Taylor was charming and affable and his face lit up when he saw us. "Welcome to Tehran," he said, his hand outstretched. He was wearing his mod-style glasses and had on a pair of jeans and cowboy boots. He was hardly the uptight government bureaucrat I was expecting. He introduced us to his secretary, a small elderly woman named Laverna, and then took us into his inner office.

The office was sleek and very modern. There were glass cases full of books, framed photos, as well as a fully stocked bar. The floor was covered with several high-quality Persian rugs and a Canadian flag hung in the corner. The room's most striking feature was Taylor's desk, which wasn't really a desk at all but a stylish round glass-topped table.

We sat down and Taylor explained that they were just about ready to shut down the embassy in preparation for the coming exfiltration. In fact, later that afternoon he was going to see his family off at the airport. Only five Canadian staffers remained, and these would depart on Monday, January 28, just hours after the Swissair flight we hoped to board was scheduled to depart. He explained that he would send a diplomatic letter to the foreign ministry on Monday morning informing the Iranian government that the Canadian embassy would temporarily be closed. With that out of the way, he then asked us if there was anything he could do to help. I was struck by the casual and relaxed manner of the whole encounter.

The first thing we would need to do, I told him, was to meet with the houseguests and brief them on the various options for escape. This would also give me a chance to assess whether or not they'd be able to pull it off. We all agreed that the meeting should take place later that evening at John Sheardown's home. After that, we would need to get to work on the visas and documents, which would most likely happen the following day. I had brought my kit of watercolors along with me, which I planned on using to put the final stamps into the passports. Taylor retrieved the first set of bogus documents along with the second pouch. This sealed pouch contained the second set of passports and several of the other secondary documents that we had included. Julio and I then examined the contents and were happy to see that everything had made it through. We showed the second set of passports to Taylor, and he seemed quite pleased by their authenticity. In order to make them looked used, our OTS techs in Ottawa had stomped on them repeatedly and rubbed them into the floor.

When the meeting was finished, Taylor introduced us to Roger Lucy, who seemed like a capable and quiet leader. Lucy had already made several trips through Mehrabad on behalf of Taylor and had earned us a great amount of intelligence on the controls there. Next we were properly introduced to Claude, a Québécois who was the embassy's chief of security. Claude had been given the nickname "Sledge" as a result of wielding a sledgehammer to destroy all but the most sensitive cryptographic and communications equipment at the Canadian embassy in preparation for their departure. It was a nickname that he would come to relish.

Before he left to see his family off, we asked Taylor's permission to send a cable to Washington through Ottawa, confirming our arrival and the plans to meet the houseguests later that night. I'll admit that it was gratifying that both Taylor and Lucy were excited by all the progress we'd made on the Argo cover story. They told me it had a sort of dash that they could both identify with. When I opened the portfolio and showed them the ad in *Variety*, they were both impressed. Some people have suggested that there was a kind of competition between the CIA and Ottawa, but Taylor and I never saw it that way. This was a collegial cooperation from the beginning and I can say unequivocally that both of us had only one goal in mind: to get the six Americans safely out of Tehran.

The houseguests had been told by Lucy that they should expect some visitors. Of course he didn't tell them we were CIA—just that we were coming to help. In preparation for their escape, Taylor and Lucy had organized a set of luggage and extra clothes since the houseguests had neither. It would be awkward to have them enter the airport without any bags.

After we finished up at the Canadian embassy, Claude agreed to take us over to the Sheardowns', and Julio and I piled into the embassy's Mercedes. By the time we pulled out it was five o'clock and the streets were snarled with traffic. Claude took it in stride and used his horn liberally, a device he said it would be impossible to drive in the city without. Not much had changed since the last time I'd been to Tehran. Large sections of the city were still shut down. Under the shah, Tehran had been famous for its nightlife. All of that had vanished after the revolution, replaced by blacked-out storefronts, boarded-up restaurants, and sandbagged bunkers manned by machine-gun-toting youths. The city was basically divided into north and south, with the more affluent residents living in the higher-elevated and cooler north, and the poor in the hot and overcrowded pan-flat south.

It took us about thirty minutes to clear the central part of the city, and when we finally made it to the Shemiran district, it was like being in a different universe. It reminded me a lot of places like Bel Air in Los Angeles, where the rich and powerful lived safely cloistered behind their walled compounds.

Since Ken had gone to the airport, Lucy had driven over to his place to pick up the Staffords, arriving at the Sheardowns' slightly before we did. As they waited inside, some of the houseguests had played a little game about what we might look like. I'll never forget the face of Lee Schatz as he opened the door. It was the face of an overgrown kid, full of mischief with a swooping mustache overtaking everything else. He took one look at us and said, "Trench coats! You guys are wearing trench coats?" He shook his head in dismay.

It might have seemed clichéd, but then again it fit with our cover. The others rushed forward to meet us, brimming with nervous excitement and anticipation.

As I entered the house I was confronted by a bizarre sight. A fire burned merrily in the hearth and the houseguests had laid out hors d'oeuvres. The group seemed rested and eager, even fit. Bob Anders actually had a nice tan. Lucy went into the kitchen to mix us drinks and it wasn't long before we were sipping happily on our cocktails and getting to know one another. If not for the roaming bands of murderous Revolutionary Guards and komiteh patrolling the streets outside, it felt just like any other dinner party I had been to in Washington, D.C.

When I felt that we'd sufficiently broken the ice, I stood up to brief them on the various cover stories. "Now, you guys have worked long enough in the government to know that we didn't get here without some questions," I said. "We've got three different options, each with their own passports and supporting documents. You will ultimately have to decide which one you like best, but Julio and I can certainly advise you."

I then laid down the different sets of passports and went through the various cover stories—American teachers, Canadian nutritionists, Hollywood option. I explained that regardless of which option they chose, the plan was to leave through Mehrabad Airport on Monday morning.

The houseguests were obviously concerned about the security at the airport and wondered what might happen if they were stopped and taken into secondary, a form of interrogation reserved for those individuals deemed suspicious enough to warrant it. I could tell that Joe Stafford, of all the houseguests, was perhaps the most concerned. He struck me as being highly analytical, the kind of person who has trouble letting go in the moment. Since the success of any disguise is predicated on confidence, I hoped he would come around.

Lee pointed to the U.S. documents. "Traveling though the airport as Americans seems like a pretty lame idea to me," he said. The others nodded, noting as I had that the English schools had been closed for many months. I could tell they were wrapping their heads around the whole concept of their escape, trying to take it all in. I felt this was a perfect time to present my case for Argo.

"I've managed a lot of these kinds of operations in the past," I said. "And I'm confident that the Hollywood option will work."

I opened the Studio Six portfolio and took out the issue of *Variety*, which had the Argo ad in it. I then handed Cora Lijek her Studio Six business card and indicated the ad. " 'From a story by Teresa Harris'—that's you," I said. I picked up her Canadian alias passport with her picture and handed it to her. Cora studied her photo and forged signature with obvious wonderment. Next I picked up the sketch pad and handed it to Kathy Stafford. "Here," I said. "We saw that you have a little art in your background and decided to make you the art director." I passed out the remaining business cards, which indicated the various roles the other houseguests would be playing: Joe Stafford was an associate producer; Mark Lijek was "Joseph Earl Harris," the transportation coordinator; Lee Schatz was "Henry W. Collins," the cameraman; and Bob Anders was "Robert Baker," the locations manager.

I explained that we had rented an office in Hollywood and that right now we had a staff of people manning the phones. "If anybody calls, they'll be told that Teresa Harris is with a location scouting team in the Middle East but will be back next week."

The six Americans stared at me for a long second, perhaps understanding for the first time the lengths to which we had gone to get them out, including setting up a fake movie production with offices staffed by real Hollywood insiders. This on top of all the hours spent by my team at Foggy Bottom working on perfecting their cover stories and documentation to "prove" they were who they said they were.

Finally Mark spoke up. "It doesn't sound totally crazy," he said.

"What's the movie?" Anders asked.

I tried my best to explain, using the jargon that Calloway had coached me on. "It's like *Buck Rogers* in the desert," I said. "The story mixes Middle Eastern myths with spaceships and far-off worlds. Believe me when I say the Iranians won't be able to understand a word of it, which is great."

I could see they were still on the fence. "Whatever option you decide on," I said, "this has to be something you can see yourself doing, something you can believe in."

With that, I instructed them to go into the dining room and discuss it among themselves. They also needed to figure out whether they wanted to leave as a group or individually.

Later, I would talk with the houseguests about how this discussion went. The group had gathered around the table and immediately launched into the pros and cons of the various plans. For Lee, who was an agricultural attaché, the idea of nutritionists seemed like a nonstarter from the beginning, which wasn't high praise given his background. The others felt that the schoolteachers and nutritionists just didn't feel right. Cora pictured somebody stopping her and asking her a question about crops, and the thought worried her. She knew zero about agriculture and had no idea what she'd say. However, she knew a little something about Hollywood, just like everyone else. She pictured herself as a Hollywood screenwriter. All she would have to do would be to read the script and she would be good to go. The others began to come around as well. Mark realized that it made perfect sense that a person from Hollywood would be crazy enough to come to Iran in the middle of a revolution. Anders, for one, was instantly sold. He envisioned himself on the set of a film, rubbing elbows with Faye Dunaway and Warren Beatty. It seemed like a role he was born to play. "It sounded like we were going to have one hell of a good time, and I couldn't wait to get going," he later told me. Lee, for his part, knew almost nothing about operating a movie camera, but he imagined the adventurous life of a Hollywood cinematographer traveling all over the world. He had been to some exotic places himself and figured he could easily wing it. The biggest factor for all of them was that it was clearly the option with the most supporting documentation, not to mention that there was an office actually staffed with people to back up the story.

In the end the only dissenter seemed to be Joe, who kept saying, "I just don't see it." Joe, it appears, was against all of the plans and instead wanted to remain in Iran. Mark knew Joe quite well by now, and he saw Joe's response as being more emotional than rational. To Mark, it appeared that he was feeling guilty at the prospect of escaping while their colleagues languished down at the embassy. "What if they retaliate against the hostages if we leave?" Joe asked everyone. It was a good point, and one that I had considered myself, but with Canada closing down their embassy and the Iranians getting closer and closer to discovering the fugitive Americans, there was really no other option but to leave. The other house-guests certainly felt that way. "Well, what do you want us to do—stay here? How is that going to help them?" Anders asked him. Joe then proposed that they go down to the U.S. embassy and try to reason with the militants. It might have been a noble gesture, but both Anders and Schatz were adamant. "You can forget about it," they said.

It was as they were debating Joe's plan that I decided to walk in and see how things were going. I could sense the electric tension in the room, so I decided to use some parlor magic. "Let me show you how an operation like this works," I said. I picked up two corks off a nearby counter, interlocking them between my thumbs and forefingers to form two D shapes. I had used this trick many times to illustrate how to set up a deception operation. "Here's us and here are the bad guys," I said. "And this is how we are going to get out of each other's way." With a little sleight of hand I pulled my two hands apart and the corks appeared to move through each other. It was a simple trick, but the goal was to show them that they were involved with professionals in the art of deception. That everything had been thought of.

It must have worked, because after that they voted five to one in favor of using the Argo cover option and leaving as a group.

With that out of the way, the six gave Julio and me a tour of the house, which was truly palatial. While we were making our rounds, Chris Beeby, the New Zealand ambassador, showed up along with his second secretary, Richard Sewell. Sewell would prove to be in-credibly valuable over the coming days. He explained to me that he had a close contact down at Mehrabad who worked for British Air-ways, and Julio asked him if he would be willing to help us out by grabbing some more of the yellow and white disembarkation/embarkation forms. Sewell readily agreed and we set up a time to meet at the Canadian embassy the following day.

Before leaving, I sat down with the houseguests once again to go over their cover stories. I handed each of them the personal résumé that Joe Missouri had created for them and told them to memorize them backward and forward. "If anyone stops you or hassles you in any way, just act confident and look them in the eye. Think about how someone from Hollywood would react. Remember, Julio and I will be right beside you, so if anything goes wrong let us do the talking."

The last thing I wanted to go over was their disguises. I had brought with me the materials that Doris had included and I spread them out on the table. Since thousands of Iranians had passed through the consular section of the embassy, where the majority of the houseguests had worked, there was a chance that one of the Americans might be easily recognized.

I explained to them that the key to a good disguise was to identify the various salient features or qualities that make them who they are, and then alter those, rather than try to go overboard in one area. Often, it is the subtle things that give people away, such as the way they walk, or a particular mole. If this operation were taking place in Moscow, we would have had a whole crew of OTS disguise experts working with us. Instead, we would have to make do with what we had.

"Each of you is going to need to make yourself look a little flashier, a little more Hollywood," I said. I handed Schatz his view-finder and gave Cora the script.

"Julio and I will be back here on Sunday night to go through a little dress rehearsal," I told them. "But in the meantime, learn your parts. You will be tested!"

Since they knew the stakes, I didn't have to tell them what would happen if they didn't. I only hoped that Joe would come around and get into the spirit as the others had. Despite all the hard work and energy we'd put into the Argo cover story, one lackluster performance and the whole plot would come crashing down.

14

FINAL PREPARATIONS

Julio and I returned to the Canadian embassy on Saturday morning. The building, which was normally empty on the weekend, was buzzing with activity as the Canadians went through their last-minute preparations for shutting down on Monday. The first thing I did was send an updated ops plan and situation report to Ottawa and CIA headquarters. In it I elaborated on their cover, explaining that "six Canadians from Studio Six Productions" had called on the ambassador in Tehran. They were hoping that he could set up an appointment with the Ministry of National Guidance to present their case for leasing the local bazaar for their film "Argo." I then went on to explain that the ambassador had advised them to look elsewhere for locations and that, following his advice, they would probably depart the country on Monday, January 28.

This would give us the option of bringing the six to the airport in an embassy vehicle with an embassy driver, saving us the difficulty of having to arrange reliable transportation to the airport.

After this was done, Julio and I sat down to work on the documents package. As gracious as ever, Taylor offered to let us use his office.

Julio immediately got to work on the disembarkation/embarkation forms. Sewell had dropped by with a stack of extras, which gave us a nice cushion. Julio completed the Farsi and English annotations on about twenty of these, using the wording on our own yellow sheets to guide him.

While this was going on, I turned my attention to the passports. My main task was to insert the Iranian visas that we had collected in Toronto and complete the back travel, including stamping in the arrival cachet entry for Mehrabad. The prime exemplar for the Mehrabad arrival cachet was the stamped impression we had received in our own passports upon arrival.

The worst thing that can happen when you're falsifying a cachet entry is to forge the signature of an immigration officer before arriving in the country, only to discover this same person is about to stamp you out. He would obviously know that he was not working on the day your passport says you arrived. Another mistake, of course, would be putting in a stamp that was no longer in use. Our careful monitoring and collection of the cachets at Mehrabad, as well as the diligence of our OTS ink experts from the graphics division, allowed us to produce an exact match.

I then slowly and carefully placed the cachets in the passports, using a technique I'd learned from my days in the bullpen to make it look as if they'd been done hastily by an immigration officer.

As with operating in disguise, there are two types of validators: those who do it by feel and those who work in a controlled manner. The former tend to work better after lunch when they've had a few martinis to loosen them up. I, on the other hand, was definitely a member of the second group. My approach to validating was to make it look as offhand as I could but to control it. That way, if I ever got in a tight spot, I didn't have to rely on my instincts and reflexes, but could rely on my mechanical talents. There were several tools I'd been given in training to help me, such as the forger's bridge, a technique using one hand to steady the other while writing. And of course there were many other tricks I'd learned on my own.

Over the course of my career I'd had plenty of opportunities to practice my skills as a forger. Being an artist-validator is anything but routine—there were times when I found myself holed up in some safe house on the other side the world, working long hours under the glare of a watchmaker's lamp.

Among the first jobs that our new artist-validators typically will get are reproducing border cachets. The actual impressions of these stamps tend to be a little messy to begin with and so it's okay if their work is not so perfect. In fact, perfection can sometimes be a detriment, as a document's very perfection is often what sets it apart from the common variety. There is nothing more suspicious to an immigration officer than seeing a perfectly inked cachet impression in the midst of all the clutter in a travel document. After mastering the skill of creating realistic clutter, an artist can then move up to working on secondary documents: driver's licenses, military ID cards, health cards—anything that would accompany a primary document. At the top of the food chain are major documents, such as a travel document. Some artists could work years in the bullpen before getting a crack at one of these, and it was considered a major insult if a less experienced artist was assigned one before a more experienced artist.

On some occasions, we would have the whole department working on something together. I can remember one time when someone had access to a rarely seen communist country's passport but had to return it the next day. A whole crew of experts was brought in on the weekend. It took all the process photographers we had on board just to photograph the different elements we had to make in order to duplicate it.

As an OTS traveling tech officer, you have to be ready to work at any time and under any condition. Once I was even forced to improvise in the bathroom of an airplane. This was on a mission to the subcontinent to help out with an exfiltration of a Russian defector and his family. (This same Russian had been smuggled overland from a neighboring country in the trunk of a car.) A cable had gone out asking for the services of an artist-validator and I'd hopped on the next flight. As the plane was descending to land, however, the flight attendant announced that there had been an outbreak of yellow fever in the country and anyone who was not currently vaccinated could expect to be put in quarantine for who knew how long. We had less than twenty-four hours to get the Russian and his family out of the country, so this was not an option. In addition, I had several incriminating rubber stamps and forging tools, not to mention thousands of dollars in cash hidden in a concealment inside my briefcase. With so much on the line, I couldn't risk being held up. I quickly stepped into the toilet and upgraded my shot record to include a yellow fever notation good for ten years. I had to do this in a matter of minutes as the flight began its final approach. The turbulence made it difficult, but I was able to make it back to my seat just before the plane's wheels touched the ground. We were able to get the Russian and his family out the following morning.

As Julio and I worked on the documents, Taylor took a break from his activities and joined us in the office. Not wishing to bother us, he took a seat on a white sofa across the room while Julio and I continued to go about our business. Taylor sat and listened as we asked each other questions and discussed the finer points of our counterfeiting skills. He was clearly enjoying being in the midst of this clandestine skullduggery. A few minutes later, Taylor's secretary entered the office to inform him that a rug wallah had arrived in the outer office. "Oh, right," said Taylor. The wallah entered with a flourish. "I have brought only my finest rugs for you, Mr. Ambassador!" he called out. He unfurled several rugs, laying them about the floor. Taylor bent down to examine them with an expert eye. It was clear that he was hoping to purchase a few more antique Persian carpets to take home with him. They were having a quiet discussion about the goods, discreetly so as not to disturb us.

While this was going on, Claude "Sledge" Gauthier was busy slamming away with his sledgehammer, destroying sensitive equipment in a far-off room of the embassy, the reverberations of each impact echoing through the halls.

Julio and I were too engrossed to notice any of this. I was busy stippling in a date on one of the cachets with a sharpened stick, similar to a manicure stick my wife often used. When I'd finished with the cachets showing the houseguests' back travel, it was time to move on to the visas. We had had somebody from Ottawa pick up an exemplar for us in Toronto, which we'd then sent to OTS in Washington so that the techs could reproduce the stamp. However, as I opened the inkpad I noticed that the ink had completely dried up. Our ink chemist had painstakingly formulated this ink especially for its fluorescent quality. These visas were, in fact, the operative entries in the whole package. They would be subject to the closest scrutiny at immigration departure controls. Without these, it didn't matter what cover story we used—we wouldn't be able to get out of Iran. Looking about for a solution, my eyes fell on Taylor's liquor cabinet. I walked over and scanned the labels, selecting a single-malt scotch that I thought would have a high-octane quality alcohol as one of its ingredients. I poured two fingers of scotch into a highball glass and brought both the bottle and the glass back to our workspace. Julio looked mildly amused as I set them down. "Thirsty?" he asked. I poured some of the scotch onto the inkpad to moisten it and without skipping a beat began stamping the visas into the passports. Julio shook his head and smiled his smile. "Why not?" he said. "This whole operation is being fueled by alcohol anyway."

It took a good part of the morning to complete the entries in all six passports. The only thing left to be done was to tidy up our document packages and destroy any evidence of the dark arts of a forger. The spurious Canadian passports, the fallback set with the error in the visas, were sent to the shredder. So were the alias U.S. documents we had included in the diplomatic pouch just in case we needed them. Our tools, inkpads, ink supplies, and so on were fed into the flames of the embassy incinerator. The schoolteachers and nutritionists went up in smoke. It was Argo or nothing.

M eanwhile, back in Hollywood, Bob and Andi Sidell were busy manning the phones at Studio Six. We hadn't given them a timetable as to when the exfiltration was going to happen, so Bob assumed it could be at any moment.

In the beginning, Bob and Andi had gotten a thrill out of playing amateur spies. It wasn't long, though, before this initial excitement was replaced by worry and fear. It suddenly dawned on them that the lives of eight individuals, possibly more, were in their hands. Later Bob told me that in the evenings they would crowd around the TV, hoping they wouldn't see my face paraded across the evening news as the latest captive tied up and blindfolded. Down at the office, Andi began dreading the sound of the telephone, worrying each time she heard it ring that it would be someone calling to report bad news. Instead most of the calls were about business.

Even though Sidell had been in the film business for nearly twenty-five years, he was still amazed by how easily the myth of Studio Six had taken off. After our initial ad had run in the industry trades, the *Hollywood Reporter* had called asking for comment. Hollywood is a small town and word had gotten around that Calloway was connected to the picture. A reporter wanted to know who would be starring in the film. Sidell was quoted in the article as saying, "We will use substantial names. At the moment we are sworn to secrecy." It wasn't long before he began to get calls from friends who were looking for work. After two weeks, the office had been inundated with scripts and headshots. "This is crazy!" Bob said to Andi one day as they sifted through it all.

In addition, several credible people in the industry pitched him ideas and he even scheduled meetings. One writer wanted to know if he would be interested in producing a little-known Arthur Conan Doyle horror story titled "Lot No. 249," about a college student who uses Egyptian magic to reanimate a mummy that ends up going on a murderous rampage. Sidell was so intrigued that he actually looked into purchasing the rights to the story from the Doyle estate, even though he knew full well that as soon as we got out of Iran, Studio Six would cease to exist.

It was like a lie that had taken on a life of its own, and now he was forced to go along for the ride. In Hollywood terms, it was the role of a lifetime, but he wasn't sure for how long he could keep it up.

On Sunday night, Julio and I returned to the Sheardown house to go through a dress rehearsal. The houseguests had spent the previous day learning their covers and perfecting their disguises. Now came the moment of truth. Lucy had brought the Staffords over and everyone was waiting for us in the den. When we got there, I couldn't believe my eyes. All of the houseguests had borrowed clothes, assembled some personal items, and completely restyled their appearance in order to fit their new roles. Mark had used some black eyeliner to darken his beard, while Lee fiddled confidently with the viewfinder hanging around his neck. "Call me Woody!" he said. He had decided that any Hollywood cameraman worth his salt would have a nickname, and Woody was his. Cora, meanwhile, had used some sponge rollers to curl her hair, which she normally wore straight. She'd also taken off her glasses and used a lot more makeup than she was accustomed to. She flipped though the script absentmindedly. Our art director, Kathy, had pulled her long brunette hair up into a ponytail and put on a set of dark, thick-rimmed Truman Capote–esque glasses to go along with the Argo sketchbook. But the most surprising transformation came from Bob Anders, who had blow-dried his hair mod-style and donned tight pants and a blue shirt two sizes too small, unbuttoned down to his chest. To complete the ensemble, he wore a gold chain and medallion and threw a topcoat across his shoulders like a cape. "Check this out," he said, sauntering self-importantly through the room. I found it hard not to smile.

The best thing about the show was the relaxed and easy way the houseguests had adopted their new personalities. As I'd hoped, they were having fun and didn't seem the least bit worried about the trip through the airport the following day. Joe hadn't really done anything to change himself, but by virtue of the rest of the crew, I felt we could get by.

In addition to their disguises, Roger Lucy had coached the houseguests on their accent to help them sound more Canadian. Cora gave me an example of the proper way a Canadian would say Toronto: "It's *Toronna*, like *piranha*," she said. Lucy joked that he told them to just say "eh?" a lot after every sentence and everything would be fine.

Then there were the maple leaf stickers, lapel pins, and luggage tags Joe Missouri and I had purchased in Ottawa to be used for final window dressing for our travelers. As anyone who's traveled abroad knows, real Canadians do tend to plaster their bags with maple leafs so they won't be mistaken for Americans.

After the dress rehearsal, Julio and I handed each of them their freshly stamped documents and their round-trip airline tickets, which reflected the travel itinerary we'd concocted for them as well as the origin of their visas. These latter details were extremely important. One of the first things an immigration officer would be apt to ask is where their visa had been issued and what was the route of their travel. Joe Missouri had purchased the round-trip tickets in Toronto on the appropriate dates and we had removed the coupons from their tickets for the legs they would have traveled. To not know the details and the route of travel would be the quickest way to capture.

We also gave them some money, which would help them to feel slightly more normal under the circumstances.

Soon Taylor arrived at the house with a response from Canada to an earlier cable I had written that morning containing the final operations plan. He handed it over to me and smiled. The powers that be in Ottawa and Washington had signed off on our ops plan and we were good to go for the following morning. They closed their message on a upbeat note: "See you later, exfiltrator!"

We then retired to the dining room for what can only be described as a feast. Not wanting to leave anything behind for the Iranians, the houseguests had prepared a seven-course meal, complete with fine wine, champagne, coffee, and liqueurs. Ambassadors Munk, from Denmark, and Beeby joined us and the mood quickly grew festive. I reminded the houseguests not to drink too much as they would be facing a "hostile interrogation" by Lucy after dinner. I could see right away, however, that they had plans of their own. In fact the six had gotten together earlier and decided that in order to keep things as relaxed as possible, they were going to leave on adrenaline. The house still had a sizable selection of liquor and the houseguests seemed intent on drinking it all.

As we ate, I regaled the guests with some of the lore of past operations in places known as "denied areas," like Moscow, where the surveillance teams could sometimes number more than one hundred people. Julio joked that he would never again visit that country. Moscow had become an important proving ground for us, and many of the techniques we were utilizing on the Argo mission had at one point been tested out under the watchful eye of the KGB.

Everyone was curious about the idea behind Studio Six and I clued them in on the origin of the Argo knock-knock joke. It wasn't long before we all raised our glasses and gave a hearty "Argo!" cheer. I then got serious for a moment and asked them not to publish any details of the rescue mission in order to protect our sources and methods, which are the lifeblood of our secret operations.

"After this is over you all are going to want to write a book," I said. "Don't do it. Julio and I need to stay in business."

After dinner, everyone met back in the den for the mock interrogations. In order to make it as realistic as possible, Lucy wore large jackboots and an army fatigue jacket, and carried a swagger stick. He looked to me like something right out of *The Man Who Would Be King*.

He moved slowly to the center of the room and took on the posture of an officious immigration officer. "Who's first?" he barked.

The houseguests shifted in their seats. Taylor and I stood in the back of the room along with Julio, Beeby, and Munk.

Lee shot up and walked over to Lucy, who stared him down. "Your passport, please," he said, affecting the accent of a Persian speaker speaking English. Lee handed over his documents, and Lucy flipped through them. "And where visa you get?" he asked.

Lee, who'd been playing it cool, suddenly went blank. "You know, funny thing . . . I don't remember."

Lucy jumped down his throat. "What you mean you not remember?" He got right in Lee's face. "You big liar! You American spy!"

Taylor turned to me. "Is this really necessary?" he asked.

"Absolutely. The more they get into their roles the better off they'll be tomorrow," I said.

When Lee was finished, I turned to the group. "Listen," I said. "We didn't give you these cover stories for you not to learn them. Woody here just showed you how easy it is to trip up. You may get these questions and you may not. But if they come up you have to be comfortable answering them."

While the interrogations continued, one of the two foreign ambassadors asked me to step into the dining room. He'd been in contact with Mike Howland, one of the three American diplomats at the foreign ministry along with Vic Tomseth and Bruce Laingen. He told me that Howland had confided in him that he was planning an escape. In fact Howland said he'd already been outside of the foreign ministry and was asking for a glass cutter and a gun. The ambassador asked me what I thought he should do. I told him it would be okay to give Howland a glass cutter but definitely not a gun. (As it turns out I'm not sure he gave him either, as Howland,

Laingen, and Tomseth would all remain in captivity at the Iranian foreign ministry for the duration of the hostage crisis.)

When the mock interrogations were over, Julio and I sat down with the houseguests one last time to go over the final arrangements. I had drawn a diagram of the airport and took them through the various phases of the plan so there would be no confusion. "It's all about misdirection. We're going to use the same tricks that a magician uses to fool his audience," I said. The plan was to be as follows: I would arrive at the airport thirty minutes before everyone else, driven by Sewell, who would pick me up from the hotel at three a.m. Once I had arrived, I would recon the airport and confirm that our flight to Zurich was on time. At that point, if all went well, I would check my bag in through customs, then take my position inside the large windows to give an all-clear signal.

The houseguests, along with Julio, meanwhile, would be driven to the airport in the embassy van. When Julio spotted my signal, he would then lead the houseguests through customs and meet me at the check-in counter.

Ideally, in an operation of this kind, if anything went wrong, we would have a couple of cars waiting outside in case we needed to bug out in a hurry. We had no such backup—no backup plan at all, in fact. Once we got inside the airport and into the teeth of their security, there would be no chance to turn back.

All of the houseguests had been through the airport, but I wanted to make sure there were no surprises. Despite being almost like a chicken coop, the airport was pretty well organized, thanks in large part to the draconian controls instituted under the shah.

The first control point was just outside the main door: two national police officers checking passengers as they walked through. At this control only a picture ID was required. After this came the customs station. Unlike most Western airports, where people are allowed to take their bags unhindered right up to the airline counter, thanks to the fear of Iranians smuggling goods out of the country, there was a customs station almost immediately inside the front door. "After that we will proceed to the check-in counters," I said. I didn't envision we'd encounter a problem there. Immigration controls, however, were another matter. "Here is the choke point," I said, pointing to the immigration desk on my diagram. I knew the houseguests still had some concerns about the disembarkation/embarkation forms, but I reassured them that the authorities hadn't been matching up the white and yellow copies for months. "It's much better to not have something than to include something you shouldn't have," I told them. "You can always bluff your way out if you are missing something. 'How should I know where the white form is? It's your form!'"

At midnight Julio and I finally said good-bye, and as we walked out the door the houseguests gave a hearty "Argo!" salute to see us off. I paused before leaving. "You guys are going to do great tomorrow," I said, looking at each of their six faces. "Just remember to go with the flow and have fun and you'll be fine."

After Julio and I left, Lee and Joe stayed up drinking and talking. The scorched-earth policy had worked and by this time the only liquor left in the house was a bottle of Cointreau. Joe continued to stew about the plan and kept coming up with ways in which things could go wrong. He was concerned that because the Ministry of National Guidance was in charge of filming permits, they were going to simply pull everybody off the plane and hold them until they could confirm that the Argo story was true. Lee countered by telling him that the flight would be full of foreigners, and that the ministry didn't open until nine in the morning—an hour and a half after our flight was scheduled to leave. "There is no way they are going to pull us off that flight and hold us for two hours." Joe then returned to the problem of the yellow and white forms. Lee shook his head, getting frustrated. The Cointreau was working on him and he knew he should get to bed. "The bottom line," he said before turning in, "is that I am going to get on that plane tomorrow. I hope you decide to make the trip, but if you don't want to come then that's your choice. But if you do come, then don't screw it up for me and the others."

15

THE ESCAPE

The phone woke me at three o'clock the following morning.

"It's me, Richard," said the voice on the other end. "I'm down in the lobby."

It was Richard Sewell, right on time. I showered and threw my few remaining things together and was down in the lobby in less than fifteen minutes. Sewell had come to pick me up in the ambassador's Mercedes and drove carefully through the still sleeping town. The streets were dark and nearly deserted at that hour—both restful and alien—and by four thirty a.m. we had arrived at Mehrabad Airport.

Sewell parked the car and the two of us proceeded through the initial security checkpoint without a problem. As I'd expected, the airport was relatively empty. There were only a couple of passengers in the hall and several airport personnel were slumped over dozing at their desks. Only a few Revolutionary Guards leaned against the counters, looking lonely and bored. I knew by late morning the scene would be completely different, with crowds of Iranians mobbing the controls and a larger force of Revolutionary Guards to keep them in line. This was one of the main reasons I'd picked this early departure time.

I breezed through customs without incident. Richard had gone his own way; we were not necessarily planning on meeting up again, unless a problem presented itself. Richard had in his possession a diplomatic ID card that pretty much gave him run of the airport. At this point he was going to check with his contact at British Airways in case we needed a fallback plan. I then went over to the airline counters, where the Swissair clerk confirmed that our plane would arrive on time at five a.m. I pulled out a magazine and browsed the headlines while hanging around to wait for Julio and the rest.

Meanwhile, back at the Sheardowns', Roger Lucy was doing his best to get the houseguests up and moving. It wasn't easy. The group had barely slept and several were suffering from hangovers. Cora recalls walking down the hallway and seeing Lee make a mad dash for the bathroom in his underwear. Lucy put on a pot of fresh coffee and everyone began the process of getting into character, putting the finishing touches on their disguises. Bob Anders had found a navy blue beret in one of the Sheardowns' closets and added it to his getup. He checked out his appearance in the mirror and was pleased with the results. When it was time to leave, Lucy wished them well and herded them off into the waiting embassy van. Lee noted that Joe had decided to make the trip.

As the van transited the city, the driver, an Iranian employee of the Canadian embassy, thought it was just another routine run to the airport. The houseguests were well aware of that fact and had to be guarded in what they said while in the van. Mostly they sat in silence. Mark remembers how peaceful, almost serene, the drive was. It felt comforting to be ensconced in the darkness of the van's interior. He thought about how nice it would be if they could just drive, bundled together, all the way to Washington, D.C. Sitting next to him, Cora was going through a checklist in her head. She decided to search through her purse one last time for anything that might have her real name on it. She was surprised to come up with a receipt from the dry cleaners, and quickly stuffed it into the seat. The others were mentally going through their cover stories, reviewing the details, psyching themselves up.

When the driver missed the correct turn for the Sheraton, Anders reminded him that they were supposed to pick up somebody at the hotel. The driver quickly backtracked and sped up so as not to lose time. Unflappable as always, Julio had spent the time waiting in the lobby reading the newspaper. He told me later how relieved he was when he saw the van pull up outside. By the time they got to Mehrabad it was a little after five a.m.

Inside the terminal, I wandered over to a set of floor-to-ceiling windows near the main entrance and stopped where I knew I would be clearly visible from the outside. As nonchalantly as I could, I folded up my magazine and put it in my briefcase, pulled out the rather large Argo portfolio, and began flipping through it. As planned, I'd gone ahead and was signaling to the others that it was okay to enter the airport. The signal was for me to stand where they could see me, just on the other side of the windows, examining my portfolio.

Outside, the houseguests sat waiting in the van. Because of the driver's presence, they still could not talk freely. Julio kept his eyes on the windows, and when he saw me he turned to the others. "Okay," he said. "Let's go."

The seven of them approached the national policemen standing outside the terminal and handed over their IDs. A cop flipped through them, noted their airline tickets, and waved everybody through. They looked good, confident, like world travelers on the move. *One down,* I thought.

I walked across the airport to the check-in counters, where I could better observe Julio and the houseguests spill into the bright interior of Mehrabad. They seemed to be in good spirits but also a little overwhelmed. After all, they'd been at the Sheardowns' for nearly ninety days and I knew it must feel strange to suddenly be surrounded by so many people. I marveled at Bob Anders, who sashayed through the doors carrying a cigarette between his thumb and forefinger. He looked like a character out of a Fellini film. *I hope he doesn't overdo it,* I thought, watching him smooth his hair in a gesture that seemed almost feminine. Despite the Canadians' help, the houseguests had had some difficulty putting together luggage and appeared to a trained eye to be traveling a little light for a Hollywood location scouting party on an around-the-world trip.

The trip through customs, however, went smoothly and they soon joined me at the check-in counter. As we came together for the first time in the airport I could see the corners of their eyes were ratcheted with tension and fatigue. Still, there was a good feeling of camaraderie. We were in this together and we were going to get through it together. We were a team. We were a location scouting party on our way to the next stop, then home to Hollywood. We were in the moment. They appeared to have listened to everything I had told them in our rehearsals. *All right,* I thought. *They can do this.*

The plan I had briefed the houseguests on had one key element: stay together. In the event that anything should go wrong, this would give me the opportunity, as the production manager, to jump in with the Argo portfolio. Lee, however, had other ideas. Even more than Anders, I could see that Lee had embraced the adventurous spirit of the Argo mission. Back then, airlines had two lines for checking in: smoking and nonsmoking—it seems incredible, but back in 1980 it was still permissible to smoke on airplanes. Out of habit Lee had jumped into the much shorter nonsmoking line, while the rest of us were in the smoking line. This meant that by the time we got our boarding passes, Lee had already checked in and was on his way to the immigration controls.

When Lee reached the front of the line, we were still a little ways behind him. I noted that a uniformed officer, and not some untrained komiteh thug, was manning the controls, as I had warned them. I watched as Lee handed over his passport and yellow form. As a CIA officer with years of experience using alias documents, I can tell you that the first time you put one down on the immigration officer's desk, there is always a little twinge. *Here we go,* I thought to myself. *This is the moment of truth.* Lee was playing it cool, but I knew inside his stomach must be cinching itself into knots. If anything was going to go wrong, it was most likely going to happen here. And now.

The immigration officer studied Lee's passport. "Is this your photo?" I could barely hear the officer ask. I cocked my head to hear Lee's reply.

"Of course," Lee said. He was trying to remain calm, but I could see his nervousness was starting to show. A pair of scruffy Revolutionary Guards leaned against a nearby wall, looking on with a mixture of boredom and menace.

The immigration officer left his post and quickly disappeared into a back room. Lee glanced back in our direction. We stood transfixed, our eyes glued on the door where the officer had disappeared. Had we missed something in Lee's passport? Was the official looking for Lee's matching white disembarkation sheet? The seconds dragged on until finally the officer returned. "It doesn't look like you," he said in heavily accented English. He showed Lee the photo, which had been taken several months before. In it, Lee had a bushy Yosemite Sam mustache that completely covered his upper lip. Realizing what the problem was, Lee pulled a serious expression to match the one in the photo, then used his fingers to mimic a pair of scissors clipping the ends of his mustache. "It's shorter now," he said.

The immigration officer glanced at the photo, then back at Lee, and finally shrugged. With that, he stamped his passport and Lee disappeared into the departure lounge. I studied the houseguests and was happy to see that despite this close call, no one had panicked.

The line inched forward, stalling occasionally as arguments broke out between the passengers and the immigration officer. Several Iranians were trying to travel on false documents, and one woman was pulled into secondary when she refused to cooperate. A few weeks earlier, Cora had read an article in the local paper about a woman who had been caught trying to smuggle money in her vagina. As she watched the woman being pulled from the line, she suddenly worried that the authorities might be subjecting random female passengers to full-body searches.

When we finally got to the counter, everyone lined up to present their passports as a group. The immigration clerk, however, had mysteriously disappeared. We stood there for several minutes, doing nothing. Mark and Cora, who were at the front of our group, had a quick discussion about whether or not they should just walk past the checkpoint. They quickly realized it would be a bad idea. If they were caught trying to sneak past, it would only arouse suspicions that they had something to hide. Mark was confident enough in the quality of the documents and the plan to wait it out. After a few more minutes, the immigration officer returned to his desk, stirring a cup of tea. He scooped up our passports and without further delay gave us our exit stamps and waved us through. He also collected our yellow forms, and as he tamped their edges down on the counter, one of them floated onto the floor. As we walked past, I couldn't resist, and I surreptitiously picked it up and stuck it in among my papers. It was Bob Anders's form.

Each one of us breathed a huge sigh of relief as we entered the departure lounge. Technically, we weren't out of the woods yet, as there was still one final security checkpoint before we had to board the plane, but with immigration behind us, it felt like the worst had passed. A few Revolutionary Guards roamed about the lounge eyeing people suspiciously, but their interest seemed dulled by the early hour. We had about twenty minutes until our flight was called, so all we had to do was sit tight, keep our heads down, and wait it out.

Lee and Bob paired off and wandered over in the direction of a row of seats. The lounge was about half full, but I knew it wouldn't be long before it was jammed to the rafters. The two of them eyed a spot and then sat down, noticing as they did that sitting right across from them was Junior, the Canadian MP who had helped to house-sit after Roger Lucy had taken over for John Sheardown.

With the embassy closing, the Canadians had been scheduled to fly out in two shifts, with several departing on early morning flights and the rest, including Ambassador Taylor, leaving in the afternoon. In fact, Laverna, Taylor's secretary, was sitting right beside Junior. As soon as Lee sat down, Junior happened to see Lee's bag, which was covered with Canadian maple leaf pins. After spotting the pins, Junior's eyes then moved up from the bag until they rested on the beaming faces of Lee Schatz and Bob Anders. Junior took one look at the two Americans and did a double take. Laverna was just as surprised. She'd seen Anders at a few embassy functions in the past, but it took her a moment to realize that the bare-chested man wearing the flamboyant medallion and beret was the same as the buttoned-up senior diplomat she knew from before.

Junior leaned forward. "What are you doing here?" he asked Lee.

Lee didn't hesitate. "Goin' home, eh," he said in his best Canadian accent. Junior was floored. He shook his head in amazement.

While this was going on, I had gone to find Sewell, who was standing in the corner of the lounge with his friend from British Airways. The friend asked me why we hadn't chosen to fly with them. "We would have given you the royal treatment," he said. "First class, champagne, you name it."

"I appreciate that," I said. I told him it was great knowing that we had a fallback in case something went wrong with the Swissair flight. It's very rare to have an inside contact at the airport for an exfiltration and it definitely bolstered my confidence.

I noticed that Joe and Kathy were over at the duty-free boutique but couldn't see what they were doing. Then suddenly Kathy was tugging at my jacket and Joe approached me with a sealed bag from the duty-free shop. His mouth split into a wide grin as he handed it to me with a flourish, standing at attention as if he were presenting a trophy. "We would like you to have this as a token of our esteem," he said somewhat formally.

I found it a little bit awkward but it was heartfelt. It was clear they'd purchased a huge container of Iranian beluga caviar—I could see it through the plastic bag and could measure its heft. It was not inexpensive. It seemed like an odd moment, before we actually had "wheels up." I felt that with this gift Joe was saying: "I'm with you on this plan, your plan, and I think we are going to make it out of here." We were still "a mile from home," as Jerome would say, and so it seemed a little premature, but the thought was genuine, especially coming from Joe, the reluctant warrior all along. It seemed that Joe had finally completed his own gut check and had found the confidence to push forward.

It was at this moment that a voice announced over the intercom that Swissair Flight 363 was ready to board. The houseguests instantly leapt to their feet and I shepherded everyone toward the gate. We passed through the metal detectors and final security check without incident, and took our place in the tiny glassed-in room at the gate. Looking around, I could see that everyone was excited, barely holding it together. All that was left was to get on the tarmac bus. But before we knew it there came a second announcement over the PA system: "We are sorry to inform you that Swissair Flight 363 will be delayed due to mechanical problems." It appeared that Murphy was not done with us yet. Our entire group formed a tight knot around me. "Everybody relax," I told them. "This happens all the time. I'll check this out and find out what kind of a mechanical problem it is, and what kind of a delay they are talking about."

We filed back into the departure lounge trying to stay upbeat. Once again I met with Richard and his British Airways contact to see what could be done. As it turns out, they'd already spoken with Swissair and found out that the problem was only a minor technical one. "It's just a faulty air speed indicator. It should only take an hour to fix," Sewell reported. The three of us then discussed the possibility of switching to a British Airways flight but decided in the end that it would probably only draw unnecessary attention. We had already checked our bags on Swissair and to switch would have meant pulling them off the plane and going through the process of checking them again.

I met with the six and filled them in on what I'd learned from Richard. Everyone agreed it would be best to stick it out. "We just need to be patient," I told them. Mark and Cora exchanged looks. "I know you are worried," I said quietly to all of them, catching Joe and Kathy's eyes as well. "You'd be crazy not to worry. But I've been here before. Mechanical problems happen all the time. This one is minor." Bob Anders seemed to relax immediately. Lee, ever vigilant and vocal, was momentarily speechless.

The wait became agonizing. Dawn had broken and the sky outside was just beginning to show a filtered gray light. Piles of snow were scattered around the tarmac like icebergs afloat on a steel gray sea. Inside the airport, the departure lounge was rapidly filling up with passengers as numerous flights began arriving from Europe and Asia. Several teams of Revolutionary Guards were now present in the lounge, moving among the passengers. Growing tired of picking on Iranians, they turned their attention to foreigners, addressing them rudely in broken English or German. It seemed almost like a sport to them.

I wondered how long we could last before some overzealous komiteh member turned his attention toward one of us. I looked around to see how the houseguests were faring and was startled to see Joe reading a Farsi-language newspaper. I thought he had lost his mind—nobody would believe that a Hollywood producer would be able to read Farsi. It seemed that Joe had just had the same thought, though, and he suddenly put the newspaper down.

Time seemed to stand still. The lounge became hot and stuffy and the haze of cigarette smoke filled the air. The noise grew louder. The press of the crowd became uncomfortable. What had started out almost as a game had turned into a grueling mental ordeal. Then, just when I thought one of the houseguests might crack, the PA announced that Swissair Flight 363 was now ready to board. Once again we filed past the security check and into the glassed-in room. This time, we were not turned back. As we scrambled onto the old airport bus, I could see that everyone was exhausted, myself included. We were so close now and we could all feel it.

Out on the tarmac, we disembarked from the bus and headed for the stairs. The cold air was a welcome change after the stifling heat of the departure lounge. Then, as we climbed up to the plane, Bob Anders punched me in the arm. "You guys think of every-thing," he said, smiling ear to ear.

Turning, I saw what he was pointing at. There, painted on the side of the plane's nose was the canton in Switzerland where it had come from. In big letters it read, AARGAU. I let myself smile, and took it as an omen that everything would be all right.

As the DC8 roared down the runway and into the air, I felt eu-phoric. As we say in the business, there is no sweeter feeling than wheels up. We still had two hours to go before we would cross out of Iranian airspace, but it seemed like a formality now. When the captain finally announced that we had passed out of Iran and into Turkish skies, the plane erupted into cheers (there were several escaping Iranians who had no doubt gone through their own private ordeals that morning). For the houseguests, it was as if a terrific weight had been lifted from their shoulders. I could see elation on their faces as the realization hit. We'd done it. Their long ordeal was finally over—they were going home.

When the flight attendants wheeled out the bar cart, everyone ordered Bloody Marys to celebrate. I raised my glass in a toast to the others. "Argo! We're home free," I said.

Back at the Canadian embassy, Ambassador Taylor sent word of the mission's success to Ottawa via cable. Afterward, he asked Claude to wield his sledgehammer one last time to smash the communications equipment, which the MP did with gusto. Taylor then hung a TEMPORARILY CLOSED sign on the door to the Canadian embassy, and he, Lucy, Claude, and a fourth Canadian official went out to lunch. By the time the eight of us would land in Zurich, Taylor's cable had made its way from Ottawa to Washington, where an anxious President Carter received a rare piece of good news from Iran—the six Americans had gotten out.

will always remember the looks of joy on the faces of the houseguests as they descended the stairs in Zurich. Lee and Bob stomped their feet on the tarmac and raised their arms in triumph. Surprisingly, there was no one to meet us at the gate, and so we were forced to go through immigration controls, bogus documents and all. As we emerged into the parking lot, a group of U.S. State Department officials quickly approached. Without so much as a hello, they grabbed the houseguests and put them into a waiting van, then sped off. I would later find out that they were whisked to a mountain lodge where they were fed pizza and given six-packs of Heineken.

Julio and I, meanwhile, were left standing alone in the cold parking lot. Like any covert operative who values his or her anonymity, we hadn't expected a ticker tape parade upon our return. Most CIA officers are quiet professionals who never get the recognition they deserve. For us it was just part of the job. I was happy to have done my part in helping to get the six Americans out of Iran, but I knew there was more work to be done. There were still fifty-three Americans being held hostage who needed our help.

"It's time we talked about your future in the film business," I said to Julio, my words wafting in the frosty night air. I explained that since the Argo cover story had worked so well, there was a real chance it would be used to infiltrate the Delta Force commandos into Tehran in the event of a rescue attempt. "They are going to want you to take some classes in international finance."

"You think I can pull it off?" he asked me. He seemed younger for a second, saying it.

"My only doubt is what language you should do it in," I said.

A cold wind knifed through the parking lot and I shivered, suddenly realizing I no longer had my coat. "Let's get out of here," I said. "I'm freezing."

"Where's your coat?" Julio asked me.

"I lent it to Joe."

He laughed. "B&F is going to have your ass for that one."

"Don't I know it. Come on," I said. We turned and walked toward a line of waiting taxis. It was time to get back to work.

16

AFTERMATH

None of the houseguests had given much thought as to what would happen after they got out of Iran. They probably assumed they would go back to their normal lives, but in Switzerland they would find out the truth. The State Department informed them that if news of their escape were to get out, there was a good chance the hostages could suffer reprisals. In addition, since there was the chance that the Argo cover story might be reused to help rescue the hostages, it would be important to keep the operational details of their rescue secret. So rather than being allowed to return home, they were going to be hidden away on a U.S. Air Force base in Florida until the fifty-three hostages were released. When they learned that they wouldn't even be able to call their families to let them know they were safe, they began to grumble. Of course, Lee being Lee, he asked if they could be sent to Fiji instead.

They spent the night at the mountain lodge, eating pizza,

drinking beer, and being observed by the senior medical officer from the local embassy. They were told there was no precedent for a group of State Department staffers being held in captivity for such a long period of time. The State Department was eager to learn all it could so as to be better prepared to deal with the hostages once that situation was resolved. At some point they would be asked to take an air force stress test for air traffic controllers, the results of which determined that most of them were very "high strung." After being debriefed, they were told to hand over all of their alias documents as well as the Argo material. However, several of them held on to their Studio Six business cards and still have them today.

Despite the State Department's best attempts to keep the escape of the six under wraps, it wouldn't take long for the whole world to know what had happened.

Jean Pelletier of Montreal's *La Presse* had been sitting on the story for over a month. When he found out on January 28 that the Canadian government was closing its embassy in Tehran, he concluded that the missing Americans must have gotten out. Since he'd originally agreed not to publish the story until after the danger had passed, he felt that he'd more than fulfilled his part of the bargain. He called the Canadian embassy in Washington once again for confirmation and was told by officials there that they would prefer if he held off publishing until after the entire crisis was over. Pelletier, however, claimed that his "instincts" were telling him that he had to publish it now. Worried that some other enterprising journalist would scoop him and pressured in part by his senior editors, he decided to finally run with it. The newspaper published the piece on the morning of January 29. Soon after, the story was picked up by radio and TV stations, and before lunch it was all over the world.

Now that the news was out, there was no longer any need to keep the houseguests in seclusion. Worried that the story might be connected to the Swiss government, which still had a functioning embassy in Tehran, State Department officials hastily loaded the houseguests into a van and drove them to Ramstein Air Force Base in Germany.

I was back in Frankfurt working on my after-action report when the news broke. Reports outlined how the Canadians had sheltered the six Americans for nearly three months before organizing their escape. No mention was made of the CIA, or Argo, which was just fine. The last thing the White House or headquarters needed was for the Iranians to know that the CIA had been conducting operations in Tehran, which would almost certainly have put the lives of the hostages in jeopardy. Eventually a vague reference would be made in a *New York Times* article, saying that the CIA had provided technical assistance, but for the next seventeen years the world would never know the truth about Argo.

In the wake of Pelletier's article and subsequent news pieces, the outpouring of gratitude by Americans toward the Canadian government was unprecedented. I remember landing at JFK on February 1 and picking up a copy of the *New York Post*, which had a massive three-inch headline on the front page that read: "Thanks, Canada!" In diners and bars, Canadians were treated to backslaps and free drinks. Just about everywhere you looked there were maple leaf flags, signs, even billboards expressing America's gratitude toward our neighbor to the north.

On January 30, the U.S. Congress passed a resolution honoring

Canada, while the following day President Carter called to personally thank Canada's prime minister, Joe Clark.

With the CIA's involvement a secret, the lion's share of the credit for the operation went to Ken Taylor. He became an overnight sensation and was nicknamed the "Scarlet Pimpernel" of diplomacy. After flying from Tehran to Copenhagen, he eventually arrived in Paris, where he was mobbed at Charles de Gaulle Airport by a horde of photographers and reporters. He would give a press conference the next day and follow that up with an eleven-month public relations tour that would take him to practically every major city in the United States and Canada. He would receive both Canada's and the United States' highest honors, including the Congressional Gold Medal (an award shared by the likes of the Dalai Lama and Pope John Paul II). Wherever he went he was always gracious in trying to defer credit onto others, but he clearly didn't shun the limelight. Of course Taylor was only doing what we wanted him to do, which was to deflect attention away from the United States and onto Canada. Even if he had wanted to, he couldn't have mentioned the CIA's role. And in a way, what he was doing was carrying off another cover story that shifted the blame away from America and onto Canada.

Among those in the know, however, the idea that Canada had acted alone became an opportunity to have a little fun. I later heard that, typical of the man, Jerome Calloway had taken out a full-page ad in the local Burbank newspaper that said: "Thanks, Canada—we needed that!"

As word of the rescue reached Iran, reactions there were predictable. At the foreign ministry, Bruce Laingen, Vic Tomseth, and Mike Howland were accused of somehow aiding and abetting the escape and had their telephone and telex privileges permanently taken away. Down at the U.S. embassy, meanwhile, it was reported that one of the militants had called the rescue "illegal." Though perhaps the most famous response came from Sadegh Ghotbzadeh, Iran's foreign minister, who said, "Sooner or later, here or anywhere in the world, Canada will pay for this violation of the sovereignty of Iran." Ghotbzadeh, as it turns out, would eventually be executed by the Iranian government, shot by a firing squad for suspicions of colluding with the West.

Now that the rescue was the worst-kept secret in the world, the houseguests were finally told they could go home. They spent a few more nights at the military base in Germany, then flew back to Dover Air Force Base in Delaware on an Executive 707 that belonged to the commander of NATO, dining on filet mignon and fresh pineapple flown in from Hawaii.

When they arrived at the State Department, they were met in the lobby by a cheering mob. One woman held up a sign that read, WE LOVE YOU BOB ANDERS, AND CANADA TOO! The atmosphere was electric. After hearing nothing but bad news about their colleagues trapped at the embassy, here at last was a chance to finally celebrate a victory. All their pent-up emotions came pouring out: they clapped, whistled, waved signs, and cheered with abandon. When asked about it later, Lee described the moment as one of the few times he felt like crying in public.

Their next stop was at an auditorium in the State Department, where Bob Anders read a prepared statement, saying that due to the sensitivity of the situation, neither he nor any of the other houseguests could go into any details about their escape. When discussing their time at the Sheardowns', Bob said that the majority of their days had been spent playing Scrabble and following the news of the world. Eventually, each of them would be sent a deluxe Scrabble set and a letter from the president of Hasbro.

After the press conference, they would meet with Cyrus Vance, and then later with President Carter at the White House. For the houseguests, who had vilified Carter while discussing the stalemate of the hostage crisis at their nightly dinners with the Sheardowns, it was an awkward meeting. Some of them, like Mark, still felt that the president had mishandled the whole affair by allowing the shah to enter the United States without first doing more to protect the embassy. In the end, Carter's southern charm won them over and they left feeling that the president was genuinely concerned for the well-being of the hostages.

It was around this time that I landed at JFK in New York. I'd flown over on a TWA flight from Frankfurt and had trouble getting them to refrigerate the huge tin of caviar that Joe Stafford had given me. The stewardess took one look at the tin and said, "Sir, that caviar is either Iranian or Russian. If it's Iranian, I am not refrigerating it until the hostages are released. If it's Russian, after they get out of Afghanistan and the Olympics are rescheduled, we would be glad to find room for it in our fridge." I looked at her with newfound admiration. I took all of my laundry out of my carry-on bag and swaddled the tin in my American underwear.

Before hopping on my connecting flight, I called my family from JFK to let them know that I was going to be arriving on time.

I had an emotional reunion with my family at Dulles when Karen and the kids came to pick me up. Much was left unsaid, but I think all of them could tell that I was relieved to be home. Later that night, when Karen and I were going to bed, the two of us lapsed into a minute or two of silence. Eventually she turned to me. "You're a national hero," she said, and then, after a short pause, "but nobody will ever know."

About a week later, I went to Los Angeles with Hal and our wives to meet with Calloway and Sidell and their spouses. In the wake of the story being published, Studio Six had quietly faded away and it was time to express our gratitude. Dave, the CIA officer I had handed the ten thousand dollars to in LA, had come down for the celebration with his wife as well. As we pulled into the parking lot at the Universal Studios Sheraton, we saw on the marquee the now familiar slogan THANKS, CANADA! and as we checked in we were given round metal Sheraton lapel buttons emblazoned with the same expression. We each proudly pinned them to our lapels. Our "wrap" party, the Hollywood tradition celebrating the last day of filming, was being held secretly in the midst of the celebration of Canada's great rescue operation. A casual observer might have thought we were Canadians, from the way we were celebrating.

At the end of the evening I proposed one last toast. Standing at the end of the table and swaying only slightly, I raised my glass and uttered a word that few outside of our group would hear or understand. "Argo!"

On March 11, Stansfield Turner invited me to join him at the White House for his morning meeting with President Carter. I was told I had two and a half minutes with the president to tell him briefly the story of Argo and how we were able to pull it off. The only other person in the Oval Office was Zbigniew Brzezinski, the president's national security adviser. The president was on the phone when we entered the office, standing in his shirtsleeves poring over a memo. He was telling someone to change the word "hate" on the bottom of page two to "abhor." Classic Jimmy Carter—all about the details. Turner introduced me to the president and he shook my hand, but looked perplexed as to who I might be or what I might have done. Turner attempted to clarify, but I was prompted to move through my story quickly while trying to keep the president on schedule. When it came time for the obligatory photo, the White House photographer came forward and snapped several frames. Admiral Turner immediately threw himself in front of the camera. "No, no," he said, "we can't show his face. He's undercover!" The president asked if it couldn't be just between the two of us. "Sure," I said. It would only take me seventeen years, but eventually I would be allowed to have the photo. Today it hangs in my library.

When I got back to Foggy Bottom, I went to Fred Graves's office and he immediately took me to see the director of OTS, Dave Brandwein. I tried to tell them about my meeting with President Carter, but they seemed uninterested. "Here," they said, "this is more important." They told me I had been promoted to GS15, the equivalent of a full-bird colonel in the U.S. Army.

After I walked out of South Building and went up to the third floor of Central Building to my office, I caught my secretary elbows deep in her safe drawer. "Guess what, Elaine?" I said. "I got promoted and I saw the president, but not in that order."

"Did you get my message?" she asked. "You're having dinner at the White House tonight. Call Jacques Dumas. You're supposed to be there at five o'clock."

I called Jacques on the green phone, the secure line between our offices and headquarters, to ask him what was going on. "Oh, yeah," he said, "I put that part about having dinner at the White House to be sure you'd call me back. Actually, you're going to meet with Hamilton Jordan, White House chief of staff, at five o'clock."

My instructions were to go to the West Wing and meet Jordan in his office. I found my way back to 1600 Pennsylvania Avenue for the second time that day. I was ushered into Jordan's office by his secretary, Eleanor, who informed me that "Ham" would be there shortly. Eventually the door opened and a smiling face came bobbing into the room. Hamilton Jordan shook my hand and we settled into a couple of chairs in his sitting area while he proceeded to tell me what he needed. Jordan wanted a disguise, the best disguise that we could build in a short time. He then explained why. He'd arranged a secret back-channel meeting with Sadegh Ghotbzadeh in Paris to discuss the release of the hostages. However, the slightest hint that Ghotbzadeh was meeting with Jordan would throw the whole thing out the window.

The following day, Eleanor escorted me to the White House basement barbershop. It was still light out when we went downstairs. The shop was closed but Eleanor let me in. I was surprised to see that it looked just like every barbershop I have ever been in: two chairs, two mirrors, two sinks. She pulled the shades on the garden-level windows and turned on the lights. When Jordan arrived, I sat him in one of the chairs and used a custom-made wig, mustache, and pair of glasses to completely alter his appearance. When I was finished, I had transformed him from a brightly polished American bureaucrat into what he came to call his "sleazy Latin American businessman" look. I took the description as high praise.

Jordan's meeting had been part of a scenario worked out by two men, Christian Bourguet and Hector Villalon, two adventurers with access to Iran's secular government. Bourguet was a French lawyer involved in radical causes while Villalon was a businessman from Argentina, whom Carter would later describe as having the reputation of a "South American riverboat gambler." Both were old friends of Ghotbzadeh's and claimed they could open a direct line between Iran's secular leadership and the White House. It was always a long shot, but Carter was desperate. Up until this point, there had been no direct talks on any level between the White House and Iran. So Carter sent Jordan and Hal Saunders to meet with the two men in Paris, and over the course of a few weeks they were able to hash out a plan that was said to have the support of both Ghotbzadeh and Iran's newly elected president, Abulhassan Bani-Sadr. The convoluted idea would involve a multistep process that started with the creation of a five-person UN commission that would listen to Iran's grievances. Eventually this commission would take control of the hostages after they had been transferred to a hospital in Tehran. Many thought the plan was nothing but a distraction. Ghotbzadeh was a natural schemer who talked a good game, but who in the end had little clout when it came to the hostages. When Khomeini refused to give the UN commission permission to meet with the hostages, the whole thing fell apart.

No one was more frustrated by this than President Carter. By early April it appeared as if diplomacy had run its course. On April 7 he expelled all Iranian diplomats from the United States and enacted unilateral trade sanctions against Iran. Then, five days later, at a meeting of his National Security Council, he announced that he was ready to launch Operation Eagle Claw.

From the beginning, my office had some grave reservations about the viability of Eagle Claw. By the winter of 1980, RAPTOR had settled into his new life in the West and had aligned himself with the intelligence community. As an Iranian ex-colonel, RAPTOR had intimate knowledge of the country's topography, including the geography of the area that Colonel Beckwith's men called Desert One. The plan, which had evolved slightly, called for eight helicopters to fly into Desert One from an American aircraft carrier in the Arabian Sea. There, they would link up with six C130 aircraft. The C130s would bring in Beckwith and his team of Delta Force commandos and Army Rangers, as well as large packets of fuel for the helicopters. After being refueled, the helicopters would then ferry the soldiers on to Desert Two, the second site outside of Tehran. From there they would launch their assault on the U.S. embassy. With his local knowledge, RAPTOR could see right away that there was a problem. The site picked for Desert One was on a smugglers' route used only at night, and he believed that the U.S. military had a good chance of being discovered if they tried to use it as a staging area. Reportedly, he warned the planners and Beckwith about this but was rebuffed.

The history of Eagle Claw has now been written, and the world knows that the helicopters never made it to the U.S. embassy in Tehran. In fact, they never even made it to Desert Two. The problems began almost as soon as the mission got under way. When the C130s made it to Desert One, RAPTOR's prediction turned out to be true. Upon landing, Beckwith and his team immediately encountered several unknown vehicles racing through the area. Even worse, a firefight erupted. It turned out that one of the smugglers' trucks was carrying fuel, and when a soldier tried to knock it out with an antitank rocket the fireball lit up the desert sky for miles. It appeared as if one of the men in the truck had escaped and made it into a second truck, which then sped away. If that wasn't bad enough, as Beckwith was contemplating this new development, a large Mercedes bus carrying nearly forty Iranians swung into view, and the Army Rangers were forced to stop it at gunpoint. This put Beckwith on the horns of a major dilemma and forced him to divide his forces. So much for the element of surprise.

While this unfolded, the eight helicopters en route from the aircraft carrier were having their own problems. Two had mechanical failures and were forced to turn back, while a third made it to Desert One but became inoperable upon landing. Five helicopters weren't enough to complete the mission, and President Carter made the decision to abort. In the ensuing confusion, one of the helicopters collided with a C130 gunship full of fuel. Eight U.S. servicemen tragically lost their lives while several others were wounded. The remaining helicopters and C130s returned safely.

By almost any metric, the aftermath of the failed rescue was the lowest point for America during the 444-day Iranian hostage crisis. In his book *Keeping Faith*, Carter describes it as one of the worst days of his life.

A few days later, Cyrus Vance, who had been against Eagle Claw from the beginning, resigned as secretary of state.

In May of 1980, for our role in helping to rescue the six houseguests, Julio and I received the Intelligence Star, which was one of the CIA's highest honors. The medals and certificates were presented in the Agency's secure bubble, on a stage in front of a few hundred of our colleagues. Admiral Stansfield Turner did the honors. Since the operation had been a secret, my family was not allowed to attend the ceremony.

After a brief stay in Panama, the shah had moved on to Egypt, where he died on July 27. Strangely, this was more or less the exact scenario that Jerome and I had envisioned for our body double operation at the beginning of the crisis. With the shah now dead, Russian armies on the march in Afghanistan, and Iran tiring of the American embargo, Khomeini finally signaled his willingness to negotiate. The United States was also inadvertently helped in this matter by Iraq, which had invaded Iran in September of 1980. Needing American parts and ammunition for their weapons was just one more incentive to bring the Iranians to the table.

On January 21, 1981, the fifty-two remaining American hostages were finally released. Jimmy Carter flew to Germany to meet with them personally, but by this time the damage to his political career was irreversible. His failure to resolve the crisis caused him to be seen as a weak and ineffective leader, and Ronald Reagan had easily defeated him in the 1980 presidential election. Rubbing salt into the wound, the Iranians had chosen the date of Reagan's inauguration as the day they would hand over the hostages. In all, the hostages had spent almost fifteen months in captivity with the United States government unable to do anything to effect their release.

Obviously, diplomatic relations with the Iranian government ceased the day that the American embassy was overrun. But nobody could have predicted that more than thirty years later the United States and Iran would still have no formal contact. Iran, a country once considered our long-term friend and strategic ally, has now segued into a rogue state governed by Islamic fundamentalist zealots. During the hostage crisis, America was frustrated by its inability to negotiate with a regime that placed the ideals of theocratic bigotry before those of reason and the rule of international law. Unfortunately, not much has changed. Today, the United States and Iran are as far apart as they have ever been, while the population of Iran suffers under a corrupt and ineffective regime.

We now know that when the militant students overran the American embassy, they did not expect to stay for any length of time. But as the crisis stretched on, and as Ayatollah Khomeini seemingly endorsed their actions, they discovered that they had invented a new tool of statecraft: hostage taking. In no other civilized country in the world would such an undertaking be tolerated by the host government. And therein lay the power of the technique. Once Khomeini approved of their plan, the students had no need to negotiate.

Iran has followed its own example in the interim, taking hostages almost whimsically whenever it felt a need for international attention or had a cause that needed leveraging. In 2007, fifteen British Royal Navy sailors were taken hostage and held for two weeks. In 2009, a British ship with five sailors was boarded in international waters and the sailors held hostage for over a week before being released. Three American hikers who wandered into Iranian territory, famously known as the "hiker-spies," were taken hostage and two of them held for over two years, released only after a million-dollar bail was paid. The British embassy was overrun in 2011, its files burned, its flag desecrated, and the building pillaged. Six hostages were taken briefly before the government stepped in. The Iranians have never had to pay a price either for ignoring the conventions of international diplomacy or for taking foreign civilian citizens hostage under the most questionable of circumstances.

And there is no reason to believe that they will let up on this behavior anytime soon.

Iran today is considered a hot spot, one where the next international crisis may well be brewing. The country's insistence on pursuing a nuclear capability has put it near the top of the list of rogue states and earned it a series of international sanctions by the rest of the world. And Iran's capricious foreign policy relationship with Israel is much like a low-grade fever that could spike at any time.

Following the Arab Spring in 2011, which saw turmoil across the region, I was reminded that Iranians are not Arabs. They are Persians, a different race with a different history. On June 12, 2009, supporters of the opposition party candidate Mir-Hossein Mousavi took to the streets of Tehran en masse in what has come to be known as the Green Revolution. Their aim was to protest the reelection of Mahmoud Ahmadinejad. Turnout was incredibly high and many Iranians suspected that Ahmadinejad had rigged the election. In a scene eerily reminiscent of the violence that rocked the nation in 1978, protestors clashed with riot police and were met with tear gas. In the ensuing struggle, nearly forty Iranians were killed. This was followed up in February 2011 with what is commonly referred to as the Day of Rage, when loyalists of the rival candidate, Mousavi, decided to hold a rally in support of the recent Arab Spring. But the spark was quickly extinguished by the mullahs and the heavy hand of the Iranian Revolutionary Guard in a bloody crackdown. Several demonstrators were beaten and arrested and the young activists retreated, perhaps to protest another day.

As an intelligence officer I am not confident that our old rules of engagement will work any longer. It is difficult to negotiate with an adversary who does not want to come to the table. And it is impossible to find common ground with another government that does not respect the rules of international diplomacy. When the rules of governance flow only from the religious tracts of Islam, there is little room for agreement or compromise. The best that our intelligence community can hope for is to keep a watchful eye on the mullahs and the Iranian government and try to forestall any serious mischief they may be planning. A daunting task to say the least.

When I think about how long the story of Argo remained secret, I am reminded of the Sunday night dinner at the Sheardowns', when I told the houseguests that even though they might be tempted to do so, they were not allowed to tell anyone about what had really happened in Tehran. And for the most part we succeeded. The only leak of any significance came shortly after the story broke, when Jack Anderson said on his syndicated radio show that two CIA officers acting as "mother hens" had led the six through Mehrabad Airport. We assumed that Anderson had a source inside of the CIA, but the story never gained traction—either domestically or internationally—and we breathed a sigh of relief. Jean Pelletier would eventually go on to cowrite a book about the rescue titled *The Canadian Caper*, which turned out to be wildly off the mark given that he basically stuck to the letter of the cover story that Canada had done everything. The CIA could not have been happier.

No other books were written—not by me, not by the houseguests. And none would have been, except for the fact that the CIA saw fit to honor me in 1997.

On the fiftieth anniversary of the CIA, the Agency sought out a publicist to look for a way to celebrate the milestone. The CIA was advised to shrug off its cloak of secrecy ever so slightly and have a public event. This, in turn, morphed into an internal nomination of the top fifty officers in the CIA's first fifty years. Amazingly, I was selected as one of them.

The Trailblazer Award was presented with a citation that read in part that I had been chosen out of those "of any grade, in any field, at any point in the CIA's history, who distinguished themselves as leaders, made a real difference in CIA's pursuit of its mission, and who served as a standard of excellence for others to follow." There was, indeed, a public ceremony, to which the media was invited. There were Trailblazer Medals struck and presented to each of us, or in some instances next of kin.

It was the media, in the form of Tim Weiner of the *New York Times*, who requested the first interview. Someone had leaked the story of the rescue of the houseguests to him, but I told him that he couldn't use it. "People could get hurt," I said. He wrote a story, but did not use the Iranian operation. Then, when I checked with senior CIA officials, I was overruled and asked to tell the story of the Iranian operation to Dan Rather of *CBS Evening News*. When I protested, saying, "But this is one of our best-kept secrets," I was contradicted. "Tenet wants to do it," I was told. And so I did it. But I must say it was difficult for my lips to form the words the first time I actually verbalized what we had done.

I was worried about the safety of my family and about the Iranian reaction once they realized that they had been fooled. The suits on the seventh floor of headquarters assured me that there was no danger. "They could never even find your driveway," said one senior officer, a man who had visited my art studio over the years and knew that coming down my mile-long unpaved road was a challenge for anybody.

Once the truth came out, there was no longer a reason not to celebrate the story with the public at large. Cora remembers that when she was finally able to tell her mother-in-law, the woman was furious. "Why didn't you tell me before?" she asked Cora. "Because," Cora explained, "you tell one person, you tell a hundred."

Back in the summer of 1980, I invited the houseguests to my home for a picnic. I happened to run into Bob Anders in the Foggy Bottom metro station and he called out, "Kevin!" from across the platform. We embraced, like two long-lost friends. The houseguests were so busy that it was difficult for them to find a day when we could get together. Somehow they wedged me in before their appearance at Yankee Stadium, where that evening's game would be dedicated to them.

I invited them to my forty-acre patch in the woods for a clandestine barbecue. Nobody could know. It wasn't until I issued the invitation that they learned my true name. At the barbecue they often forgot, though, and fell back into the habit of calling me Kevin. The get-together was a warm reunion. Joe and Kathy did not come, but the others were there. Jack Kerry and his wife, and Dan, from my team, were able to come too. Karen finally had the opportunity to meet these famous folks. We played tennis on our grass court and Lee, not surprisingly, was the star of the game, although Bob was no slouch.

Some of them had changed; most hadn't. Lee was still his old mischievous self. Cora seemed to have been affected most by her time with the Sheardowns. Before going to Iran she had always envisioned herself as a career woman and so had told Mark that she didn't plan on having kids. During the time they'd spent at the Sheardowns', however, she'd felt as if she belonged to a family. The experience gave her an entirely new outlook on life, and upon returning she realized that her priorities had slightly shifted.

Years later I visited Jerome Calloway at the Motion Picture and Television Country House, on Mulholland Drive in Burbank. Calloway and his wife had retired there following a stroke that he had suffered some time before. He was in a wheelchair now, with limited mobility, and his speech was slurred. But he still had the old sparkle in his eyes and was clearly glad to see me again.

He wanted to show me his room. He and his wife had separate apartments, and once I entered his it became clear why. His room was cluttered, festooned with mementos from a long and successful career in Hollywood. One long wall, maybe twenty feet long, was hung floor to ceiling, salon-style, with framed black-and-white glossy photos of Jerome with every movie legend you could name: Shirley Temple, Audrey Hepburn, Katharine Hepburn, Walter Matthau, Elizabeth Taylor, Bob Hope . . . It was a walk down memory lane, as if Memory Lane existed on the set of a Hollywood movie.

His trophies were lined up on a shelf on the same wall, from one end to the other. Gold statuettes of his most prestigious awards were all in a row. And, front and center, hanging with a bit of white space around it, was the CIA's Medal of Merit, one of only two ever given to a non-CIA staffer. It was a special recognition of a very special man.

Calloway turned his wheelchair to face me and rolled over

closer so that I could hear him more easily. "I've thought about it," he began, "and I've decided that if this place ever catches fire and we have to get out of here fast, the only thing I'm taking with me is that." He pointed to the medal. "It's hanging low, you see, so that I can grab it from this damn chair." He wheeled himself over to the wall to show me how he could reach it if he ever needed to.

It was the last time I ever saw Jerome. It's a great memory of a man who did a lot for his country and who was a good, true friend.

The first rule in any deception operation is to understand who your audience is. In the case of Argo, the audience was not the Iranians but the houseguests themselves. While we'd backstopped the cover story to the hilt, the people we really wanted to convince were those six American diplomats. Of course, if any Iranian officials had actually checked, their story would have seemed legitimate. But knowing that is what sold the cover story to the houseguests in the first place. They believed in it, which gave them the confidence to carry it off.

The second reason Argo worked was its overall outlandishness. It was the proverbial too-crazy-to-be-a-lie story that was impossible to check. It was something that no intelligence officer in his right mind would ever choose for a cover story. And therein was its beauty.

Most films nowadays are judged to be a success or failure based on the box office receipts. In a way, even though our fake science fiction film never made a dime, in my mind it had had the most successful opening in the history of the cinema. We'd saved the lives of six people—not a bad haul for a film that never existed.

ACKNOWLEDGMENTS

I have told the story of the 1980 rescue of six "houseguests" from revolutionary Iran scores if not hundreds of times over the years. The details of the role of the Canadian government plus significant Hollywood and CIA involvement in planning and conducting the operation were a well-kept secret until 1997. Then, at the CIA's request, I began to speak out as a way of celebrating the fiftieth anniversary of the Agency. The story became a chapter in my first book, *The Master of Disguise*, then it became an article in *Wired* magazine, and then a movie script titled *Argo*, and now it has become a book in its own right.

The story of *Argo* seems to have captured the public's imagination. Those in Hollywood involved in making the movie have expressed enormous enthusiasm for this story, and audiences across the United States have sat rapt as I told them how the CIA went into Iran in the middle of a revolution to rescue six innocent American diplomats hiding in the care of the Canadians.

In this book I have set forth the actual account of how that rescue was planned and executed. It is an honor to be able to tell this story. To that end I would like to acknowledge those who played a role in the operation.

First, I would like to thank my wife, Jonna, who is not only my muse, my comrade in arms, and my inspiration, but also a font of ideas and my most insightful and unyielding adviser. I could not have done this without her.

Equally important, I must nod to a good friend and a true patriot, "Jerome Calloway," who was responsible for mustering the Hollywood component of these events and many of the good ideas. Unfortunately, even in death we cannot name him, but he was a bona fide genius in his own right.

I must thank my son Jesse Lee Mendez for the weekends he has given up while home from college. We put this book together on a tight deadline, and although I would wave hello as he arrived and hug him good-bye as he left, we all missed hanging out and catching up. The same goes for his older siblings, Toby and Amanda. We promise to do better.

I was fortunate to be able to work with Matt Baglio on this project. A seasoned journalist and author, he now divides his time between Rome and California with his wife, Sara, and young son. Matt is a tireless investigative writer, researching the history of Iran that was the backdrop to the story of this rescue operation, interviewing the houseguests, and gaining an outsider's view of the story unencumbered by the proverbial wilderness of mirrors, the classified details. It was a pleasure to work with him. During the writing of this book Matt and his wife lost her father, Fernando Di Bari, and my heart was and is with them.

This book would not have happened without the very direct participation of Christy Fletcher of Fletcher and Company in New

York. She was a vital part of the making of this book at every turn, and she and her assistant Alyssa Wolff made it a pleasure to move forward each day. Likewise, Joshua Kendall at Viking, assisted by Maggie Riggs, was an enthusiastic editor who cared deeply about the material and gave it careful attention in the editing process. It shows. He took something that was good and made it even better. My thanks to them both.

My former colleagues at the CIA will, of course, pretty much remain nameless. There are enough details in the book that CIA employees of a certain age will be able to identify their former colleagues and sometimes themselves. Others, at the same time, have been assigned vague, generic names, like "Bob" (sorry Bob), but they know who they are. Unsung heroes, one and all. I hope that the reader will have a better and greater appreciation for the work of the CIA and the people doing that work.

The houseguests were perhaps the greatest source of new information for this book. Their insights, their points of view, and their experiences bring the human element to an operation that has heretofore been only known as "The Canadian Caper" or "The Rescue of Six Diplomats." Getting their feelings and experiences down on paper was something that the team managed with great finesse.

And then, of course, there were the Canadians. We have reached out to many of the Canadians involved in this rescue operation to revisit the history. It was a wonderful experience to work with them to achieve a common goal. From Ken Taylor and his secretary Laverna, recently deceased, to Roger Lucy and on down through the working levels, it was a pleasure to work with our neighbors to the north. While we like to say that "Small Is Beautiful," it is much,

much more. Canada is a true friend to America and I will never forget the pleasure of working with a foreign government that felt so much like my own.

Thanks, Canada!

Antonio J. Mendez

NOTES

Chapter 1: Welcome to the Revolution

11: **The final straw for the Eisenhower administration:** Eisenhower, *Mandate for Change*, p. 163.

12: **Upon meeting him, the shah famously said:** Roosevelt, *Countercoup*, p. 199.

14: **Even the U.S. Ambassador to Iran at the time:** Sick, *All Fall Down*, p. 94.

15: **Ironically, the shah was said to be somewhat nervous:** Ibid., p. 25.

15: **President Carter visited Iran and reassured:** Carter, *Keeping Faith*, p. 437.

16: **In a breakfast meeting at the White House:** Ibid., p. 455.

17: **As Graves stood by the window:** John Graves interviewed by Wells, *444 Days*, p. 39.

18: **To complicate matters, the militants had chosen to launch:** Bowden, *Guests of the Ayatollah*, p. 8.

18: **It seemed as if the students were just going:** Bill Belk interviewed by Wells, *444 Days*, pp. 40–41.

19: **The plan was to occupy the embassy for three days:** Bowden, *Guests of the Ayatollah*, p. 14.

19: **One lay down in one of the offices on his belly:** Bill Belk interviewed by Wells, *444 Days*, p. 40.

20: **The last thing Laingen told Golacinski before signing off:** Laingen, *Yellow Ribbon*, p. 13.

20: **Don Hohman, an army medic**: Don Hohman interviewed by Wells, *444 Days*, pp. 46–47.

20: **the militants had found the structure's one weak spot**: Bill Belk interviewed by Wells, ibid., p. 53.

21: **Golacinski then asked Laingen over the radio if he could go outside**: Bowden, *Guests of the Ayatollah*, p. 42.

21: **The order to do so had been slow in coming from Laingen**: Cort Barnes interviewed by Wells, *444 Days*, p. 48.

21: **Besides housing the communications equipment**: Daugherty, *In the Shadow of the Ayatollah*, p. 108.

22: **Someone waved a burning magazine in front of his face**: Mark Bowden, *Guests of the Ayatollah*, p. 58.

22: **Golacinski shouted through the metal door**: Ibid., p. 58.

22: **John Limbert, a political officer who spoke fluent Farsi**: John Limbert interviewed by Wells, *444 Days*, pp. 66–67.

23: **Carter was "deeply disturbed but reasonably confident"**: Carter, *Keeping Faith*, p. 457.

Chapter 3: Diplomacy

46: **Then, on November 12, he cut off**: Sick, *All Fall Down*, pp. 266–67.

46: **In a speech given before a roaring crowd of supporters**: Jordan, *Crisis*, p. 54.

48: **One local radio station in Ohio**: Bowden, *Guests of the Ayatollah*, p. 210.

48: **At another radio station in the Midwest**: Ibid., p. 243.

48: **Throughout the interview, Wallace**: Ibid., p 200.

49: **In a fit of frustration, Carter told his press secretary**: Ibid., p. 139.

49: **The imam was reported to have told the emissary**: Sick, *All Fall Down*, p. 263.

50: **Early on the militants were convinced**: Bowden, *Guests of the Ayatollah*, p. 246.

50: **For instance, when NBC aired the Gallegos interview**: Ibid., p. 246.

51: **They seemed eager to believe any conspiracy theory**: Sick, *All Fall Down*, p. 38; Bowden, *Guests of the Ayatollah*, p. 159.

51: **On another occasion, Colonel Dave Roeder**: Bowden, *Guests of the Ayatollah*, p. 318.

NOTES

Chapter 4: Nowhere to Run

65: **Undeterred, the militants smashed through the glass**: James Lopez interviewed by Wells, *444 Days*, p. 51.

66: **Before entering, he pulled out his pistol**: Ibid.; Harris, *The Iran Hostage Crisis*.

68: **After unlocking the door, Richard Queen**: Richard Queen interviewed by Wells, *444 Days*, pp. 72–73.

69: **Morefield turned to him and explained**: Harris, *The Iran Hostage Crisis*.

74: **On the morning of November 4, Koob**: Koob, *Guest of the Revolution*, p. 11.

75: **An Iranian voice came through the phone**: Ibid., p. 18.

76: **Koob tried hiding in a women's bathroom**: Ibid., pp. 30–31.

77: **It was clear now that the Iranians were hunting down the Americans**: Victor Tomseth interviewed by Wells, *444 Days*, p. 118.

77: **Tomseth had called the British chargé d'affaires**: Ibid.; author interview with Victor Tomseth.

77–78: **Finally, at about five o'clock, Joe called the British embassy**: Cora Lijek interviewed by Wells, ibid., p. 118.

81: **At the foreign ministry, meanwhile**: Laingen, *Yellow Ribbon*, p. 19.

81: **On the morning of November 6, they were told**: Wells, *441 Days*, p. 141.

81: **Tomseth had suspected that their phone conversations**: Author interview with Victor Tomseth.

84: **Sam had gotten the news**: Ibid.; Victor Tomseth interviewed by Wells, *444 Days*, p. 144.

Chapter 5: Canada to the Rescue

90: **In addition, a few days after the takeover**: Wells, *441 Days*, p. 226.

96: **On November 21, Taylor received a curious phone call**: Triffo, *Escape from Iran*; author interview with Ken Taylor.

105: **Amazingly, the local newspaper in Lee Schatz's hometown**: Harris, *The Iran Hostage Crisis*.

105: **In another instance, during a telephone interview**: "Embassy Escape: American Escaped During Takeover," *Free Lance Star*, Nov. 14, 1979; "9 Got Out of Embassy," *Milwaukee Journal*, Nov. 14, 1979.

106: **Not five days after the houseguests had left Koob's**: Harris, *The Iran Hostage Crisis*; author interview with Victor Tomseth.

NOTES

Chapter 7: Assembling the Team

133: **The various ideas being floated for the houseguests ranged**: Harris, *The Iran Hostage Crisis*; author interview with Roger Lucy.

133: **she would put them on bicycles and have them ride for the Turkish border**: Triffo, *Escape from Iran: The Hollywood Option*.

Chapter 8: Cover Story

145: **As President Carter wrote in *Keeping Faith***: Carter, *Keeping Faith*, p. 478.

147: **Of course, while this seemingly innocuous scene**: Robert Ode interviewed by Wells, *444 Days*, p. 208.

147: **A few were annoyed when one of the ministers**: Sgt. Paul Lewis interviewed by Wells, *444 Days*, p. 208.

Chapter 9: Hollywood

161: **in looking for help to design a new miniature camera**: Wallace and Melton, *Spycraft*, pp. 89–90.

161: **Another example saw OTS techs working with**: Ibid., p. 198.

Chapter 11: A Cosmic Conflagration

199: **On one occasion, Ken Taylor's wife, Pat**: Author Interview with Ken Taylor.

Chapter 15: The Escape

276: **Back at the Canadian embassy, Ambassador Taylor**: Author interview with Ken Taylor.

Chapter 16: Aftermath

280: **Jean Pelletier of Montreal's *La Presse***: Pelletier and Adams, *The Canadian Caper*, p. 224.

280: **Pelletier, however, claimed that his "instincts" were**: Ibid., p. 225.

280–81: **Soon after, the story was picked up by**: Ibid., p. 228.

NOTES

281: **Eventually a vague reference would be made**: Gwertzman, "6 American Diplomats, Hidden by Canada, Leave Iran," *New York Times.*

281: **On January 30, the U.S. Congress**: "Canada to the Rescue," *Time.*

283: **Down at the U.S. embassy, meanwhile, it was reported**: Ibid.

283: **Though perhaps the most famous response**: Harris, *The Iran Hostage Crisis.*

283: **When asked about it later, Lee described the moment**: Ibid.

288: **whom Carter would later describe as having the reputation**: Carter, *Keeping Faith*, p. 485.

BIBLIOGRAPHY

Associated Press. "Embassy Escape: American Escaped During Takeover," *Free Lance Star* (Fredericksburg, VA), November 14, 1979.

———. "9 Got Out of Embassy," *Milwaukee Journal*, November 14, 1979.

Axworthy, Michael. *Iran: Empire of the Mind: A History From Zoroaster to the Present Day*. London: Penguin Books, 2007.

Bowden, Mark. *Guests of the Ayatollah*. New York: Atlantic Monthly Press, 2006.

"Canada to the Rescue," *Time*, February 11, 1980.

Carter, Jimmy. *Keeping Faith: Memoirs of a President*. New York: Bantam, 1982.

Christopher, Warren, Harold Saunders, Gary Sick, and Paul H. Kreisberg. *American Hostages in Iran: The Conduct of a Crisis*. New Haven, CT: Yale University Press, 1985.

Daugherty, William. *In the Shadow of the Ayatollah: A CIA Hostage in Iran*. Annapolis, MD: Naval Institute Press, 2001.

Eisenhower, Dwight D. *Mandate for Change*. Garden City, NY: Doubleday, 1963.

Gwertsman, Bernard. "6 American Diplomats, Hidden by Canada, Leave Iran," *New York Times*, January 30, 1980.

Harris, Les (director). *The Iran Hostage Crisis: 444 Days to Freedom (What Really Happened in Iran)*. Documentary. Canamedia, 1997.

Jordan, Hamilton. *Crisis: The True Story of an Unforgettable Year in the White House*. New York: Berkley Books, 1982.

Koob, Kathryn. *Guest of the Revolution*. Nashville: Nelson, 1982.

Laingen, Bruce. *Yellow Ribbon: The Secret Journal of Bruce Laingen*. New York: Brassey's, 1992.

BIBLIOGRAPHY

Mendez, Antonio J., with Malcolm McConnell. *The Master of Disguise: My Secret Life in the CIA*. New York: Morrow, 1999.

Pelletier, Jean, and Claude Adams. *The Canadian Caper*. Toronto: Paperjacks, 1981.

Roosevelt, Kermit. *Countercoup: The Struggle for Control of Iran*. New York: McGraw-Hill, 1979.

Sick, Gary. *All Fall Down: America's Tragic Encounter with Iran*. New York: Random House, 1985.

Triffo, Chris (director). *Escape from Iran: The Hollywood Option*. Documentary. Harmony Documentary Inc., 2004.

Vance, Cyrus. *Hard Choices: Critical Years in America's Foreign Policy*. New York: Simon and Schuster, 1983.

Wallace, Robert, and H. Keith Melton. *Spycraft: The Secret History of the CIA's Spytechs from Communism to Al-Qaeda*. New York: Plume, 2008.

Wells, Tim. *444 Days: The Hostages Remember*. Orlando, FL: Harcourt Brace Jovanovich, 1985.